IDENTITY, SELF-DETERMINATION AND SECESSION

Identity, Self-Determination and Secession

Edited by
IGOR PRIMORATZ
The University of Melbourne, Australia
and
ALEKSANDAR PAVKOVIĆ
Macquarie University, Australia

Routledge
Taylor & Francis Group

LONDON AND NEW YORK

First published 2006 by Ashgate Publishing

Reissued 2018 by Routledge
2 Park Square, Milton Park, Abingdon, Oxon OX14 4RN
605 Third Avenue, New York, NY 10017

First issued in paperback 2021

Routledge is an imprint of the Taylor & Francis Group, an informa business

Typeset by Saxon Graphics Ltd, Derby

A Library of Congress record exists under LC control number: 2005021764

Notice:
Product or corporate names may be trademarks or registered trademarks, and are used only for identification and explanation without intent to infringe.

Publisher's Note
The publisher has gone to great lengths to ensure the quality of this reprint but points out that some imperfections in the original copies may be apparent.

Disclaimer
The publisher has made every effort to trace copyright holders and welcomes correspondence from those they have been unable to contact.

ISBN 13: 978-0-815-38961-3 (hbk)
ISBN 13: 978-1-351-15608-0 (ebk)
ISBN 13: 978-1-138-35604-7 (pbk)

DOI: 10.4324/9781351156080

Contents

List of Contributors

Allen Buchanan is James B. Duke Professor of Philosophy and Public Policy at Duke University. His research is mainly in two areas, bioethics and political philosophy. His books include *Secession: The Morality of Political Divorce from Fort Sumner to Lithuania and Quebec* (Westview, 1991), *Justice, Legitimacy, and Self-Determination: Moral Foundations for International Law* (Oxford University Press, 2003) and *States, Nations, and Borders: The Ethics of Making Boundaries*, co-edited with Margaret Moore (Cambridge University Press, 2003).

C.A.J. (Tony) Coady is Professorial Fellow at the University of Melbourne division of the Centre for Applied Philosophy and Public Ethics. He was Boyce Gibson Professor of Philosophy at the University of Melbourne from 1990 to 1998. His publications include *Testimony: A Philosophical Inquiry* (Oxford University Press, 1992) and *Terrorism and Justice: Moral Argument in a Threatened World*, co-edited with Michael O'Keefe (Melbourne University Press, 2002). He is writing a book on morality and political violence.

Simon Keller is Assistant Professor of Philosophy at Boston University. He received a PhD from Princeton University in 2002. Most of his work is in moral and political philosophy; he is currently working on a book about the nature and ethical significance of different kinds of love and loyalty. He has also published on the philosophy of time, and on Plato. His work has appeared in such journals as *Australasian Journal of Philosophy*, *Ethics*, *Phronesis* and *Social Theory and Practice*.

Geoffrey Brahm Levey is Senior Lecturer in Politics and International Relations, and Coordinator of the Program in Jewish Studies, University of New South Wales, Sydney. His research is in contemporary political theory and political sociology, with publications in such journals as *Political Theory*, *Political Studies* and *Philosophy of the Social Sciences*. He is co-editor (with Philip Mendes) of *Jews and Australian Politics* (Sussex Academic Press, 2004) and editor of *Political Theory and Australian Multiculturalism* (Berghahn Books, 2006). He is completing a book on autonomy and the right to culture.

Margaret Moore is Professor in the Political Studies department at Queen's University, Kingston, Ontario (Canada). She is the author of *Foundations of Liberalism* (Oxford University Press, 1993) and *Ethics of Nationalism* (Oxford University Press,

2001), editor of *National Self-Determination and Secession* (Oxford University Press, 1998) and co-editor (with Allen Buchanan) of *States, Nations, and Borders: The Ethics of Making Boundaries* (Cambridge University Press, 2003).

Aleksandar Pavković is Associate Professor of Politics at Macquarie University, Sydney and an Honorary Research Fellow at the Centre for Applied Philosophy and Public Ethics in Melbourne. In the past ten years he has mostly written on the nationalist movements and ideologies of former Yugoslavia, including *The Fragmentation of Yugoslavia: Nationalism and War in the Balkans* (Palgrave, Macmillan 1997). He has also written on More's *Utopia*, on terrorism and liberation ideologies, on humanitarian military interventions and on normative theories of secession; the last topic is the subject of his current research.

Igor Primoratz is Professor Emeritus of Philosophy at the Hebrew University, Jerusalem, and Principal Research Fellow at the Centre for Applied Philosophy and Public Ethics, University of Melbourne. He is the author of *Justifying Legal Punishment* (Humanities Press International, 1989) and *Ethics and Sex* (Routledge, 1999) and editor of *Human Sexuality* (Ashgate, 1997), *Patriotism* (Humanity Books, 2002) and *Terrorism: The Philosophical Issues* (Palgrave Macmillan, 2004).

Peter Radan is Associate Professor of Law at Macquarie University, Sydney, where his primary teaching is in the fields of international law, law and religion, and contract law. His research focuses on the area of self-determination and secession, equity and contract law. He has published a variety of articles on these topics in scholarly journals in Australia, Canada and the United States. He is the author of *The Break-up of Yugoslavia and International Law* (Routledge, 2002), co-editor of *Law and Religion: God, the State and the Common Law* (Routledge, 2005) and co-author of *Equity and Trusts*, 2nd edn (LexisNexis, 2005) and *Principles of Australian Contract Law* (LexisNexis, 2006).

Janna Thompson is Associate Professor of Philosophy at La Trobe University in Melbourne and Head of the Melbourne University division of the Centre for Applied Philosophy and Public Ethics. She has written books on international justice, discourse ethics and, most recently, on historical obligations. Her book *Taking Responsibility for the Past: Reparation and Historical Justice* was published in 2002 by Polity Press. She has written many articles on topics in political philosophy and ethics.

Daniel Weinstock is Professor of Philosophy at the Université de Montréal, where he holds the Canada Research Chair in Ethics and Political Philosophy. He is the Founding Director of the Centre de recherche en éthique de l'Université de Montréal. He has published many articles in political philosophy on topics such as the ethics of secession, the relationship between nationalism and liberalism, and on the concept of public reason, in volumes and in journals such as the *Journal of Political Philosophy*, *The Monist* and *Ethics and International Affairs*. He is currently launching a new research project on the family as a political institution.

Introduction

Igor Primoratz and Aleksandar Pavković

This book engages with a range of interconnected and highly topical issues of identity, self-determination and secession. It examines the import and implications of 'identity claims', and looks into 'identity politics' motivated by such claims, which are becoming ever more salient in democratic and culturally and ethnically heterogeneous states. It discusses nationalism as an important component of identity of individuals and groups, and a position that generates claims of self-determination and secession on the part of ethnic and cultural groups. It also examines patriotism, which had been on the wane before the terrorist attacks in the United States on 11 September 2001 and the start of the global 'war on terrorism', but has undergone a dramatic revival since. The book offers a typology of patriotism, an assessment of its moral standing, and a critique of the beliefs about the *patria* it characteristically involves. Also discussed are topics such as the ways a liberal society should treat nonliberal communities within it, the role of heritage and remembrance in national identity, the status of national minorities as an issue of equality, the legality of secession, and arrangements concerning indigenous peoples and intrastate autonomy as an alternative to secession. These are some of the issues to do with identity, individual and collective, in the focus of current debates at the intersection of philosophy and political theory.

Identity and Identity Politics

According to the traditional understanding of the nature and aims of politics in a liberal and democratic polity, politics is about articulating and accommodating interests of different groups. This portrays politics as dealing with largely mundane matters, most of which are negotiable, and as a process of negotiation that needs to be as rational as possible in order to be as fruitful as possible. However, in recent decades, political life in a number of liberal and democratic countries has also been informed by a different approach: that of 'identity politics'. The aims sought and the arguments advanced are no longer couched in terms of what a certain group wants, or what would be in its interest, but rather in terms of the identity of the group: who and what its members are, and what recognizing and respecting their identity would require or rule out. This development is welcomed by some, and met with suspicion and apprehension by others, both with regard to the impact of identity politics on democratic processes and practices and with regard to the ways in

1

which it affects the individual. While some see identity politics as indifferent at best, and inimical at worst, to the requirements of universal and impartial justice and equality, others point out that quite a few political organizations representing identity groups have in fact actively and successfully promoted justice and equality for all. While some, focusing on 'ascriptive', that is, unchosen, identities, highlight the ways in which group identities constrain the individual, rather than promoting his or her autonomy, others emphasize the importance of the sense of belonging and security such identities provide.

For better or worse, identity politics is an inescapable feature of liberal democracy. As Amy Gutmann has recently written,

> Identity groups are an inevitable byproduct of according individuals freedom of association. As long as individuals are free to associate, identity groups of many kinds will exist. This is because free people mutually identify in many politically relevant ways, and a society that prevents identity groups from forming is a tyranny.[1]

The first two contributions to this volume present two mutually opposed views of the nature and significance of identity politics in liberal democracies. In Chapter 1, Daniel Weinstock argues that identity claims and the kind of politics they generate are indeed dangerous to democracy or, more accurately, to the ideal of 'deliberative democracy' that has been propounded by a number of political theorists and that he, too, finds attractive. Advocates of 'deliberative democracy' reject the understanding of democratic politics as a search for a *modus vivendi* that is based on the balance of power, and urge us to aim higher, for a consensus among participants in the process of common, public deliberation on political matters. Weinstock rejects the balance of power/consensus dichotomy, and suggests that these are rather poles of a continuum. He also argues that consensus may not be a realistic aim in ethnically and culturally pluralistic polities, and that we should rather seek a middle-of-the-road solution, which is compromise. Given compromise as the aim of politics, Weinstock goes on to argue, we should desist from both making and admitting identity claims in the political give and take, as they make compromise more difficult than it would be if all parties were to deploy only arguments in terms of preferences, interests and even values. Identity claims are obstructive because they bring into play people's sense of integrity and self-respect. Once one party has made such a claim, it tends to perceive further call for compromise by the other party as a call for compromising her identity and integrity. Moreover, while satisfaction of preferences, promotion of interests and realization of values are matters of degree, recognition of and respect for identity are not. Making identity claims invokes an 'all or nothing' logic, which cannot be good for the prospects of reaching a compromise. Finally, while claims regarding satisfaction of preferences or realization of interests or values are predicated on empirical considerations that are open to falsification, identity claims are not. They tend to bring the debate to a dead end, rather than to promote it.

The other side of the issue is argued in Margaret Moore's contribution (Chapter 2). Moore does not tackle directly Weinstock's central argument, but some of what she says does tend to undermine it. She sees identity claims as making legitimate political demands, and engages the critique of identity politics by writers such as Brian Barry and Jeremy Waldron. She tries to show how the worries about the subjective character of identity claims, about their inflationary tendencies, and about their potential to undermine just and equal social and political arrangements and disrupt proper functioning of the political process can be laid to rest, or at least considerably alleviated. Identities are indeed subjective in an important sense, but that does not mean that any preference or interest can be arbitrarily proclaimed a part of one's identity and made the basis for making demands, or seeking exemptions, in the public arena. Identities have an objective aspect too, and cannot be changed at will, the way one changes hats. Moreover, politics of identity does not trade in mere personal identity claims; to accord special accommodation to all such claims would obviously not be feasible. It rather advances claims of collective identity, which is more likely to be central to the person, both morally and psychologically. Such claims do not, and could not, tend to proliferate quite as much. What Waldron has termed 'the incompossibility problem', namely the impossibility of recognizing, respecting, and protecting all different and sometimes conflicting collective identities, is to be solved, or at least mitigated, by Moore's thesis that identity claims involve an implicit limitation. When I claim that my polity should exempt me from a certain requirement, or provide me with a certain benefit, because that is required by my identity, by who and what I am (say, a Catholic), I thereby implicitly commit myself to acknowledging that others have *their* identities, different from mine (they are Moslems, or Jewish, or whatever), and that those identities, too, generate similar claims that need to be attended to. Accordingly, the demands I make on the basis of *my* collective identity have to do with what *I* (and others sharing this identity) may be required to do, and not about what *people with different identities* may be obliged to do. Identity politics need not be a recipe for friction and discord; when properly understood and circumscribed, it is rather a plea for toleration.

Within the liberal tradition, a standard way of arguing for toleration (and for exploring its limits) is in terms of individual autonomy. The individual is conceived as having a basic interest in being able to develop her own conception of the good life, to revise it, if need be, and to conduct her life accordingly. This is the basis of the rights of the individual, and also of liberal political morality, including its requirement of toleration. However, various identity groups living in liberal society without being of it look upon this way of grounding the principle of toleration with increasing unease and suspicion. They suspect that liberal insistence on personal autonomy and rational, critical thinking about all subjects, including fundamental religious, moral and cultural issues, is subversive of their way of life. They reject the claim of the liberal state to be neutral with regard to competing conceptions of the good, and perceive it as actually favouring a distinctive – namely, liberal – conception. How, then, should our society, characterized by far-reaching ethnic, religious and cultural diversity, maintain its liberal commitments, and at the same time accommodate nonliberal communities within it?

In Chapter 3, Geoffrey Brahm Levey examines two approaches to this problem. One is 'identity liberalism', advanced by authors such as Bhikhu Parekh or William

Galston. This approach proposes to replace the value of autonomy by some other basic value, such as identity or diversity. Levey argues that 'identity liberals' set out to dethrone autonomy as the governing value only to reinstate it under some other heading, for instance, as bound up with the political virtues of good citizenship. The other approach discussed is that of political liberalism, whose classic statement is the book by John Rawls with the same title. Here autonomy is retained as a basic value, but only as a purely political ideal, valid within the public sphere. It determines the public status of individuals, their human and civil rights and obligations. At the same time, political liberalism refrains from endorsing autonomy as a comprehensive ideal, a conception of the good aiming to regulate human life in all its aspects. Individuals are left free to pursue their own conceptions of the good in their private lives, and within their families and identity groups they belong to. Levey finds this position too unsatisfactory, at least so far as the liberal understanding of the self is concerned. One cannot very well be a communitarian in private life and a liberal in public life: one's self cannot be both embedded in one's collective identity, unable to stand back from it and judge it and its requirements critically, and also maintain one's autonomy in relation to that identity, one's capability of assessing and reassessing it rationally and critically. At the same time, Levey concedes that political liberalism may prove more accommodating to nonliberal identities at the level of legislation and public policy.

Can there be further latitude for nonliberal identities within liberalism? The self, as understood by liberals, is characterized by the capacity of 'rational revisability'. No end is exempt from critical examination and revision; in the words of Will Kymlicka, 'I can always envisage my self without its *present* ends'.[2] Does this mean that the liberal self not only has to be characterized by rational revisability, but also has to understand itself as so characterized? Levey argues that rational revisability need not be self-conscious. He is thus advancing a thesis that has an air of paradox: there is some space for nonliberal identities and ways of life in the murky area of nonliberal attachments and practices that *are* revisable, but are not *known* to be so by the individual concerned. One may wonder whether members of communities adhering to nonliberal values and practices are likely to see this as the kind of toleration they are hoping for.

Identity, Country and Nation

When asked who and what one is, one usually mentions one's nationality, the country one stems from or lives in, the polity whose citizen one is. These are normally important parts of one's identity, and discussions of identity need to provide some account of the ways in which we relate to them, as individuals and as groups. This means that such discussions need to include the topics of nationalism and patriotism. Both subjects were almost completely neglected in philosophy and political theory for a long time. The renewed interest in them is due to several reasons, some theoretical and some practical. Both nationalism and patriotism present good test cases for pursuing the debates in moral philosophy between advocates of universal morality and adherents of more particular, local attachments and commitments, and the debates in political theory between liberals and communitarians. At a more practical, political level, the last decades of the twentieth century were marked by a dramatic revival of nationalism in several parts of the world. More recently, there has been a resurgence of patriotism in the United States and some other countries that see themselves as being under attack by global terrorism.

Discussions of nationalism and patriotism are often made even more difficult than they have to be by a confused and confusing usage of the two terms. Nationalism, in particular, means many different things to different people. Igor Primoratz (Chapter 6) suggests a simple way of distinguishing between nationalism and patriotism in terms of the object of the identification, loyalty and special concern involved. That is either *natio* or *patria*: either one's nation (in the ethnic, rather than political sense of the term), or one's country and polity. This, of course, still does not tell us just what a nation (in the ethnic sense) is; on that, too, there is a wide range of views, some of which are discussed in the contribution by Tony Coady (Chapter 4), together with the normative, moral and political implications these views are taken to have. Coady finds the variety of answers to the question 'What is a nation?' so confounding that it leads him to doubt the very existence of what the word is presumed to stand for. Such doubts are not laid to rest when some advocates of nationalism write that 'a nationality exists when its members believe that it does'.[3] What cannot be doubted is the attachment of the nationalist. Now this attachment, whether to something real or to a fiction, is often taken to ground far-reaching moral and political claims. It is claimed that the individual has highly important moral duties to his nation: to live in accordance with, promote and defend its values and traditions, and to exhibit special concern for its welfare, beyond whatever concern he may have for humanity at large. It is also claimed that a nation is entitled to self-determination, meaning its own independent, sovereign state. This, in turn, is taken to generate further duties on the part of the individual: to help strengthen and defend the nation-state, if it is in place, or to help set it up, if it is not. Coady examines these moral and political claims on behalf of the nation and nation-state, and finds them all implausible.

Beyond that, both Coady and Simon Keller take to task nationalism and patriotism, respectively, for offending against the ethics of belief. Even if the existence of a nation is not a fiction, many of the beliefs a nationalist holds about it – about its virtues and achievements, about its present and its history – are deeply flawed in various ways. They are typically driven by interest, above all political interest, rather than attained and maintained in a rational way. Unsurprisingly, some are pure myth, and many are half-truths. Unlike nineteenth-century proponents of nationalism, who tended to be rather literal about nationalist beliefs, its present-day advocates often concede that such beliefs cannot be taken seriously from the epistemological point of view, and go on to give them a pragmatic justification of one sort or another. Coady looks into these justifications and finds them unconvincing, resting, as they do, on dubious empirical premises.

In Chapter 5, Keller undertakes a critical analysis of the relation of patriotism to the sort of beliefs about the *patria* a patriot characteristically holds. While one's love of and loyalty to a family member or a friend may coexist with a low estimate of that person's qualities, love of and loyalty to one's country involves pride in, or endorsement of, that country. This, Keller argues, leads the patriot to indulge in bad faith: to hide from herself the true source of some of the beliefs involved. If the patriot is to have the right sort of pride in the *patria*, she must consider her beliefs about the country's virtues and achievements to be based on some objectively valid standards of value, and on an unbiased examination of her country's past and present record, leading to the conclusion that the country lives up to those standards. However, the patriot's love and loyalty are not focused on her country simply because it happens to instantiate a set of virtues a country can have, so that, if a neighbouring country were found to possess such virtues to an even higher degree, the patriot's love and loyalty would be redirected accordingly. She rather loves her country and is loyal to it because that country, and that country only, is *her* country; as Keller puts it, hers is a love and a loyalty 'in the first instance'. Thus the patriot is motivated to see the *patria* as blessed by all manner of virtues and achievements whether the evidence, interpreted objectively, warrants that or not. Accordingly, she forms beliefs about her country in ways different from the ways in which she forms beliefs about other countries. Moreover, she cannot admit this motivation while at the same time remaining a patriot. This is bad faith, both in one of the senses the term has in common usage, and in terms of Jean-Paul Sartre's classic account. Bad faith is bad; if Keller's argument succeeds, so is patriotism, as well as every identity, individual and collective, constituted, in part, by patriotic loyalty.

The next contribution, too, discusses patriotism, but from a different angle. Igor Primoratz (Chapter 6) offers a typology of patriotism, classifying its types or facets in terms of the object of patriotic attachment, reasons for it, its motive, strength, dominant vicarious feeling and moral import. Along the last of these dimensions, he introduces a distinction between worldly and ethical type of patriotism. While the former is concerned with the worldly interests of the *patria*, such as its political stability and power, its economic strength, or its cultural vibrancy, the latter focuses on its moral record: it seeks to ensure that the country's institutions, laws and policies are just, and that they are in accord with other pertinent moral considerations, such as basic human solidarity. It would seem that, unlike the more usual, mundane type of patriotism, this distinctively ethical type of attachment to one's country and polity is not vulnerable to Keller's critique of patriotism as bound up with bad faith. Moreover, while Primoratz holds that worldly patriotism lacks positive moral significance – that it is, at best, morally permissible – he argues that the distinctively moral type of patriotism is, under certain fairly common circumstances, a stance we ought to adopt. An individual is normally in a much better position to identify, criticize and try to change immoral policies and practices in his own country, among his people, than in a foreign country, among strangers. The acceptance of benefits resulting from immoral policies or practices of one's own country, or from membership in one's polity, generates a certain kind of collective moral responsibility. Democracy, too, imposes a certain kind of collective responsibility for the laws passed and enforced and policies devised and implemented on behalf of all full-fledged citizens. In these ways, the moral identity and integrity of the individual are bound up with the moral identity and integrity of his country and polity.

In the shaping and reshaping of collective identities, an important role is played by the past: by facts of the past, and by our beliefs about them, the way we relate to them, practical conclusions we draw from them. One aspect of this large subject is touched upon in Coady's chapter on nationalism, in the course of his analysis of the way the nationalist understands and interprets the nation's history. Another, interesting yet somewhat neglected aspect is taken up by Janna Thompson (Chapter 7). Is our group identity as members of a nation or citizens of a polity bound up with some obligations to our predecessors? In view of the transgenerational, historical character of these identities and the practices pertaining to them, do we now have some obligations to acknowledge the misdeeds of our ancestors, offer apology to the descendants of those our ancestors had wronged, or offer such restitution as the passage of time and present circumstances make possible? Thompson's answer to these questions is, yes, we do have certain obligations generated by the history of our communities, by deeds and misdeeds of our predecessors. We have an obligation to remember and honour our predecessors for their contribution to the nation or polity, just as we are entitled to expect future generations to acknowledge our own labour and achievement. We also have an obligation to appreciate the things our ancestors worked to provide for us. In some cases, we have a duty to preserve this heritage and transmit it to our successors. This, of course, does not include traditional practices we have come to judge as completely pointless or morally flawed. Most importantly, perhaps, at least from the moral point of view, we may be obliged to offer apologies and make amends for the injustices perpetrated by our forebears. These obligations, in Thompson's view, can be explained by the fact that people have 'lifetime-transcending interests' and that they subscribe to the intergenerational practice of making commitments which successors are expected to honour. If we propose to bind our successors to make good our commitments, we thereby commit ourselves to this practice, which also binds us in relation to our predecessors. This is part and parcel of membership in historical communities such as nations or polities. Other obligations such communities seek to impose on the state are further explored in Chapters 8, 9 and 10.

Self-Determination and Secession

By proclaiming the nation to be the sole source of sovereignty, the Declaration of the Rights of Man and of Citizens of 1789 ushered in the era of national self-determination. If nations are the basic units of governance, every nation appears to have the right to political self-determination or self-government. Indeed, many hold this connection between nationality and self-government to be quite obvious. As John Stuart Mill famously wrote,

> Where the sentiment of nationality exists in any force, there is a *prima facie* case for uniting all members of the nationality under the same government, and a government to

themselves apart. This is merely saying that the question of government ought to be decided by the governed. One hardly knows what any division of the human race should be free to do if not to determine with which of the various collective bodies of human beings they choose to associate themselves.[4]

Democratic theory can easily explain what self-government is: a group governs itself if its government represents the governed and is accountable to them. Still, just what is the 'self' here – what is the group that is governing itself? Democratic theory offers no ready-made answer to this question. The group can consist of all adults within specified territorial borders, or of all members of an ethnically or culturally defined group, for example of the French speakers. The tension, and often the conflict, between these, the territorial and ethnic or cultural conceptions of the 'self', is at the root of much of the recent political conflict as well as philosophical debate regarding self-determination.

Since the point of contention is the identity of this 'self', the politics of identity has shaped both the political conflict and, to some extent, theoretical debate on self-determination. A growing number of groups, defined by their ethnic or cultural identity, are demanding self-government, both within economically developed and liberal–democratic states and within undeveloped states with authoritarian, single-party or military regimes. Moreover, the type of political regime and level of economic development of the host state does not appear to affect the kind of self-determination that these movements demand: identity-based political movements demand independence, that is, secession, both from liberal–democratic and from authoritarian or single-party states. Identity-based movements also make demands that fall short of independent statehood: demands for political and cultural autonomy within the host states of both kinds. However varied their scope, these demands are supported by one or more of the following three types of claims: the group demanding self-determination claims to deserve self-government because, first, it has been exposed to injustice or discrimination within the host state (in the past or in the present); second, it is ethnically or culturally distinct from the dominant group or groups in the state; or, finally, it has freely chosen, in an appropriate way, to seek self-determination.

Do claims of these three types present valid sources or grounds of the *right* of self-determination? Some theorists have argued that a majority of any territorially concentrated group acquires the right to secede from the host state, provided that this decision is reached through a democratic procedure (such as a referendum) or for the right reason (for example, the group wants to establish a superior type of political regime, such as that of direct or deliberative democracy). Others have maintained that the right of secession, as well as a broader right to self-determination within the host state, is acquired in virtue of being a minority group distinct from the majority group or groups in the host state in virtue of its unique culture and historical memory. Yet others have argued that the right of secession and of autonomy within a state is acquired if the group has been exposed to specific types of grave injustice whose appropriate remedy is the establishment of a separate state or intrastate autonomy for the group. An argument of this type is advanced by Allen

Buchanan in Chapter 9. These arguments have been advanced within the framework of a wide variety of liberal and democratic theories as well as within the framework of communitarian, republican and deliberative democratic theories. Yet most of the theorists of self-determination or secession, whatever their theoretical background, share the assumption that some groups, concentrated on a bounded territory, have a collective right to self-government which overrides the sovereign rights of the host state within which they live, regardless of type of political regime in power in that state. Therefore, most of the theorists would assume that, even if a host state is a liberal–democratic state, which does not discriminate against any group of its citizens, some groups of its citizens may have or acquire a right to self-government which is *not* derived from the constitutional principles and documents of the host state and which can be exercised outside its institutional framework. In their view this right of self-determination has an extrainstitutional status similar to fundamental human or natural rights.

The argument presented by Aleksandar Pavković in Chapter 8 challenges this view of self-determination as an extrainstitutional right. The thesis that national minorities have a right to have state-like institutions (that is, a degree of intrastate autonomy) within a state implies that national minorities have an extrainstitutional right to restricted self-determination. Pavković argues that the liberal principle of equality of citizens cannot provide any justification of such a thesis. In particular, a liberal state, in his view, is not obliged to grant state-like institutions to its national minority groups in order to protect and promote their languages and cultures. There are equally effective instruments for this purpose which do not invoke or require the right of self-determination. The liberal principle of equality, he maintains, does not require that every national (or any other) group within a liberal–democratic state should be granted equal political power within that state. It is rather the fundamental principle of nationalism – that each nation *deserves* a state or state-like institution – that can justify such a distribution of political power among national groups. Yet a demand for national self-determination of national minorities is often a demand for the parity of political power among various national groups within the state, and not a demand for the protection of equality or liberty of its individual citizens. Liberalism, Pavković argues, cannot justify or support the former demand.

The contribution of Allen Buchanan (Chapter 9) explores a similar issue of the right to intrastate autonomy: the right of groups to political autonomy within the state. Like Pavković, Buchanan believes that national or cultural groups within a state are not entitled to autonomy or an independent state simply because they are nations or partake of a distinct culture. But, in contrast to Pavković, he maintains that international law should recognize the right to intrastate autonomy in the following four kinds of case: first, when the group has the right to independence (because its has been subjected to persistent human rights violations) but has chosen autonomy within the host state; second, when the group has been granted autonomy but has then suffered persistent violations of that autonomy by the host state; third, when the granting of autonomy offers the best prospect for stopping persistent rights violations by the host state; and, fourth, where autonomy would secure the rights of the indigenous peoples who have suffered injustices at the hands of the colonizers. The indigenous peoples' right to self-government, Buchanan argues, is also a remedial right because it restores the self-governance to groups deprived of it by conquest and colonization, offers a non-paternalist mechanism for the protection against human rights violations and for counteracting the detrimental effects of past violations, facilitates the implementation of land settlements for these groups, and enables these groups to use and develop their customary law practices. In the same way one can also justify the right to self-government of the groups which were not classified as indigenous. Buchanan also holds that the host states can largely obviate the need for intrastate autonomy by better protection of individual human rights, by better access to political participation, by counteracting detrimental effects of past violations and by becoming as 'culturally neutral' as possible. If so, the recognition of the right to intrastate autonomy by international law which he proposes is, in effect, a recognition of the failure of individual states *effectively* to protect, through their central government institutions, human rights of their citizens and to counteract the detrimental effects of past injustices.

In an ideally effective and just liberal state, there would be no need either for intrastate autonomy or for secession. But we live in a non-ideal world, plagued by violent conflict and massive human rights violations, where these rights may well need to be protected by a more consistent application of international law. In contrast to Buchanan, who is seeking to reform and to augment the existing international law on secession and intrastate autonomy, Peter Radan explores the existing domestic law. He attempts to find out whether, and under what conditions, an act of secession is deemed legal (Chapter 10). In the first case he examines, the US Supreme Court decision in *Texas* v. *White* (1869), he finds that the Court held only that *unilateral* secession of a state from the USA is illegal, but that a secession of a state from the US 'with the consent of the [other] States' would be legal. Likewise, the Constitutional Court of the Socialist Federal Republic of Yugoslavia, in 1990, in a series of cases regarding Slovenia, Croatia and Kosovo, ruled unilateral secessions of its federal units (republics) to be unconstitutional, although, unlike the US Constitution, the Yugoslav Constitution of 1974 recognized the right of secession of the peoples of Yugoslavia. The Supreme Court of Canada in *Reference re: Secession of Quebec* (1998) ruled that a unilateral secession of Quebec would be illegal, but that an amendment to the Canadian Constitution, resulting from the negotiations following a successful referendum in Quebec, would make the mutually agreed secession legal. In all three cases, in spite of very different legal and constitutional traditions, the courts, Radan argues, essentially reached the same decision: that unilateral secession is constitutionally illegal and that an agreement of other federal units is necessary for a secession to be legal. These three courts reached the same decision because secession is not only a concern for the federal unit wishing to secede, but also a concern for other units in the host state.

These three chapters thus exhibit some of the limitations the principle of national self-determination faces when used (as it often is) to justify intrastate autonomy or secession. While Pavković is concerned to show that liberal principles do not countenance the use of this principle in justifying intrastate autonomy, Buchanan argues that unilateral secession as well as intrastate autonomy need not, and should not, be justified by reference to this principle at all. Radan, on the other hand, shows that, for a secession from a host state to be accepted as legal within its domestic constitutional law, an agreement of other parts of the host state needs to be secured. Taken together, these three chapters systematically question the utility of the right of national self-determination in normative examinations of intrastate autonomy or of secession, as well as its primacy over other rights, interests and identities of individuals.

Acknowledgments

The papers collected in this volume were generated by the workshop on 'Identity, self-determination and secession', organized by the editors and held under the auspices of the Centre for Applied Philosophy and Public Ethics (CAPPE), University of Melbourne division, and Department of Politics and International Relations and Division of Law, Macquarie University. It was held on 22 and 23 August 2003 at the University of Melbourne. Papers presented at the workshop were subsequently revised for publication in the light of the detailed critical discussion each paper had received at the workshop.

The editors would like to thank Ms Irena Blonder, Manager of the Melbourne division of CAPPE, for invaluable help in organizing the workshop.

Notes

1   A. Gutmann, *Identity in Democracy*, Princeton, NJ: Princeton University Press, 2003, p.4.
2   W. Kymlicka, *Liberalism, Community and Culture*, Oxford: Oxford University Press, 1991, p.52.
3   David Miller, 'In Defence of Nationality', *Journal of Applied Philosophy*, vol.10 (1993), p.6.
4   J.S. Mill, *Utilitarianism. On Liberty. Considerations on Representative Government*, ed. H.B. Acton, London: J.M. Dent & Sons, 1972, pp.360–1.

I
IDENTITY AND IDENTITY POLITICS

Chapter 1

Is 'Identity' a Danger to Democracy?

Daniel Weinstock

The concept of 'identity' has played a very important role in political philosophy over the course of the last few years. It has also been taken up in ordinary political discourse. We often hear protagonists in a political conflict justifying their position or demands by exclaiming: 'It is a question of identity!'

Now, it is important to note that the concept of identity, as it is often employed in political philosophy and everyday debates, refers to many quite different considerations. Sometimes, the term simply refers to an individual's values. Someone who considers environmental protection important will say, for example, that engaging in this or that controversial practice represents, for her, an issue of identity. More often, the term is not used to designate abstract values with which the individual identifies, but rather more particular human attachments, those which link us to a community, an ethnic group or a nation. Following the recent sale of a Canadian hockey club to an American businessman, the idea of identity was invoked on all fronts by commentators, either to indicate the population's level of 'identification' with the team, or to note the degree to which the team is part of the Montreal, Quebecois or Canadian identity.

The concept of identity is therefore quite poorly circumscribed. Nothing in the nature of things dictates a particular usage and no convention has been elaborated to constrain its application.[1]

In spite of this imprecision, the term has considerable rhetorical force in political debate. My intention in this chapter is therefore not to propose a conceptual analysis of the notion of identity, but rather to attempt to understand its *use* and its *effect*. I want to understand what people do when, in the context of a political debate, they invoke considerations of identity with the end of justifying their position. To borrow a couple of terms from the English philosopher J.L. Austin, I want to understand at least an aspect of the *illocutionary* and *perlocutionary* speech acts of which identity arguments consist.[2]

My thesis will be that, whatever the intentions of those who use them, identity arguments (which I characterize more precisely below) represent a danger for democracy. I will proceed in the following manner. I shall first define three types of results that can in principle emerge from deliberative democratic forums. I will term them 'consensus', 'balance of power' and 'compromise'. I shall try to demonstrate that compromise, rather than consensus or balance of power, represents the appropriate goal for most deliberative forums. Next, I will show that advancing identity arguments has the effect of changing the nature of deliberative democracy in a way that causes compromise to become less likely than it might have otherwise been. I conclude that our democratic institutions should to the greatest extent possible be organized in a way that discourages the use of identity arguments or, at least, renders their usage less problematic. In the third and last section, I consider whether these restrictions impose an unacceptable burden on certain actors within pluralistic and multicultural societies, by preventing them from presenting legitimate claims that could not be put forward in other ways. In other words, I ask the following question: are identity claims irreducible?

The Search for Compromise

The last few years have witnessed an impressive revival of interest in the normative foundations of democracy, as well as in the precise institutional forms which democracy should adopt. Questions of institutional design have for a long time been monopolized by the liberal project formulated by thinkers like John Rawls and Ronald Dworkin. However, many political thinkers have of late reached the conclusion that it was necessary to submit the nature and the conditions of democratic debate to a theoretical examination as sustained and profound as that which, after the publication of Rawls's book *A Theory of Justice* in 1971, had been devoted to questions about the nature of laws and their institutionalization.

A consensus is beginning to emerge in the normative literature on democracy, suggesting that we ought to make our democracies more 'deliberative'. According to one well-known model of democracy, the democratic arena is nothing more than the space where the prepolitical interests of individuals and collectives confront each other, and democracy consists only of aggregating these interests with the aim of satisfying as many people as possible. This model has been strongly denounced in recent years by thinkers who call themselves partisans of deliberative democracy. According to these authors, democracy should permit citizens to form political preferences by taking into consideration the interests and points of view of all citizens. It aims for the ideal described by Rousseau in *The Social Contract* of a truly general will. In order to arrive at this goal, participants in democratic forums should engage in the exchange of reasons, rather than the simple confrontation of desires and brute interests. Democratic deliberation, at the bare minimum, demands that we explain why we take a political position, and that we debate in a way that makes the values that motivate our viewpoints clear.

What are the types of outcomes that deliberative democracy can achieve? The vast majority of thinkers who have considered the question privilege *consensus* as the regulative ideal that orients both the participants' approach and the institutional structures appropriate to deliberation. There is a consensus when, at the end of deliberation, the participants reach a position that they consider better than, or at least normatively equivalent to, the one from which they began. Consensus can be formed in two distinct manners. First, one of the participants can convince the others of the soundness of her position. It might be that, during a deliberation, all participants are sincerely persuaded by the force of the better argument and that one position was, from the beginning, superior. Second, they can, departing from the initially divergent viewpoints, formulate a new position, judged by all to improve on the initial claims.

The search for consensus represents a regulative ideal for partisans of deliberative democracy since they believe that the only other possible result is one that reflects relations of raw power. In this case, a political disagreement is resolved, not by the normative reconciliation that an exchange of reasons brings about, but rather by the strongest participant imposing her will on weaker protagonists. Whatever the moral costs involved in resolving a debate through force or the threat of force, it is claimed that such a result risks instability. Indeed, those who find themselves obliged to sacrifice their interests in a confrontation will inevitably search to reactivate the conflict as soon as the balance of forces falls in their favour. In addition, since the losers have no reason other than that which stems from considerations of power to accept the winner's verdict, confrontations are hardly compatible with the conditions of civic friendship. That said, democracy cannot be entirely immunized against conflict and relations of power. Majority rule is based on the idea that, in the final analysis, it is the force of number that should prevail, whether it be in the elections where we elect our representatives, in the votes that take place in legislative assemblies or in deliberations by superior or supreme court judges. But it is in the interest of democratic societies that democratic deliberation precede voting in order to reduce, to a certain extent, the distance that separates protagonists, and to affirm the value of civic friendship that must obtain even among political opponents. The civic friendship on which a society's stability arguably depends is severely tested when political debates become a zero-sum game. If we are to resolve the differences that persist after a deliberation has taken place, the balance of power represented by a majority decision will always be necessary in order to arrive at final decisions. But it is also important for social cohesion that the initial conflict, if it is not eliminated by deliberation, at least be reduced.

The thesis the partisans of deliberative democracy support is that this result can only be achieved if the participants hold consensus as their regulative ideal. Unless participants to a debate set out to eliminate disagreement altogether, power will always, according to this view, end up deciding the outcome.

I have in other writing given reasons to question this thesis.[3] Above all in a pluralistic moral and cultural context, the normative gulf that separates different social groups is too significant to plausibly hope for consensus. The insistence on consensus reveals a trivialization of pluralism that is all the more surprising given that partisans of deliberative democracy often present their theory as a more adequate response to the problem of social pluralism than traditional liberal constitutionalism.

In addition, it may be that the quest for consensus in the context of pluralism will tend to generate perverse consequences. If the participants in a democratic deliberation consider themselves successful only if they have reached consensus, they will tend to undervalue more limited results that fall short of this threshold. As I will try to show in what follows, compromise can represent real moral progress, and can narrow normative differences, while preserving the conditions of civic friendship. But because it falls short of consensus, it risks being perceived by deliberative democrats as at best a quantitative, rather than a qualitative, improvement on mere balance of power.

I would argue that we should view consensus and balance of power as marking the poles of a continuum rather than as constituting a dichotomy. Between these two poles, there exists a third kind of result that deliberative democracy can yield, which I will refer to as 'compromise'. There is a compromise when, at the end of deliberation, the parties remain convinced of their starting positions' normative superiority but, preferring to resolve their differences instead of perpetuating conflict, they choose not to press certain aspects of their initial position that they know will make agreement difficult or impossible. Compromise as I have just briefly defined it represents, in numerous contexts, a true deliberative success, which in my view should not be belittled in the name of an often unachievable and overly inflated ideal of consensus. In addition, it respects the conditions of civic friendship. Compromise, as I understand it, does not imply that a concession has been extorted. If a participant decides not to insist on an aspect of her initial position, she does so freely, guided by her desire to reduce conflict, rather than by the threat advantage of her opponents. In order to reach a compromise, it is necessary that each of the participants interpret her initial position in order to distinguish what is essential and non-negotiable within it from the components that can be considered secondary.[4] In addition, it is essential that all participants view the compromise as issuing from a process of reciprocal concessions.

Consensus, balance of power and compromise are ideal types, in Max Weber's sense. In reality, these three types of processes are often subtly mingled in the resolution of most political conflicts. My brief consideration of these three possible results of deliberative democracy is however sufficient to advance tentatively two conclusions. First, it is false to think, as a good number of the supporters of deliberative democracy appear to do, that the only alternative to consensus is a *modus vivendi* arising from a balance of power. Compromise represents a result distinct from these two extremes. It has its own moral dignity and is compatible with the conditions of civic friendship, since it does not result in the simple imposition of the will of one party on another.

Second, it is reasonable to think that, in the context of value pluralism, compromise is a more appropriate regulative ideal than consensus. Indeed, if the pluralism of modern societies is as deep as many modern political thinkers, including the supporters of deliberative democracy, seem to believe, it will be necessary to find ways of resolving important conflicts without eliminating the deep normative differences that underlie them. This deliberative attitude is more appropriately oriented towards compromise than consensus since the quest for compromise does not exclude the possibility of discovering an unexpected consensus in participants' different conceptions of the good life. On the other hand, the tendency to evaluate all conflicts in terms of consensus risks the unfortunate consequence of participants being unable to recognize the real progress compromise represents. Compromise and consensus are, so to speak, asymmetrically related on this point: the quest for consensus risks leaving the participants unable to recognize a compromise, while nothing in their search for compromise prevents them from achieving consensus if it presents itself.[5]

For these reasons, it appears to me that compromise represents the most appropriate regulative ideal for deliberative democracy.

The Identity Problem

While we may wish that our democratic institutions would function more as forums for the exchange of reasons than as arenas of combat, it would be unwise to want completely to eliminate the 'agonic' dimension of deliberative democracy. Even if democracy allows us to discover what Jürgen Habermas calls 'generalizable interests', the fact remains that conflicts of interest and values are unavoidable aspects of all human societies, and that the will to transcend this conflict in the name of an ideal unanimity risks degenerating into authoritarianism.[6]

In particular, we should never forget that deliberative democracy is, among other things, a site of strategic interaction. Everyone who participates in the democratic 'game' does so with the aim of satisfying their interests, or the interests of those they represent, against the backdrop of the shared understanding that all interests and values at stake cannot be satisfied.

Participants in deliberative democracy exist after all in Humean circumstances of justice: it is in their interest to live in a society where they can take advantage of peaceful, favourable conditions of cooperation, but both their sympathy and available resources are limited. In other words, we can attribute to actors on the democratic scene two sets of preferences that are often in tension. On one hand, they want their interests to be satisfied and their values realized to the greatest degree possible. But on the other, they also want their social ties with others to remain viable. They realize, if they are rational, that pressing for too great a satisfaction of their interests might damage the quality of their social relations. They want to win, but they want to be able to continue to count on the voluntary cooperation of 'losers' in future shared endeavours. This requires weighing the goods of short-term interest satisfaction and those of longer-term social amity. Basically, it will be rational for each party in an interaction to try to achieve as much interest satisfaction as is compatible with the maintenance of viable social relations.

Now, part of the evidence that parties will use in order to determine how far to push the promotion of their interests will be other parties' avowals of their tolerance levels. We need to know where and when our pursuit of our own interests will harm our relationship with others, and one way of acquiring this knowledge is simply to listen to what others say. The problem is that others' avowals will be determined by strategic as well as by epistemic considerations. To the extent that they too want to realize their interests, they have reason to overstate their susceptibility, to make us believe that they are less tolerant of loss than they may in fact be. Even if I am willing at the end of the day to accept a 30–70 split in some strategic interaction with you rather than returning to a state of nature in which my losses might be far greater, I have reason to make you think that I will accept nothing less than 40–60. Of course, I must in my self-presentation not overstep the point at which *you* might think that it is in your interest to return to the state of nature. So the calculations in such contexts will be complex. Both parties must balance the goods of civic amity and of individual preference satisfaction, and they must do so in a context where the information they receive from others is distorted by their own strategic purposes. Compromise arises when we all feel we have done as well as we can given our abiding desire to maintain workable relations with our fellow citizens, and given what we are able to make out about the dispositions of others to preserve civic amity in conditions of divergent interest.

How does all this relate to the question of the use to which identity arguments are put? My claim is that, regardless of the actual intentions of the agents that put them forward, claims formulated in terms of identity convey the impression that their proponents are reluctant to compromise. When I claim that my identity is at stake in a given debate, I indicate that I am not willing to accept *any* compromise what-soever or, at any rate, that my threshold of tolerance for the non-satisfaction of my interests is in fact very low. But if, as I claimed above, compromise is essential to democracy, in the sense that it is what participants in a democratic debate should strive to achieve, then it follows that identity arguments are dangerous for democ-racy. If democracy requires compromise, and identity arguments make that more difficult to achieve, democratic institutions should seek to minimize the occurrence of such arguments.

But what is an *identity* argument? I define an identity argument as a type of argu-ment that defends a position on a given political issue by invoking the consequences this position has for the identity of the individual or the group in question. Examples of arguments couched in terms of identity abound in modern political discourse. (Allow me to invoke local Canadian examples. I am sure that the reader will be able to supply examples of such arguments drawn from her own political context.) An ongoing debate in Montreal concerns the legitimacy of municipal mergers. The island of Montreal has until recently been divided among independent municipali-ties sharing urban space with the City of Montreal. When the provincial govern-ment decided to merge all of these municipalities into a single island-wide city, arguments from identity were legion. By removing the semi-autonomous status of municipalities and turning them into boroughs of one large city, the government had, or so it was claimed, done immeasurable harm to civic identities. Or again, debates among native and non-native fishermen as to who should and should not be subjected to fishing quotas are often pitched in terms of the centrality of fishing to local identities. Finally, debates about language laws in Quebec are invariably framed in terms of identity. Anglo-Quebeckers view the Quebec language charter as an affront to English–Quebec identity, whereas old-stock French-speaking Quebeckers view any attempt at moderating its strictures as an attack upon their identity.

Now, as I will suggest below, identity-based arguments can be framed in terms of values and interests without loss of meaning. As far as their locutionary content is concerned, identity arguments are just shorthand for arguments that could more fully be spelled out in terms of values and interests. My point here is to claim that the *effects* of pitching arguments at the level of identity are different from those that are given rise to by talk of values and interests.

Why do I feel entitled to claim that identity arguments make compromise less likely than arguments couched in terms of values and interests? Three aspects of identity arguments, in my opinion, make compromise more difficult to reach. First, the notion of identity is rhetorically and symbolically very close to those of integrity and of self-esteem. A just and decent society will try, as far as possible, to create social institutions and laws that are not perceived by citizens as demeaning.[7] Political institutions must ensure that the social conditions of self-respect are in place. An individual who perceives, rightly or wrongly, that she must compromise a dimension of her identity in order to accept this or that law might come to think that, in demanding this compromise, the society to which she belongs falls short of its obligations of justice and decency. This would not be true, it seems to me, if she were asked merely to sacrifice one of her preferences or only partially realize one of her values. She might decide, in virtue of the type of calculation we briefly mentioned above, that it is more important to insist on the value or preference, even at the risk of paying the price where others will be less willing to continue cooperating with her. But it seems to me she would be less inclined to see the demand of compromise at the level of value and interest as an attack on her integrity, assuming her society's capacity to provide the political and institutional conditions that support her self-esteem. We *hold* values and we *possess* interests, whereas that around which we construct our identity constitutes who we *are*. Attacks upon my values and interests will thus be perceived less as attacks upon who I am than will attacks upon my very *identity*.

This asymmetry explains, in my opinion, a second way in which identity arguments are particularly detrimental to democratic debate. It concerns what we might call the *monolithic* character of the concept of identity. We can appreciate that, in the context of democratic life, we might have to accept political outcomes that only partly conform to our interests. We view the satisfaction of values and interests as lying on a continuum, rather than being all-or-nothing. If I am a convinced environmentalist, I would prefer that the use of private cars be severely limited, but I will understand, in view of other preferences and values present, that I should be satisfied with more moderate measures (prohibiting driving in the city's centre at certain hours, the obligation to equip one's vehicle with certain anti-pollution devices, dissuasive taxes on fuel and so on) that will allow me to realize my views to a certain degree. Or, if I own property in a certain neighbourhood, I might prefer that the government completely refrain from building a detoxication centre nearby, but I would understand in spite of everything that I should be satisfied if its construction respects certain spatial limits. Briefly, our interests and values do not invoke an 'all-or-nothing' logic. Often we have to accept that some will only be partially realized, or that, in order to realize an interest we hold strongly, we must give another interest less consideration. In sum, the satisfaction of our interests and values admits of degrees.

Identity functions differently in deliberative contexts. In effect, simply in virtue of the symbolic force and rhetoric of the concept, and independently of any question of *content*, it is more difficult[8] to accept that compromise might be required where identity stakes are concerned. In this context, reaching a compromise is rapidly perceived as requiring that one compromise one's identity. Values and interests can be satisfied to greater and lesser degrees. The integrity that one's identity confers seems more of an all-or-nothing affair.

Finally, identity arguments, because of their vague conceptual contents, are not falsifiable. A claim according to which one of my interests cannot be well served by a piece of public policy can be put up for public discussion. Such a claim wears on its sleeve, as it were, the conditions of its own falsifiability. If someone can spin out a convincing story according to which the implementation of the policy in question would have consequences that I had not foreseen, and that might go some signifi- cant way toward satisfying my interest, then even a minimalist set of rules of delib- erative engagement will require that I withdraw my claim. For instance, to return to my environmentalist example, we can imagine an environmentalist participant in a democratic exchange thinking that the only way of keeping pollution within reason- able limits is to impose very strong restrictions on the use of automobiles. Someone else might attempt to convince her that the same objective could be attained with less coercive measures (for example free public transport or tax deductions for bus or metro passes). If it turns out that the latter claim is borne out, rationality requires that the environmentalist withdraw the initial claim.

Identity arguments do not allow for this type of empirical debate. Since they do not possess clear semantic reference, or rather, since they refer only opaquely to the values and interests that alone make them meaningful, it is difficult if not impossible to adduce empirical evidence in order to controvert a claim to the effect that a given item of public policy ought to be withdrawn because it exacts an intolerable toll upon one's identity. To the extent that democratic debates (like many other types of norma- tive debates) often involve resolving empirical questions (what measures will favour environmental protection? what economic policy will promote growth?), the non- falsifiable aspect of identity arguments is a problem for deliberative democracy.

The symbolic and rhetorical relation of the concept of identity with that of integ- rity and self-esteem, the 'monolithic' character of arguments expressed in terms of identity, as well as their non-falsifiable character, render identity arguments particu- larly problematic from the point of view of a democratic debate. The invocation of the identity card modifies the nature of the deliberation and increases the risks asso- ciated with disagreement. When I move from the argument form 'you should rec- ognize that my interest x justifies that this proportion y of our society's resources be allocated to me' or 'you should accept my way of resolving societal debate a because you should appreciate the superiority of my set of values b', or where the justification of my position depends on the degree in which the nature of the interest or value that I legitimately defend supports my political positions, to an argument in which 'you should accept my position because it is central to my identity', I transform the normative debate into a question of recognition. I demand that my interlocutor see things my way since they represent, for me, an identity stake, even if the arguments or the considerations that support my position only have a weak independent justification.

The use of identity arguments transforms the game in which participants in dem- ocratic exchange are involved in ways that are quite dangerous for democracy.

Participants who employ identity arguments communicate to their interlocutors that, for them, all compromise represents an unacceptable loss. It is one thing to have to accept that their interests are only partially satisfied, or that the values to which they adhere can only be partially realized. It is another to have to accept an attack on their identity, since this implies calling into question the integrity of the person who is being asked to accept a compromise. The use of identity arguments therefore raises the stakes. Those who make use of them are in essence telling their interlocutors that any gain that they might make in terms of their interests and values might be offset by losses in terms of social cohesion and trust. 'By making me compromise my integrity', the party advancing an identity claim seems to be saying, 'you will have to bear important costs as far as my willingness to continue to participate in common pursuits is concerned.'

In fact, the effect of identity arguments is to communicate that compromise is much more difficult and costly than it would be were it to occur in a context in which only values and interests are at stake. Compromise is a particularly valuable result in the setting of deliberative democracy, since consensus is almost unattainable, and mere balances of power are too costly from the point of view of social cohesion. If the arguments that I have put forward above are correct and compromise is the appropriate target to set for deliberative exchanges, then it follows that identity arguments are undesirable in democratic contexts.

This conclusion should not be conflated with the very different conclusion that agents in democratic exchanges are morally prohibited from using identity arguments. As I have attempted to show, it is often rational to use such arguments in democratic contexts. If I want to immunize a particular interest or value of mine against compromise or contestation, presenting them as aspects of my identity will make it less likely that other participants will choose to require of me that I compromise. And this type of strategy risks being particularly attractive in democratic debates that oppose participants who are asymmetrically situated in terms of power or control of economic and political resources. If I am in an inferior situation in terms of resources and influence in relation to the person with whom I deliberate, a simple way of enhancing my position consists in raising the stakes of our disagreement by invoking identity considerations. It is a low-cost strategy: I do not have to increase the social and economic resources that I control in order to be able to enjoy the strategic advantage that identity arguments afford. It may be perfectly rational for a participant to use these arguments in democratic debate. And, in asymmetrical contexts, a concern for 'levelling the playing field' can lead to the conclusion that, despite their harmful effects for deliberative democracy, it is desirable that weaker groups be able to take advantage of these arguments.

However, this strategic advantage can be neutralized by the escalation that the use of identity arguments is liable to cause. Such arguments can lead to other participants also expressing their claims in identity terms, which will have the effect of bringing democratic debate to a deadlock: where two identities battle, compromise is more difficult than when the confrontation only opposes interests and values. But that is simply another reason to want to avoid the use of identity arguments in democracy.

The Open Question Argument

I have defended two claims in the preceding sections of this chapter. First, I tried to give reasons for thinking that compromise rather than consensus or 'balance of power' is the appropriate regulative idea for deliberative democracy in a pluralist society. It is preferable that citizens in a democracy display character traits that dispose them towards compromise than it is that they be geared toward consensus. Second, I tried to show that the use of identity arguments represents a danger for democracy, since these arguments lend themselves less well to compromise than do arguments couched in terms of values, interests or preferences.

Let me now consider a final question. If it turns out that identity arguments are, in terms of content, reducible to arguments formulated in terms of values and interests, with the only difference residing at the 'perlocutionary' level – that is to say at the level of effects caused by one way rather than another of formulating arguments – there is reason to attempt to adopt measures to minimize the place occupied by these arguments in public debate. We would not be preventing any semantic *contents* from entering into the fray. We would merely be guarding against the harmful effects of certain (eliminable) ways of making claims. Prohibiting identity arguments, or at the very least creating institutions that reduce the incentives to couch arguments in identity terms, would be more problematic were parties in democratic debate thus prevented or inhibited from making certain kinds of substantive claims altogether.

My intention here is not to respond to this question in a definitive way. I will propose rather a way of reflecting on the question that seems useful. The idea is to adapt G.E. Moore's famous 'open question argument' to the concept of identity. The goal of this argument, as is well known, was to show that those who believe that 'good' could be reduced to a natural concept such as utility or pleasure were mistaken. According to Moore, it is always possible to describe an agent, event or thing as useful, pleasant and so on, without the question, 'yes, but is it good?' being resolved. The fact that this question remains to our ears open even after we have accepted the agent, event or thing as being useful or pleasant, shows that a sense of the concept of 'good' has not been fully captured, and that it cannot consequently be entirely reduced to 'natural' concepts, to do for example with utility.[9]

I propose that identity arguments be put to a variation of Moore's test. Can we imagine a given political position being important for the identity of an individual or a group without its serving the non-'identity' interests, values or preferences of that individual or group? Imagine, for example, that a majority of Quebecois is convinced that all their linguistic interests could be fully realized while eschewing the coercive and restrictive aspects of the present language Charter, and relying instead on subtler incentives. What would we make of the claim that the language Charter in its present form should nonetheless be kept in place, not because of its impact on creating the conditions for the survival of a French-speaking community in North America, but because of its irreducible place at the heart of the Quebecois identity?

I recognize that intuitions may diverge on this point, and I will not attempt to show that mine are the only valid ones. It is enough for present purposes to bring out the burden of proof taken on by those who claim that identity arguments can in certain circumstances have an irreducible semantic content. They must show that the values, preferences or interests at stake in deliberative democracy are not exhaustive of all that is at stake in political debate. They must show that some policies can promote or endanger identities irreducibly. This is a tall order, though I can think of no argument that would show definitively that it cannot be made good.

Conclusion

My argument has been stated at a fairly high level of abstraction. Still, the implications for the democratic debate in rifted societies such as Canada should be sufficiently clear. In effect, it appears to me that the debates between cultural and linguistic communities in Quebec and the deliberations between Quebecois and Canadians outside Quebec are too often stated in terms of identity and, thus, in ways which do not make it possible to question the necessity of wholly preserving different clauses in Quebec's language laws without the emergency button of *lèse-identité* being pushed. Regarding cultural and linguistic minorities in Quebec, beginning with the national anglophone minority, they also have the tendency to reject political projects of the francophone majority by invoking identity considerations. This has been particularly striking following recent debates on the fusion of municipalities on the island of Montreal.

The same phenomenon can be observed on the federal scene. The Quebecois separatist claims are rarely evaluated in terms of their impact on the interests and preferences of citizens in the rest of Canada: more often we see only a threat to the Canadian 'identity'.

Maybe the recourse to identity arguments is the sign of a fundamental distrust between the different communities as much in Quebec as in Canada. This suspicion renders us incapable of arriving at an honourable compromise regarding our interests, our values and our diverse preferences that is necessary in order to save the federation. And so we resort to identity language, which is much less favourable to compromise. Those who take to heart the health of democratic deliberation, whether on a Quebecois or Canadian scale, should consider challenging the omnipresence of identity arguments in our political discourse.

Notes

1   For an interesting attempt to analyse one of the most important uses, see David Copp, 'Social Unity and the Identities of Persons', *Journal of Political Philosophy*, vol. 10 (2002).

2   In his important work *How to Do Things with Words*, Austin distinguishes three types of acts which we can perform using language. Of course, we can express an idea, describe

an object, and so on. According to Austin's typology, we can perform locutionary speech acts, whose nature is determined by the semantic content of the statement. But we can also do things with words: in certain specific contexts words constitute actions. For example, a judge can marry two people by pronouncing certain words in an appropriate judicial context. This, for Austin, is an illocutionary speech act. As well, a speech act can cause certain effects. For example, I can persuade someone with my arguments. Austin calls these speech acts perlocutionary. See J.L. Austin, *How to Do Things With Words*, Oxford: Oxford University Press, 1961.

3   See 'Démocratie et délibération', *Archives de philosophie*, vol. 63 (2000), and 'Saving Democracy from Deliberation', in R. Beiner and W. Norman (eds), *Canadian Political Philosophy*, Oxford: Oxford University Press, 2000.

4   The notion of compromise is particularly well developed by Martin Benjamin in *Splitting the Difference*, Lawrence: University Press of Kansas, 1990.

5   I treat the attitude disposed towards compromise in more detail in my essay, 'Le "raisonnable"', in A. Duhamel, L. Tremblay and D. Weinstock (eds), *La Démocratie délibérative: philosophie et droit*, Montreal: Les Éditions Thémis, 2001.

6   See on this point the important essays by Isaiah Berlin, especially those collected in *Four Essays on Liberty*, Oxford: Oxford University Press, 1969.

7   John Rawls believes that self-esteem is the most important social good, and elaborates the institutional conditions in section 67 of *A Theory of Justice*. Avishai Margalit has recently written an important work about the conditions that should be fulfilled in order that a society can qualify as a 'decent' society. He insists notably on the importance of non-humiliation. See *The Decent Society*, Cambridge, MA: Harvard University Press, 1996.

8   Difficult, but in fact not impossible. My argument does not require the absurdly strong claim that it is somehow conceptually inconceivable to compromise one's identity. It simply requires that the probability of compromise be reduced substantially by the use of identity arguments. I thank Igor Primoratz for having warned me away from the more radical reading of the central claim of this chapter.

9   This argument is developed by Moore in *Principia Ethica* (revised and augmented edition), Cambridge: Cambridge University Press, 1993.

Chapter 2

Identity Claims and Identity Politics: A Limited Defence

Margaret Moore

This chapter is concerned with the legitimacy of identity claims, by which I mean claims that take the form that 'such-and-such should not be allowed because it violates my religious or ethnic or national identity', or that 'such-and-such is required as an expression of respect for my identity'. It is not concerned with the role that such claims play in mobilizing the group. It is concerned with the issue of legitimacy of this sort of claim when it is directed to the state. It is concerned with legitimacy, both in the general sense of whether identity claims can legitimately enter political discourse (and I will argue here that they do embody a legitimate political demand) and in the more specific sense of how much can be legitimately claimed (from the state) in the name of a particular identity.

The strategy of the chapter is to take seriously the charges that identity claims are subjective, non-verifiable and greatly inflate the kinds of claims that one can make under the category of 'my identity'. These arguments have been discussed in terms of two specific criticisms of identity politics, which have been advanced principally by Jeremy Waldron and Brian Barry. The first criticism is termed by Waldron the 'incompossibility problem': the problem that respecting different people's identities in the same state may not be compossible (possible together) because respecting A's identity requires a policy or proposal that is inconsistent with respecting B's identity.[1] Further, he argues that using the language of identity renders the claims non-negotiable in a way that is detrimental to the give-and-take of democratic politics. Waldron suggests that liberals, socialists, egalitarians and others are right to be concerned about the elasticity of the concept, which he identifies as related to its subjective character, and worry about whether and how we can organize a framework of laws and rights to live under which respects everyone's identity. A second, related, criticism is advanced by Brian Barry in his book *Culture and Equality*. The principal thrust of Barry's book is that the politicization of group identities[2] is destructive of liberal egalitarian policies and polities. This argument, which takes a mainly instrumental form, depends on viewing identity arguments as establishing nothing. This is explicit in Barry: he argues that the fact that something is your identity does not constitute a justification for it. It is an anthropological observation. Indeed, Barry points out that, if somebody says, 'we've been doing this a long time', the right response might well be, 'then it's high time you stopped doing it.'[3]

To address these concerns, this chapter attempts to clarify what is meant by identity, and especially to distinguish personal identities from collective identities, which tend to be non-voluntary, and constitute the background against which personal identity formation occurs. This distinction enables us to see more clearly how some of the charges, especially those concerning the subjective nature of identity claims, can be addressed, and to suggest the limits of the concept's inflationary tendencies. The chapter does not address directly the argument that the language of identity is less open to compromise than that of interest or preference, although it is implicit in the discussion of the first claim that this criticism is greatly exaggerated, and that identity claims typically contain within them an implicit limitation.

What is Identity?

The social psychological literature on identity tends to emphasize how identity formation is important to individual self-esteem and self-respect, and to point to three different functions that identity performs for the person:[4] membership, differentiation and a subjective or inner identification. Membership indicates that identity is seen by others and the identity can be demonstrated to others. There is an objective (to the person) dimension of the identity. In the case of the ascriptive collective forms of identity that are the object of this chapter, the identity group is a feature of human interaction in the sense that people situate others according to these ascriptive features of their identities, and that identities cannot simply be chosen by anyone (randomly). For example, I may not *identify* with other women, but it would be hard not to have a female identity, in all three dimensions, if everyone who looked at me identified me as female. Conversely, I may wish I were black or Asian, but, if everyone who looks at me thinks I am white, then it is hard to sustain, because identities have to be ratified by others. The mutual identification component of an identity means that identities cannot be so multiple or so fluid that they are like changing hats. There may be some element of choice for some people concerning which identities, even of an ascriptive kind, to adopt, but there are some identities that are simply not open to one. A mixed race person may have some choice about identities, or which identity to emphasize at different times, and of course they have some choice about the role that that identity might play in their life. A Jewish person cannot (easily) become Buddhist, but they can certainly make decisions about the role their Jewishness may play in their life, from the most minimal to being a very strongly observant Jew.

The second, strongly related, dimension of identity is differentiation. The term 'differentiation' refers to the fact that a crucial feature of identities and identity groups is the creation of an Other. Identities form in contrast to others (other people, other groups or ideas or practices). There is often some kind of 'marker' around which the identity revolves, and which indicates how the identity can be demonstrated to others.

Finally, identity exists as a subjective or internalized perspective of what makes one's life intelligible and meaningful. There is an irreducibly subjective element to identity claims which generally involves a subjective orientation around the identity, a sense that it is the basis on which one makes choices, constructs preferences, and so on.

The Normative Force of (Collective) Identities

With these elements in place, it is now possible to clarify the normative force of identity claims and the type of identity that is typically at issue. There are three reasons why we might think that identity claims should be treated seriously. We can call these (1) the integrity reason, (2) the ethical commitment reason and (3) the ascriptive reason.

When someone claims that something is central to her/his identity, it suggests an integral relationship to the self. One's identity is linked, causally, with one's sense of self, or one's integrity as a person. It is the basis on which one's other (non-identity) interests, values and preferences are based. This suggests that we should think very carefully about enforcing rules and policies that violate people's identity, or require people to act contrary to what they regard as central to their sense of self. At the very least, the state should have very good reasons for avoiding policies that force people to act in ways that they experience as a violation of their very identity.

Second, and following from the integrity notion, one's identity is strongly linked with the moral core of the person. It is generally accepted that there is a strong relationship between one's sense of self and one's essential ethical commitments. It is often thought to be unreasonable for the state to demand that the person conform to rules and policies that are directly counter to his/her strongest moral beliefs, or, at least, that it should not do so for trivial or even utilitarian reasons. The liberal state's toleration of conscientious objection is instructive here. The idea here is that the state should accept reasons of conscience as good reasons for exempting the person from active participation in violent warfare. There is a difficulty for the state in distinguishing between conscientious objectors and nonconscientious objectors, and one response to this difficulty is to exempt only documented members of a pacifist religious group from universal conscription. This is partly because it helps to operationalize the real distinction – between conscientious and nonconscientious objectors, justified and unjustified cases – but also because, historically, there was a close link between religious belief and conscience. Nevertheless, the category of conscientious objector sometimes extends to non-religious people who make similar claims of conscience.[5]

Finally, the ascriptive aspect of many identities is relevant to requirements of the state that bear on people's identities. There are at least two bases for describing identities as nonvoluntary: one is whether they are hard-wired or biologically based; the second is whether they are ratified by others, regardless of whether or not the person identifies with them. One argument raised by gay men and women about the unequal treatment that they experience at the hands of the state is that their identities are biologically based; these are not *mere* preferences, but hard wired, as it were. Unequal treatment of different sexual orientations is therefore profoundly unfair. Others focus on the idea that identities have to be ratified by others: there is a limit to the identities that are genuinely available to one, and some identities are difficult to escape. This is not simply the point that the identities that one comes to have are partly the product of involuntary socialization and education by others (I think all identities may be described in this way)[6] but, in the much deeper sense, that identities depend, to a large extent, on how others see one and identify one.

Both types of non-voluntariness are morally relevant since there is a responsibility on the part of the state not to impose onerous burdens on the bearers of particular (unchosen) identities. The ascriptive character of an identity shifts the burden of responsibility from the person whose identity it is to the social context in which the person bearing the identity finds herself, and the social norms and rules that govern the society.

These three considerations – the integrity, moral commitment and ascriptive reasons – do not bear on all identities, and are not perfectly aligned. Some religious identities may be reasonably voluntary, especially in the case of a convert, but tend to rank quite high on the dimension of importance to the person and relationship to the core ethical commitments of the self. A racial or gender identity may be more ascriptive, but may not be as closely bound up with the normative commitments of the self. On the other hand, because they are rooted in some biological facts about the person, they may be experienced by the person as central to his or her sense of self, as closely bound up with his or her integrity. Although these considerations do not correspond neatly to each other, they are the kinds of reasons we have for thinking that identity-related claims should be taken seriously, and so help explain the normative force of particular identity claims.

This brings us to the point where it is possible to address Waldron's criticism that identity claims are problematic because not all identities can be accommodated: respecting A's identity may not be compossible with respecting B's identity. To address this concern, it is necessary to distinguish between two types of identities, which I call, somewhat misleadingly, personal identities and collective identities.[7] Personal identities tend to take the form of roles or types that the person identifies with, which represent certain values or attributes, and help orient the person to the world. There are many examples of personal identities – jocks, computer geeks, *Star Trek* fans – and freely associating individuals may organize groups around these personal identities. Personal identities of this kind tend to occur against the background of less voluntary forms of identity, around the axes of race, gender, sexual orientation, culture, religion, ethnicity and national communities, which are referred to in this chapter as 'collective identities'. Some form of the personal identity–collective identity distinction is implicit in most identity politics literature, which tends to focus on identities of the race/gender/sexual orientation type. It is implicit also in liberal theory, which tends to assume that personal identity claims are appropriately handled by liberal rights and rules of justice. Towards the end of this section, I will explain how the distinction between personal and collective identities bears on the three reasons offered above for treating identity claims seriously.

One response to those, like Waldron, who claim that the category of 'identity' is unhelpfully capacious, that anything could be demanded under the rubric of 'my identity', is to point out that, as a matter of fact, personal identity claims, which are indeed almost infinitely variable, are *not* the subject of identity politics demands. Identity politics activists have been, and are, almost exclusively concerned with more ascriptive and sociologically relevant identities, such as race/gender/ethnicity, which are confined to quite predictable categories of people. It is misleadingly alarmist to prohibit identity claims on the ground that identities are completely subjective and potentially infinite, when, in fact, the types of identities that pose a challenge to the liberal democratic state are collective identities, of the race/gender/sexual orientation type, which are quite predictable and not infinitely variable.

Liberalism, too, tends to operate with a personal identity/collective identity distinction, especially the type of liberalism that evinces sympathy for the claims of marginalized groups or accommodation of identities. Liberals have often stressed the centrality of the notions of authenticity and autonomy to liberalism[8] and the capacity of liberal theory to accommodate diversity.[9] Some liberals have accepted the idea that collective identities require special accommodations,[10] but personal identities are thought to require only a regime of universal rights and, pre-eminently, rights to freedom of expression, freedom of religion and freedom of association. These rights give the person a sphere of free action, attached, as it were, to the person, in which he or she is free to be an autonomous self-chooser, to create the kind of life, the type of personal identity, that he or she is comfortable with. According to liberal theory, it was not within the purview of the state to make judgments about the moral merits of people's (personal) identities, although they can prevent people from doing things (actions) that harm others.

There is, however, an important normative question here, which is not addressed merely by noting that personal identities do not tend to make demands on the state. This is the question whether personal identities could make a legitimate demand on the state for institutional recognition or accommodation beyond that of simple toleration in a political context of human rights, fair social norms and freedom of association. To put the matter another way: why are the collective identities that are typically the subject of identity politics claims not treated by the same norms, rules and principles that govern personal identity issues? Is there a strong normative basis for the distinction between personal identities and collective identities?

The answer to this series of questions lies in the general association of collective identities with the three reasons advanced earlier for thinking that the coercive apparatus of the state (to use a Marxian term) should tread lightly on people's identities. Collective identities are more likely than personal identities to be integral to the person, central to his/her moral commitments and at least partially ascriptive.

The ascriptive character of these identities is clear in the case of race, gender and ethnicity, but even language, religion and nationality – while potentially open to all persons, and the object of individual choice – tend to have quite high exit and entry costs. People can acquire facility in another language and become comfortable with the symbols and nuances of another community, but it is difficult, at least in the sense that it requires a significant investment of time. Exit is also fraught with difficulties: for most people, most of the time, it is difficult to leave family, home and friends. This suggests that even those collective identities that are not ascriptive are also not accurately described as the objects of free choice, as something that one can easily or freely adopt.

Moreover, because the sources of collective identities are less voluntary (rooted in biology or hard-wired orientation or difficult to change matters of fact of the person), they are very closely associated with personal integrity. The fact that they are often more biologically based, are not easy to renounce, means that the person associates disrespect for her racial, gender, ethnic, sexual orientation identity as disrespect for *her.* This is also because the person typically identifies with her physical being, as something that existed in the past, is in the present and extends into the future, and is the basis on which one's particular personal identity formation occurs.

There is a degree of generalization in the foregoing and a degree of fluidity between personal and collective identities that this distinction is at risk of not capturing. This is because the distinction between personal and collective identities does not perfectly track the three reasons why we might think that identities are important to the person. They are more accurately seen as proxies for the type of identities for which the three moral reasons for treating identity claims seriously are likely to be true.

Admittedly, this method of proceeding is both overinclusive and underinclusive. It grants exemptions to people on the basis of a religion, even though some of the beneficiaries may not care much about their religion, rarely go into church, or otherwise practise it. And it may fail to grant exemptions to people who care a lot about something, if their identities are classified as merely personal identities.

The problem of overinclusiveness is not a serious problem, since, as I will go on to argue, most identity claims take the form of granting an exemption to someone on the basis of an identity-related claim. Exemptions, by their very nature, do not require the person to take them up; if the person cares little for his or her religion they may not need the exemption in the first place. There may be an exemption from motorcycle helmet laws for Sikhs, to permit them to wear a turban, but one would only need the exemption if one actually did wear a turban. A non-practising Sikh, who does not conform to Sikh dress codes, would have no need of the exemption.

In his book *Culture and Equality*, Barry uses the example of someone who does not want to wear a helmet because he or she loves to ride with the wind in his or her hair. This is difficult to conceptualize as an identity, even of a personal kind, rather than a strongly held preference. But the general point that he makes is an important one: we can imagine cases where there is a rule or exemption that grants exemptions to people who fall into the appropriate collective identity category, but denies it to people with strong personal identities. Here the problem is that of underinclusiveness. I agree that this is a problem, but I think it is outweighed by the greater moral hazard of empowering the state to investigate the actual beliefs and strength of belief that people have and how it interacts in one's life; or the opposite moral problem of ignoring and riding roughshod over people's legitimate identity-related claims.

The distinction between personal and collective identities and the way that they interact with the rules of the state parallels the general position taken with conscientious objection. In the case of conscientious objection, the state admits exemptions for a whole category of people, but expects people who fall outside the category to conform to the rules and policies of the state.

Similar to conscientious objection, there are good reasons for adopting a proxy model rather than try to determine more exactly whether the three conditions hold. One consideration is the difficulty of falsifying a claim that takes the form that one should be exempted from a general rule because one bears a particular identity. The problem is overcome if we are dealing with collective identities. If Jews are exempt from the Sunday closing rule, or if non-Christians are permitted to take different holidays without penalty from work, then all that should be required is that the person demonstrate that they are a Jew or Muslim or some other (non-Christian) religion. It is not within the purview of the state to investigate how strong or observant a Jew or Muslim we have here. If we are dealing with personal identities, the case is much more problematic. It is hard to know what objective considerations could bear on the person's claim that X is central to his or her identity, and that this identity is *really* important to the person. This point bears on the possibility of falsifying or verifying claims of identity of the personal kind. Even if that were not a problem, there might be reasons connected to the impartiality and generality of state laws and regulations for permitting the state to admit people on a case-by-case basis only if the criterion of admission is itself subject to generalizable rules.

This is not simply a convenience argument. The claim here is that there might be good moral reasons for not wanting the state to deviate too far from a general position of impartiality with respect to its citizens. There may also be good reasons why we would not want the state, or agents of the state, to ask intrusive questions about the relation of one's identity to one's commitments and lifestyle. It might be problematic to adopt an institutional rule that legitimates the state in investigating the strength of people's commitments and feelings, their inner life and experience, and which empowers state officials to grant exemptions to some people and not others on the basis of these investigations.

The operative distinction here (between personal and collective identities) is fluid in the sense that it does not preclude the possibility that an identity could, at one time, be classified as a personal identity, but then be reconceptualized, on the basis of new information, say, as a collective identity. Indeed, this is precisely what has happened in the case of crossdressers. This used to be conceived as a mere personal identity, or even possibly a preference for a particular type of dress, but subsequently became reconceptualized, in part through the mobilization of crossdressers or other transgendered individuals, as a collective identity. Interestingly, the central argument for admitting crossdressers as a legitimate collective identity was that it is relevantly similar to other legitimate collective identities, particularly sexual orientation identities. The idea here is that this is not a mere preference but is biologically based or at least 'hard-wired' in the same way that sexual orientation is, and so should be the object of a more flexible treatment by the state. Of course, it is not sufficient to make this claim; it has to be accepted by many people in the population.

This fluidity does not challenge the distinction between collective and personal identities; all that is involved here is questioning the inclusion of identity X within a particular category, which is far from collapsing the distinction altogether or claiming that all identities are fair play for identity politics types of claims. Moreover, the basis of the argument for inclusion tends to reinforce the point made earlier, that collective claims on behalf of particular identities have legitimacy precisely because they tend to track (at least one of) the three moral reasons for treating identity seriously: integrity, moral commitment and ascriptiveness.

What Can be Claimed in the Name of a Particular Identity?

Even if, as I have argued, we confine ourselves to collective forms of identity (not personal identities) and to cases where there is general agreement that something represents a case of an admissible type of collective identity[11] – gender, sexual orientation, religious, cultural, ethnic, linguistic and national – there may still be a strong possibility that the identity claims will conflict, and that the significance of the claim will be enhanced by its attachment to the person's very identity. If so, Waldron's concerns about incompossibility will be realized: it will not be possible to set up a constitutional or legal regime that respects everyone's identity, since these identities give conflicting answers for the same set of questions.

In order to address this potentially serious concern, we must be clear how much can be legitimately claimed of others as required in terms of respect for one's identity. In his discussion of the incompossibility problem, Waldron suggests that incompossibility is a very real concern because of the proliferation of identity claims. 'The viability of the liberal enterprise,' he writes, 'depends on claims of this sort being fairly limited.'[12] He suggests that, under standard liberal theory, there are only a small number of interests that require the special non-negotiable treatment that is usually associated with rights.[13] This suggests that incompossibility arises because of the potential for endless proliferation of identity claims.

However, Waldron leaves entirely unexamined the type of things that can be legitimately claimed of others in the name of 'respect for my identity'. In this context, it is useful to explore the limits of an identity claim. One way to approach this is to think of the difference between saying, for example, 'X is required by my religion' and saying 'X is required by my religious identity'. The former refers to the reasons for the belief. It explains the person's motivation, and may offer a justificatory reason for his/her actions, but one which, in the context of religious diversity, is not helpful to resolving disagreements about the policies or practices of the society. The reference to religious identity is a bit different. It appeals to a generalizable interest, which everyone can understand, in having an identity of a certain kind, in having deep moral commitments and a sense of self. The appeal to this sort of interest, rather than the values implicit in the identity itself, makes sense especially in the context of diversity. It is not an argument that one would make when appealing to someone within one's identity group, an interlocutor who already accepts one's religion or the importance of one's cultural practices. But it is an argument that one would make to outsiders, who may not be convinced by the truth of the religion or the superiority of the practice, but can at least understand that it is important to you.

Both Waldron and Barry seem to think that the reference to identity is falsely self-conscious, and that it does not constitute an argument in its own right. Barry argues that the appeal to culture or identity establishes nothing. 'Some cultures [and some identities] are admirable, others are vile. Reasons for doing things that can be advanced within the former will tend to be good and reasons that can be advanced within the latter will tend to be bad. But in neither case is something's being part of the culture itself [or central to one's identity] a reason for doing anything.'[14] Waldron also introduces the charge of inauthenticity in his argument that identity claims do not represent a strong argument for or against something. He writes that identity claims 'represent quite inauthentic ways of engaging and identifying with a culture. They not only exaggerate but distort the way in which a person relates to the culture which is part of his identity. The key here is the air of self-consciousness that pervades the cultural engagements and self-presentations associated with identity politics'.[15] He then goes on to explain that the authentic relationship of the person to the culture is an unselfconscious acceptance of the mores or norms or practices of one's community: 'what one does in straightforward cultural engagement is simply speak or marry or dance or worship. In doing so, one does not say anything about the distinctive features of, say, the Irish heritage, or the peculiarities of the Maori wedding feast'.[16] And from this he goes on to argue that it is 'very odd to regard the fact that this is [our] norm – this is what we Irishmen or we French or we Maori do – as part of the reason, if not the central reason, for having the norm and for sustaining and following it'.[17] For both Barry and Waldron, a legitimate argument is in terms of the practices and norms themselves. These should be debated on their own terms and not in terms of their role in constituting someone's identity.

This attempt to rule out identity claims misunderstands what is involved in the claim to having an identity and respecting an identity. While it is true that there is a certain selfconsciousness surrounding an identity claim, this is a natural development in the context of cultural and identity diversity. The recognition that there were different people, with different cultural practices, and different religions, is far from recent: the Romans were acutely aware of the presence of Jew, Christian and pagan, Arab, Greek and barbarian, and a multitude of languages and religions within the boundaries of the Empire, and of barbarians and rival political orders beyond the Roman *limes*.[18] In any sort of multicultural context, the unselfconscious relationship of the person to the culture that Waldron celebrates is not possible. Moreover, when different kinds of people are seeking to live together amicably, it makes eminent sense not to try to convince people of the superiority of your ways over theirs but simply that a particular way of life, or a certain collective group identification, is central to your identity and as such important to you.

The argument in terms of respect for one's identity contains within it an implicit recognition that other people also have identities, which are important to them. The way the argument is formulated suggests that I could not argue for the imposition of *shariah*, for example, as a requirement of respect for my religious identity. It might be a requirement of my religion, properly understood. But an argument in terms of my religious identity refers to the importance of having an identity, and in so far as that it is a generalizable interest, it recognizes that other people, too, have identities, possibly of different kinds, and it would be wrong to require things of them that would violate their deeply held commitments and identities. For this reason, I doubt that people do argue for the imposition of *shariah* on the basis of respect for their identity. They argue for it in terms of the actual reasons for imposing it, namely, that it is required by God.[19]

Identity claims suggest a strong causal connection between the practice and the person whose identity it is. This is typically established by showing a link between what is required of the person whose identity it is, what is permitted by the state and what is enjoined by one's culture, religion, sexual orientation, gender and so on. The interaction of these elements is important to an assessment of the legitimacy of an identity claim. It is one thing to require that the member of an identity group behave, act, abstain, forbear or conform in specified ways to state-directed norms and policies and quite another for the state to enact policies or permit behaviour which directly affects other people, but not the identity group member herself, even if she disagrees with them or finds them deeply offensive. The former constitutes a violation of her identity; the latter are policies with which she deeply disagrees. To put this in terms of a concrete example, let us imagine a person with a religious identity of a certain kind, in which modest dress is enjoined by her religion, and a state that enforces a dress code that is deeply counter to her religion. It would be legitimate for her to claim that the state's requirements constituted a violation of her identity. But it would not be legitimate to claim that respect for her identity required that everyone in the society, or every woman, must dress modestly (wear a veil or *burka*). It is not a violation of 'your identity' if other people in society act in ways not enjoined by your religion, but it would be a violation of your identity if the state required that you act in ways not enjoined by your religion, and indeed, deeply counter to your religion. The appeal to one's identity has an irreducibly subjective element, and so is principally about what is required of the person having the identity, and not what is required of people in the society at large. An argument justifying a state-wide policy or directive requires that we appeal to reasons of the kind that Barry and Waldron thought ought to be appealed to – in terms of the superiority of one kind of practice over another.

This means that identity claims are principally concerned with arguing for *toleration* of certain practices, groups and so on. This is not an argument that you would make if you wanted others to adopt your identity or your cultural practices, but it is a valid argument in the face of discriminatory or assimilative policies that threaten your group. It is, importantly, an argument for toleration, not in the traditional liberal sense as grounded in a norm of individual autonomy (because obviously grounded in a claim about identity), but a practice of toleration in Walzer's sense of political toleration. In his book *On Toleration*, he defines it this way: 'My subject is toleration – or, perhaps, better, the peaceful coexistence of groups of people with different histories, cultures and identities, which is what toleration makes possible.'[20] Within that rubric, he identifies five 'regimes of toleration': multinational

empires, international society, consociation, nation-states and immigrant societies.[21] Although Walzer's definition is not helpful in identifying in what precisely
toleration consists, it is clear that the principle of toleration requires accommodation *on both sides*. It requires a preparedness to negotiate relationships, and especially to allow for forms of mutuality and accommodation, especially as regards the
imposition of power. It requires, on the part of the identity group, that it refrain
from trying to impose its own preferred option, its own way of life, on others (which
I have argued is implicit in an identity claim) and requires that the majority group,
the political authority, refrain from imposing a universal regime in the face of rival
identities and identity groups.

Of course, one striking difference between the classical regimes of religious toleration and the current claims for various forms of toleration by identity groups is
that, in the latter kind of case, toleration cannot simply be effected by the privatiza-
tion of the identity. In many cases the state has to make some decision: on which
language should be spoken in the schools, courts, bureaucracy, on what is taught in
school, on the central symbols of the state, on the territorial division of power, and
so on. Toleration can no longer be simply interpreted as 'no state interference', but
requires other mechanisms for allowing for mutual coexistence.

Although a more extensive argument is required here, involving a contextual
analysis of the different kinds of groups and the different kinds of claims that are
made, it is worth noting that many of the legal cases involving identity groups are
claims for toleration, where toleration takes the form of an exemption from a state-
wide rule or practice. Consider the 'exemption from dress codes' argument deployed
by Sikhs against motorcycle helmet laws, uniform requirements for the Royal
Canadian Mounted Police, and the school uniform case in Britain;[22] by Muslims in
the headscarves affair in France; and the Jewish demand to wear a yarmulke in the
US military. In each of these cases, the argument advanced by the identity group is
primarily an argument for toleration of a particular religiously associated form of
dress. Other kinds of cases – the exemption for *halel* and *kosher* meat from animal
cruelty laws in Europe – also involve exemptions from state-wide law to permit or
allow for certain religiously oriented practices. In each of these cases, the state-
wide law created burdens for the minority. Further, in none of these cases was
incompossibility a potential problem: these demands did not require that the rule be
scrapped in favour of a new (state-wide) rule, as a condition of *my* identity, but
merely that the rule not apply to me, that the practice or dress or ritual be tolerated
by the majority society.

The argument by gay and lesbian activist groups for a change in the definition of
the family in law to include gay and lesbian marriages might seem, at least superfi-
cially, to raise issues of incompossibility, in so far as these identity claims require a
change in the marriage law and this might conflict with a more conservative religious person's identity claim, which links their religious identity to the view that
marriage is a union of a man and a woman. In fact, however, the gay and lesbian
claim, like the multicultural claims examined above, is a claim for toleration of
their practice: not toleration in the old seventeenth- and eighteenth-century sense
that implied that one has to put up with objectionable behaviour, but toleration in

the more modern sense of being fully included, and consistent with the norm of equality.

Moreover, it is wrong to interpret the conservative religious person as making a claim about identity. The conservative Christian cannot legitimately claim that her very identity requires a heterosexist interpretation of the family: rather, such a view of the family is an important element of her religious belief. Her basic argument here is that gay marriage or, indeed, a gay way of life, is wrong. The gay person, by contrast, *is* making an identity claim, which, like the others, is centrally about toleration of his/her community's practices: he/she is accepting that there are different versions of the family and asking only that his/her type of family also be included *as a family*.

Of course, even if we accept that identity claims are primarily claims to toleration and incompossibility is not an issue, that is not the end of the matter. There may be important counterarguments or countergoods, which militate against granting the claim to toleration. The discussion thus far has not broached the thorny issue of ascertaining the limits of toleration, or where the line should be drawn, or what kind of tradeoffs, between different kinds of goods, might be involved in accepting a particular claim.[23] Consider, for example, the claims of small partial citizenship groups, such as the Hutterites or the Amish. There, the basic claim is for toleration in the sense of a measure of autonomy or freedom from state-wide rules so that they can practise their own way of life. There is no issue of incompossibility, because they are not trying to impose the Amish or Hutterite way of life on the political community as a whole. Nevertheless, in this case, in making the decision about the limits of toleration, the state must consider the tradeoff between the community member's identity-related interests and ensuring that other nonidentity-related interests of the members are met. This might involve ensuring that people within these identity groups have a valid right of exit and, relatedly, that children, who have an interest in leading a valuable life and cultivating their capacities, are not oppressed, abused or disadvantaged by their membership in the group. Indeed, debate on the issues raised by partial citizenship groups such as the Amish and the Hutterites has proceeded precisely in these terms.[24]

Conclusion

This chapter has argued that identity claims do represent a legitimate form of political discourse, and has specified the type of identity claim that poses a challenge to liberal–democratic theory. In making this argument, this chapter has addressed Waldron's and Barry's concerns that identity claims (a) do not represent an *argument* and (b) are problematic because they are subjective, potentially limitless, and raise the problem of incompossibility, which is a constraint on the type of claim that should be admissible.

The chapter also identified some general considerations in assessing the limits of identity claims, focusing on the generalizable nature of the interest in identity, and the relationship between the person, the identity group and the state. These two considerations together point to the view that identity claims are primarily claims for which toleration is a possibility, and do not admit of the kind of zero-sum relation that critics argue is a central feature of identity politics.[25]

Notes

1 Jeremy Waldron, 'Cultural Identity and Civic Responsibility', in Will Kymlicka and Wayne Norman (eds), *Citizenship in Diverse Societies*, Oxford: Oxford University Press, 2000.

2 Brian Barry, *Culture and Equality: An Egalitarian Critique of Multiculturalism*, Cambridge, MA: Harvard University Press, 2001, p.5. His description of identities is narrower than this formulation suggests. He objects to the politicization of identities, where the basis of the common identity is culture (thereby excluding cases of common identity that arise from a common relation to the labour market).

3 Barry, *Culture and Equality*, ch.7.

4 The outline of the three dimensions of identity formation is drawn from Ingrid Creppels, *Toleration and Identity: Foundations in Early Modern Thought*, New York and London: Routledge, 2003, pp.8–9. However, Creppels's treatment is not idiosyncratic: the social psychological literature on identity identifies the same elements. See Henri Tajfel, *Human Groups and Social Categories*, Cambridge: Cambridge University Press, 1981, p.256.

5 In the past, religious reasons and conscience were inextricably linked, but increasingly there is an acceptance of conscientious objections based on deep ethical principles, which are not themselves rooted in a religious belief. See Amy Gutmann, *Identity in Democracy*, Princeton, NJ: Princeton University Press, 2003, pp.151–211, where she argues for this extension.

6 See here the first chapter of G.A. Cohen, *If You're an Egalitarian, How Come You're so Rich?* Cambridge, MA: Harvard University Press, 2000, where he speculates that his political views are directly related to his upbringing by Marxist Jewish parents in Montreal.

7 The distinction between personal and collective identity is implicit in Jonathan Quong, 'Are Identity Claims Bad for Deliberative Democracy?', *Contemporary Political Theory*, vol.1 (2002). Some form of this distinction is implicit in his discussion of a *Star Trek* fan as a type of identity.

8 See Nancy Rosenblum, *Liberalism and the Moral Life*, Cambridge, MA: Harvard University Press, 1989.

9 See Allen Buchanan, 'The Making and Unmaking of Boundaries: What Liberalism Has to Say', in Allen Buchanan and Margaret Moore (eds), *States, Nations and Borders: The Ethics of Making Boundaries*, New York: Cambridge University Press, 2003, p.231.

10 Will Kymlicka, *Multicultural Citizenship: A Liberal Theory of Minority Rights*, Oxford: Oxford Univeristy Press, 1995; Jeff Spinner-Halev, *Surviving Diversity: Religion and Democratic Citizenship*, Baltimore, MD: Johns Hopkins University Press, 2000; Yael Tamir, *Liberal Nationalism*, Princeton, NJ: Princeton University Press, 1993; Charles Taylor, 'The Politics of Recognition', in Charles Taylor and Amy Gutmann (eds), *Multiculturalism and the Politics of Recognition*, Princeton, NJ: Princeton University Press, 1992.

11 Of course, within the accepted categories of religious or ethnic or sexual orientation identities there may be grey areas about what counts as an identity of the relevant type. This grey area is exploited in Brian Barry's discussion of a legal case involving Arthur Pendragon, who was caught in possession of a knife, but claimed an exemption, usually applied only to Sikhs carrying the *kirpan*. He argued that he was carrying the knife for 'religious reasons', because he was a twentieth-century incarnation of Arthur, and an official swordbearer for the Secular Order of Druids. This story is related briefly in Barry, *Culture and Equality*, pp.51–2, and could be interpreted in very different ways. The reader is left unsure whether the accused is a purely rational, self-interested and cynical actor, making use of the exemption to escape the force of the law. If so, we would not want the law to be exploited in this way. On the other hand, he could be crazy, especially in his claim to be a reincarnation of Arthur. If so, that might be a mitigating factor for his behaviour, but the law should not accept his own belief that he is Arthur-incarnate. Or it could be that he actually is a Druid, but, if so, we would expect that this could be verified in ways other than by his own claim, by attendance at pagan rituals, by knowledge of its central claims and so on. This grey area about what constitutes a religious belief or a religion is not evidence of a problem with identity politics or the inherent subjectivity of the identity claim. It arises too with respect to the liberal solution to the Hundred Years' War, which puts religious communities and religious belief on a different footing than other ethical communities or types of identities. It is therefore important to be clear about what actually constitutes a religion.

12 Waldron, 'Cultural Identity and Civic Responsibility', p.159.

13 Ibid.

14 Barry, *Culture and Equality*, p.258. I have included reference to identity, rather than simply culture, in this reference, because Barry earlier made it clear that politicized identities, where the basis of the identity was culture, were the main target of his critique.

15 Waldron, 'Cultural Identity and Civic Responsibility', p.168.

16 Ibid., p.169.

17 Ibid.

18 For a good discussion of this, see Richard Tuck, 'The Making and Unmaking of Boundaries from the Natural Law Perspective', in Allen Buchanan and Margaret Moore (eds), *States, Nations, and Borders*, pp.143–4.

19 This point is also made by Quong, 'Are Identity Claims Bad?', pp.312–13.

20 Michael Walzer, *On Toleration*, New Haven: Yale University Press, 1997, p.2.

21 Ibid., p.10.

22 These cases are discussed in Barry, *Culture and Equality*, pp.155–93.

23 I do not regard it as a *serious* embarrassment for my argument that it is unable to specify with much clarity (at least beyond the easy cases) what precisely fair treatment of identity claims requires. There is a similar lack of precision in demarcating the appropriate line between individual self-interest (individual freedom), on the one hand, and concern for others, on the other, in social justice theory. More work on this area is obviously needed.

24 It might be thought that the identity claims of minority nationalists raise a serious issue of incompossibility and represent a strong counterexample to my argument. The autonomy-related demands typical of such groups do seem to have the potential for creating an incompossibility problem, because there really is limited public space over which the identity groups contest, and the fact that the states are territorial (not personal) means that there is a potential for including or applying to people who are not members of the identity group in question, thus raising the possibility of imposition on people who do

not share the identity. Here, there are two possible lines of defence. One is to note that, here, the incompossibility problem is not a problem connected to identity-related claims in particular. It is a problem here because the modern territorial state, in its structures and policies, privileges certain kinds of identities and marginalizes others, and does not easily treat fairly all its identity groups. The problem would not go away if the demand was pitched in non-identity terms. Second, I do not think the argument that minority nationalists make is simply an identity argument. That is to say, if their argument took the form of an identity argument (and that was the only argument deployed), then I do not think it would justify the kind of autonomy arrangement that they require. Minority nationalists also need other arguments, of a democratic kind, and arguments in terms of fairness (specifically aimed at the unfairness of the current majoritarian state) to make their claims.

25 The author wishes to thank Aresh Abizadeh, Allen Buchanan, Avigail Eisenberg, John McGarry, Alan Patten, Igor Primoratz, Jeff Spinner-Halev, Christine Sypnowich, Dan Weinstock, the participants at the workshop on 'Identity, Self-Determination and Secession', Centre for Applied Philosophy and Public Ethics, University of Melbourne, August 2003, and the Montreal Political Theory Group, October 2003, for helpful comments on an earlier version of this chapter.

Chapter 3

Identity and Rational Revisability

Geoffrey Brahm Levey

1   Introduction

> By multicultural education the Swann Committee wants to impose on Muslim children
> what it considers of educational value – such as autonomy, and a critical approach to their
> own faith and culture – and is not ready, in the name of 'rationality' to accept that which is
> based on revealed truth ... This sort of multiculturalism claims to promote tolerance and
> understanding, but it tacitly justifies cultural domination by the secularist anti-religious
> majority, and at the same time, systematically undermines the basic principles of Islam.[1]

Central to much of the concern over cultural identity and diversity in liberal societies is the value of individual autonomy. For many liberals, the idea that individuals
have a basic interest in being able to make and revise their own plans in life is the
foundation of liberal political morality; it underwrites individuals' rights and liberties and sets the limits of liberal toleration. For many identity groups (and an
increasing number of liberals) however, this is just the problem, as my opening
quotation indicates. The quotation is from the British Muslim community's response
to the Swann Report on the education of children from ethnic minorities. It has
interest, for my purposes, in three respects. First, it clearly captures what many
identity groups perceive as so threatening or unfair about the liberal priority of
autonomy, rationality and a critical approach to life. Second, it effectively refutes
sophisticated liberal suggestions that autonomy is neutral among conceptions of the
good life since it only concerns 'the way in which we ought to assume and pursue
such ideals'.[2] Third, and perhaps most interesting of all, the document's level of
analysis and careful words hardly betray an absence of critical and rational reflection even as its authors call for insulation from such abilities for the rest of their
community. Indeed, most among the panel of British Muslims who drafted the
statement had a PhD.

In this chapter, I want to keep in mind the British Muslims' statement and ask
what strategic accommodation liberals can give them and other nonliberal communities that are similarly concerned about preserving their identities in liberal societies. I will consider two popular liberal approaches, in particular, and then gesture
towards a third. The first, which I will call 'identity liberalism', promises to satisfy
these communities' concerns by eschewing individual autonomy in favour of some
alternative foundational or governing value.[3] The second response, political liberalism, insists on autonomy as a foundational liberal value, but promises to limit its

normative force to the public sphere.[4] Whereas the first approach promises to dethrone autonomy as a ruling value, the second approach promises only some relief from its reign. I will argue (section 2) that identity liberals offer false hope; their proposals turn on the value of autonomy in ways and to a degree that scarcely meet the concerns of nonliberal communities. In contrast, I will argue (section 3) that, while political liberalism also fails to produce precisely the relief it promises at the level of individual personality, it does offer some at the level of law and policy. In my concluding section (section 4), I return to the apparent contradiction between the British Muslim authors' words and their own situation, and consider the liberal conception of the liberal self. I examine the assumption in current liberal theory that understanding one's rational agency is essential to being a liberal citizen, and argue that the assumption is both unwarranted and potentially illiberal.

A preliminary word is in order about the conception of autonomy I have in mind. My concern is with autonomy as the capacity of individuals to assess and revise their inherited practices and ends or what Allen Buchanan has usefully called 'rational revisability'.[5] This account of autonomy is sometimes elaborated in terms of a 'split-level self': one's desires or first-order preferences are subjected to a process of critical reflection producing 'choices' or second-order preferences. Autonomy is realized in so far as one is able to modify one's first-order preferences to accord with one's second-order preferences.[6] An important aspect is that these second-order reflections should be 'procedurally independent'; that is, be a function of the person's own critical and reflective faculties and not be the result of manipulation from without or psychological upset within.[7] This does not mean that the autonomous person must be a nonconformist or experimental individualist. It does imply, however, that she has some options, and some awareness of these options, from which to chart her course in life.[8]

2   Identity Liberals: Dethroning Autonomy?

When people claim or deny that individuals have a 'basic interest' in being able to assess and revise their ends, two issues are generally at stake. One is the philosophical anthropology or conception of the person that rational revisability presupposes. I will address aspects of this issue in sections 3 and 4. The second issue is the *value* of autonomy. Liberals value autonomy in different senses. Some, like Kant and Mill, view autonomy as having *intrinsic* value, where a morally good rational being is an unconditional good in itself or the capacity for rational self-direction is the 'distinctive endowment of a human being'.[9] Some, like Will Kymlicka, ascribe only *instrumental* value to autonomy; it is what enables us to lead the good life, as we see it.[10] Some liberals think autonomy is rather *noninstrumentally* valuable; that is, it is an end valued for its own sake, albeit one that is conditional on how it is used.[11]

Autonomy may be valued as a means (or instrumentally) also in two more mundane senses. Joseph Raz helpfully points to one of these in noting that autonomy as an ideal is 'particularly suited' to 'cope with changing technological, economic and social conditions', where there is need 'to acquire new skills, to move from one subculture to another, to come to terms with new scientific and moral views'.[12] In short, autonomy may be valuable because it allows us simply to get by and/or on in life, and, in this sense, has *functional* value. Second, autonomy may be valued as a test of the *legitimacy* of someone's way of life, in the sense of ensuring that it was freely chosen and not compelled. The assumption is that this purpose need not commit one to any further sense in which people have a basic interest in autonomy.

Identity liberals say to communities like the British Muslims that they can make room for their different traditions and value systems by refusing to privilege autonomy as a controlling liberal value. And, good to their word, no identity liberal (that I know of) advocates the view that autonomy is intrinsically valuable. However, the picture is rather more complicated and instructive regarding the other values on autonomy.

William Galston, for example, seems to rely heavily on the instrumental and functional values of autonomy in arguing for a 'Diversity State'.[13] According to Galston, the autonomous life is a legitimate mode of existence, but should not define liberal principles, since this would squeeze out communities and social practices, like those of the Amish, that respect something other than personal choice. 'Properly understood, liberalism is about the protection of legitimate diversity', not the valorization of choice.[14] Galston's solution is to focus on the state's needs for political unity and the virtues required for liberal citizenship. Yet his nominated virtues turn out to be rather considerable, and familiar, moral and intellectual capacities. The capacities to discern and respect the rights of others resemble Rawls's moral power of a 'sense of justice' and what many other writers mean by 'moral autonomy'.[15] Similarly, many liberals cite the responsibilities that appear under Galston's other 'instrumental virtues', such as the capacities to discern the talent and character of candidates vying for office and to engage in public discourse, to show how the good of liberal citizenship or political community or democratic life requires or presupposes the critical capacities of autonomy.[16]

To be sure, some of these theorists regard political or democratic participation as instantiating the good life itself, whereas Galston clearly wants to separate people's conceptions of the good from the practices and norms required to support liberal state and society. However, in both cases, citizens need to be schooled in the knowledge, talents and skills presumed under the political virtues, and it is unclear how this avoids rupturing or recalibrating the identities and value systems of nonliberal groups. Indeed, to many 'autonomy liberals', Galston's expectation that liberal citizens 'strive to narrow the gap between liberal principles and practices'[17] would seem overly demanding and intrusive.

Galston also wants to distance himself from the value of autonomy because, like our British Muslim authors, he associates it with deleterious social consequences, in particular, the undermining of tradition, faith and established social relationships. Yet, although he advocates a 'non-autonomy-based system of public education' for the Diversity State, he charges it with the mission of equipping students with 'social rationality' or that 'kind of understanding' which enables individuals to participate in the liberal 'economy, society, and polity'.[18] Life in most liberal societies today is complex, multicultural, technological and global. What could a non-autonomy-based education be in these circumstances? If it means filling students with information but shielding them from the ability to think for themselves, then what becomes of the virtues and competences necessary to negotiate life today in liberal societies? Though perhaps valued for functional reasons only, social rationality is central to that kind of education and set of life skills to which our British Muslim authors are strenuously objecting. Rather than dethroning autonomy, Galston's Diversity State dresses it in new robes.

Another identity liberal, Bhikhu Parekh, inadvertently seems to credit autonomy with a governing role in liberal societies as a noninstrumental good. Parekh begins by dismissing 'personal autonomy, uncoerced choice, capacity for independent and critical thinking, equality, etc.' along with other moral universalistic principles as either too vague or too contentious to be politically and morally feasible as guiding principles of liberal toleration.[19] What is required, he argues, is instead an 'open-minded intercommunal dialogue' governed by a society's 'operative public values'.[20] Such values are found in a society's constitution, laws and civic relations. They are public, too, in the sense that most members of society 'accept and seek to live by them, and even those who do not live by them know what they are and acknowledge their authority – at least in public'.[21] Even so, controversies arise and these values should be used as the basis of a searching dialogue rather than as a blunt instrument that forecloses their further development.

An obvious question is, what if the operative values of a liberal society are rooted in 'personal autonomy, uncoerced choice, capacity for independent and critical thinking, equality, etc.'? Parekh fully reveals his sense of the centrality of individual autonomy to liberal society in considering some controversial cases that have arisen in Britain. For example, he contends that the British Parliament rightly ruled out arranged marriages because they offend against 'the liberal values of autonomy and uncoerced choice'. And he argues against the practice of female circumcision even for adult women because the 'voluntary nature of the decision is not easy to establish'. Indeed, Parekh suggests, hypothetically, that even the banned and largely defunct Hindu practice of *sati* in India (in which a widow self-immolates on her husband's funeral pyre) might be permissible if the women 'were able to think and decide for themselves between alternative ways of understanding their religious and cultural traditions, and if they could generally be counted upon to act freely'.[22] It is hard to see how these arguments are not based on 'personal autonomy, uncoerced choice, capacity for independent and critical thinking, equality, etc.', even if they are now considered local, rather than universal, moral principles. And it is not unreasonable to assume that at least one of the British operative public values on autonomy is that the autonomous life is good for its own sake.

Parekh's proposal seems less an alternative to autonomy-based liberalism than a procedure for bringing nonliberal minorities to honour public values like autonomy, and perhaps for bringing the wider liberal society to rethink what its public values, including autonomy, might mean in any given case or conflict. These are valuable suggestions. However, as our British Muslim authors are likely to notice, the proposal does not so much dethrone autonomy as relocate the source of its authority.

A more cogent value on which to anchor liberal toleration than either diversity or operative public values is 'identity'. Its tight ontological relation to the self makes it a powerful argument for the specification of 'basic interests' and their political accommodation. Indeed, so powerful is the probative force of identity that the problem for liberals wishing to recognize it as a *primary* value is in reconciling that recognition with the basic liberal freedom of association and, especially, dissociation. This is the challenge facing Avishai Margalit and Moshe Halbertal in arguing that individuals have a fundamental right to their own culture grounded in identity or a 'right to one's way of life'.[23]

Halbertal presents a stark contrast between the identity and autonomy arguments by discussing groups, like the Amish and British Muslims, that seek to spare their children from mandatory general education. The elders fear that exposing their children to such education will entice them to leave the community for the wider society or else loosen their attachment to their own traditions. On the autonomy argument, the purpose of education is to familiarize children with alternative ways of life and to equip them with the capacity to assess these. Hence, on this model, the restrictions that groups like the Amish seek to impose on their children are a form of intolerance. But there is an alternative conception of education, one that sees it as 'concerned primarily with transmitting a particular tradition and developing a strong commitment to that particular way of life'. The Kibbutz movement and the ultra-Orthodox community in Israel, according to Halbertal, operate 'closed' education systems in this fashion. And, as long as they do not force or penalize individuals who do opt for an alternative way of life, he does not 'think there is anything intolerant in the practices of these communities'.[24]

Margalit and Halbertal's position seems to be that 'force' and 'penalize' should refer only to blatant coercion and physical threats against a member's *expressed* wishes to leave. Absent this, the right to exit might be said to apply. They frankly acknowledge, for example, that some ultra-Orthodox communities in Israel dispatch '"morality squads" that follow, report on, threaten, and sometimes act violently against members' who may deviate from the community's 'extreme puritanism'.[25] Yet, elsewhere, they suggest the inadequacy of this understanding of a right to exit. They argue that a 'cultural minority cannot be granted *control* over its members' exit'.[26] And in a side argument, Halbertal claims that Kymlicka is wrong to cite the millet system – in which the Muslim Ottoman Turks allowed the Jewish and Christian communities under their control to be largely self-governing – as a (nonliberal) form of religious toleration, 'because it was done in a framework of extreme asymmetry of power. ... The weaker parties had no choice but to be tolerant of the other parties'.[27] Clearly, when Halbertal defends education simply as the transmission of a tradition, he overlooks how the educational content and practices of many groups are built on and aim for the entrenchment of extreme asymmetrical power relations, especially between the sexes, which deny the weaker parties meaningful choice. Such control and power can mock the appearance of toleration – and Margalit and Halbertal's own deepest commitment to the consent of the individual and a right of exit – when young citizens are not equipped with some appreciation of alternative ways of life and the basic skills to assess them.

That the identity liberals presume, require or expressly acknowledge the value of autonomy in critical ways, as we have seen, does not make their theories identical to liberal theories formally grounded in the principle of autonomy. The latter theorize autonomy as valuable primarily in the intrinsic (unconditional), noninstrumental (for its own sake), and/or instrumental (for the sake of the good life) senses. Identity liberals, in contrast, tend to invoke or betray the force of autonomy for instrumental reasons of good citizenship; being able to function in modern, technological, multicultural liberal societies; and/or as a test of legitimacy for whether group members can meaningfully exercise their right of exit (although Parekh tends toward a deeper value). These are important theoretical differences. What is less clear is that, with the exception of intrinsic valorizations, these theoretical differences make a *practical* difference to the kinds of lives people are able to live in liberal societies. Certainly if judged by the concerns of the British Muslims, the identity liberals promise much in theory, but deliver little comfort *in situ*. And where practical tolerance does seem to be greatly enlarged, as in Margalit and Halbertal's right to culture, the arguments lack theoretical consistency. It is possible that in other kinds of cases, where the cultural demands are more concerned with excluding nonmembers than controlling members, the identity liberals' arguments might make a practical difference. However, as we will now see, even this much is uncertain.

3   Political Liberalism: The Promise of Relief

For many liberals who expressly value autonomy as a governing liberal principle, the problem raised by cultural diversity and identity concerns autonomy's scope. Some liberals acknowledge that autonomy is a substantive and controversial value, but believe that it may be restricted to purposes of determining our political rights and responsibilities instead of being invoked as a moral ideal for our lives in general. The distinction is thus made between 'political' and 'comprehensive' liberalism. I think this distinction collapses in terms of the liberal conception of the person, but remains potentially important in its legal and political implications. To help elucidate these points, let us consider Rawls's account of political liberalism, still the most notable example of this kind.

Whereas in his early work Rawls appeared to endorse autonomy as a comprehensive moral ideal, in his later writings he acknowledges that the ideal of the autonomous person is too controversial in democratic societies to elicit the agreement necessary to construct a stable and just political order.[28] So, rather than postulate autonomy as a comprehensive ideal, Rawls seeks to limit its scope to the political context. As a purely 'political' ideal of the person, autonomy can serve to determine individuals' *public* rights and obligations, while leaving them and their groups free to pursue their own conceptions of the good in their personal, familial and associational life. Rawls thinks that the power of autonomy for political justification can be utilized and made more acceptable if it carries no demand that people conform to its dictates in their lives generally:

This full autonomy of political life must be distinguished from the ethical values of autonomy and individuality, which may apply to the whole of life, both social and individual, as expressed by the comprehensive liberalisms of Kant and Mill. Justice as fairness emphasizes this contrast: it affirms political autonomy for all but leaves the weight of ethical autonomy to be decided by citizens severally in light of their comprehensive doctrines.[29]

The first problem with Rawls's proposal is that it is unlikely that the capacity for independent critical reflection, once introduced, will stay fixed on a given set of issues or within a given domain. It is in the nature of intellectual and moral capacities that they cannot be restricted in their exercise by proclamation. As Eamonn Callan observes, the 'attempt to understand the reasonableness of convictions that may be in deep conflict with doctrines learned in the family cannot be carried through without inviting the disturbing question that these convictions might be the framework of a better way of life, or at least one that is just as good'. And when this happens, there is a 'new psychological context that makes it implausible to say that the "same" conception of the good is affirmed before and after we have come to accept the burdens of judgement'.[30]

Rawls recognizes this tendency in his argument, but argues that it is important to distinguish between principles of justification and their unintended social effects. Requiring children to know their civil and political rights and be self-supporting may be 'in effect, though not in intention, to educate them to a comprehensive liberal conception'.[31] This distinction between 'neutrality of aim' and 'neutrality of effect', as Rawls otherwise puts it, is not unassailable. While some such distinction seems warranted in the case of effects that may incidentally follow upon the enactment of principles, matters would seem to be more complicated when certain effects are commonly or invariably related to such principles. Then, the unintendedness of these effects is morally qualified by the knowledge that one's principles are more than likely to give rise to them. In these circumstances, Rawls's counsel that 'We must accept the facts of commonsense political sociology'[32] might well be taken to heart as a refutation of the claim to neutrality, rather than, as he intends it, simply a frank recognition that one's acclaimed neutral principles have unfortunate consequences.

To be sure, Rawls does seem to think that education toward a comprehensive liberal conception is only an incidental, rather than a systemic, byproduct of his political principles. But, while he acknowledges that this effect 'may indeed happen in the case of some', he does not really explain why it will not happen in the case of most or many. Daily life in liberal societies is replete with evidence of the liberalization of groups and institutions beyond that required by law. Calls for the ordination of women in various churches and other demands for equality and non-discrimination, for example, typically come first from members of these churches, rather than from outside bodies. This liberalizing effect is also, of course, a fear of our British Muslim authors. Thus Rawls's concession that there is 'certainly ... some resemblance between the values of political liberalism and the values of the comprehensive liberalisms of Kant and Mill' understates the case.[33]

There would seem to be genuine convergence and not merely resemblance between these two liberal approaches.

But there is a second and more fundamental transitive effect plaguing Rawls's proposal. Political liberalism seems to presume or require the generalized intellectual-cum-psychological powers involved in autonomous action (critical self-detachment and rational self-direction) that it was designed to alleviate. That is, the problem is not only 'causal' in Rawls's sense above that 'exercising autonomy in the political sphere may causally promote its exercise in private life'.[34] Rather, it is that a causal relation also runs in the opposite direction: Rawls needs to assume the generalized presence of autonomous agency in citizens in order for them to exercise that agency specifically in the political context. As Kymlicka observes, political liberalism seems to assume that people are 'communitarians in private life, and liberals in public life', that is, are at once constitutive selves, unable to stand back and critically revise their social attachments and ends, and selves capable of rational self-direction.[35] The trouble with this neat bifurcation of the self is that a 'communitarian' private domain and a 'liberal' public domain are not symmetrical in their 'reach'. To be a liberal even in Rawls's public sense is to be able to differentiate and sort out one's public from one's private lives, to be ever alert to the boundaries dividing public and private spheres, to have the ability to detach oneself from the force of even one's own deepest convictions, and to affirm the canons of public reasonableness as required and when expected. To manage this, one must already be pretty much a 'full-time' or 'on call' autonomous agent, to 'already have swallowed a large dose of liberalism', as Brian Barry puts it.[36]

One might imagine versions of public reasonableness where this arguably is not the case. Consider a man from a traditional cultural group that attaches great importance to the modesty of women in dress and behaviour. One day he encounters in the street, say, a woman clad in a bikini. All of this man's traditional upbringing might move him to berate the woman, or worse, for her perceived transgression. For him to hold back venting his outrage out of some sense of the terms of liberal citizenship can take various forms. He may, for example, anticipate the legal consequences for himself if he were to lash out, and so think better of it. He may simply value civil peace as much as, or more than, he condemns women's immodesty. Both considerations are conceivably consonant with the man's traditions and require no significant alteration in his relation to them. But what if we follow Rawls and regard the man as a free and equal citizen who recognizes the fair terms of social cooperation? Then we hold him to be capable of forming, revising and rationally pursuing a conception of the good, of thinking of himself and others as being self-authenticating sources of valid claims, and of taking responsibility for his ends.[37] This would presuppose a fundamental change in the man's relation to his ends.

The two problems I have identified in Rawls's attempt to restrict the principle of autonomy to the political sphere both focus on individual personality. The first problem emphasizes how critical capacities required in the political sphere are likely to spill over and transform the nature of individuals' agency in other spheres; the second problem highlights how requiring autonomy for the political sphere already tacitly assumes its more general instantiation. In these senses, political liberalism scarcely produces the relief it promises of an 'autonomy-free' zone. But if, at the level of individual psychology, political liberalism is not only political, there is, perhaps, another level at which political liberalism may restrict the province of autonomy, and in this sense also not be metaphysical or comprehensive in scope. This is the level of law and public policy. Even if the capacity for autonomy does not evaporate beyond the borders of the political sphere, individuals are not *compelled* to exercise it there, as they are regarding their public rights and duties. This contrasts with comprehensive liberalism, where the value placed on autonomy as a general moral ideal implies much greater state scrutiny and regulation of its citizens' lives. Political liberalism thus appears to be more aptly described as what Rawls calls a 'partially comprehensive' conception of justice, one that 'comprises a number of, but by no means all, nonpolitical values and virtues and is rather loosely articulated'.[38] Though it may breach the bounds of the political, political liberalism ostensibly leaves space for practices that do not necessarily respect or reflect the value of autonomy.

But does it? Kymlicka claims not, arguing that even a political conception of the person will generate rights and obligations at odds with the traditions of nonliberal minorities and which they may find objectionable.[39] For example, liberal rights would rule out attempts by religious minorities to prohibit apostasy or to prevent children from receiving some general education and exposure to other ways of life. By prohibiting apostasy, Kymlicka presumably means compromising a member's right to exit. This said, his examples show only that political liberalism not surprisingly will carry costs and burdens for nonliberal minorities; they do not refute the suggestion that political liberalism imposes fewer such burdens on nonliberal minorities than would instantiating autonomy as a comprehensive ideal. As Donald Moon argues with great sensitivity, political liberalism will structure opportunities available to individuals and groups quite besides the authoritative commands of the state. Yet even these 'tragic choices' do not amount to the conflicts and exclusions implied by comprehensive accounts of liberal political morality.[40]

The more serious challenge to the claim that political liberalism entails less of a legal and political burden on nonliberal minorities than does comprehensive liberalism is surely that this difference is irrelevant. If, as I suggested earlier, the capacity for autonomy is unlikely to respect artificial boundaries like that defining the political, and/or if the very restriction of autonomy to a given sphere presupposes this capacity among citizens in order for them to understand and respect that demarcation, then what does it matter that autonomy is not compelled in the nonpublic sphere? It has already conquered that sphere by the force of its own value, as it were.[41] It is exactly at this juncture that the difference between the psychological and legal import of political liberalism should be insisted upon.

The fact is that many nonliberal institutions and practices have proved themselves remarkably resilient even in vigorous liberal societies. They may not have survived unchanged by their exposure to a liberal culture. Their members may well be autonomous agents in virtue of the generalization of that capacity referred to earlier. For all that, such nonliberal or traditional practices often continue to be valued and pursued by many people (as the British Muslims' statement confirms).

And it seems clear that at least some nonliberal practices would have less chance of existing, much less flourishing, under a regime that sought to impose what Nancy Rosenblum calls 'congruence' between public institutions and private associations.[42] For example, the logic of comprehensive liberalism is likely to deny religious schools exemption from anti-discrimination legislation in the employment of teachers. As an Australian federal Sex Discrimination Commissioner put it in relation to the anti-discrimination provisions, 'quite simply I'd like to see more donut, more cheese, fewer holes'.[43] In contrast, and although the specific policy implications of broad principles are rarely self-evident, one might expect a more guarded, 'political' endorsement of the autonomy principle to be more open to diversity in private associations, and more likely to view such exemptions as a *good* idea rather than a compromise of principle. Similarly, a 'political' liberal would be less likely than a 'comprehensive' liberal to legislate against discriminatory hierarchies and traditional roles within private associations, such as the prohibition on women from serving as priests, ministers or rabbis within certain faith communities. Political liberalism's invocation of autonomy for establishing our political rights and responsibilities, rather than as a moral ideal for our lives in general, can, in this way, make a practical difference.

4   Self-understanding and Liberal Selves

I have suggested that identity liberals fail to dislodge the practical import of autonomy in various ways, and that political liberalism, while not credible when judged in terms of its implications for the psychological and intellectual capacities of citizens, does have real significance for nonliberal traditions given the potential limitations in its legal and policy scope. In this final section, I want to turn to the place of self-understanding in the liberal conception of the liberal person, and explore what further latitude there might be within the heartland of liberalism for the maintenance of nonliberal identities.

How should we interpret the apparent contradiction between the words of the British Muslim scholars and their own advanced education? Perhaps they know the dangers of general education from bitter personal experience and, turning inwards, wish only to protect their coreligionists from the same fate: 'We have seen the liberal future, and it is hell.'[44] But I think it is more plausible that the authors have been changed by their education and simply do not understand their relation to Islam – and through it, the world – in the terms of rational revisability. This picture, however, challenges a key assumption in current liberal theory. Liberal accounts of the self or, at least, of the *liberal* self, place key importance on how one understands one's ends. Rawls argues that liberal persons, in their political conception, do not 'view themselves as inevitably tied to the pursuit of the particular conception of the good that they affirm at any given time'. According to Kymlicka, to be a liberal person means 'I can always envisage my self without its *present* ends', in the sense that 'no end or goal is exempt from possible re-examination'.[45] This understanding of the potential revisability of all of one's ends – which, on my reading, the British

Muslim authors lack – is a strong version of what rational revisability entails. As Buchanan notes, rational assessment may be 'only a matter of achieving and maintaining the consistency or coherence of one's own system of belief'.[46] However, before proceeding further to identify what is wrong with the strong version of the revisability principle, it is important to note a sense in which it is *more* accommodating of identity convictions than often supposed.

Liberal theory presents a static picture; it tends to imagine liberal persons fully formed, as the theory requires them to be. Fully autonomous individuals inhabit Rawls's original position, and so on. Such philosophical representations do not capture how most of us enter and become members of liberal societies. We are born into them fresh or we join them as immigrants, sometimes coming from nonliberal societies. Either way, we are socialized into being liberal citizens, which is a process over time. The capacity to stand back and assess one's ends, therefore, should also be construed as a skill and practice developed over time. Something of this more dynamic picture of revisability can be discerned in the liberal conception of the person. As Ronald Dworkin, among others, explains, the idea that the self is able to stand back and assess its ends does not mean (as some communitarian critics took it to mean) that selves stand nowhere or are totally unencumbered. Not all of one's ends can be put in question or scrutinized simultaneously. The point, rather, is that there is no 'connection or association so fundamental that it cannot be detached for inspection while holding others in place'.[47] But this means that liberal revisability is a process – at times, iterative and progressive – of holding some associations in place, while considering others. And such processes, even when working well and as they should, take time.

On this account, the British Muslim authors would be viewed as being on a curve of liberalization, which, allowing for the dynamic factor, is perfectly compatible with the liberal conception of liberal selves. Yet, as I suggested above, there is another (at least) reading of their case that is worth exploring and, I think, equally plausible: namely, that the authors are already more or less fully rational agents in their lives and in the way they relate to their ends, including Islam, although they do not think of themselves in this way. Such an account seems to be precluded by influential liberal conceptions of the liberal person, which insist that liberal citizenship requires that one views oneself as not being inevitably tied to a particular conception of the good. So we need to ask, is knowing oneself to be a rational agent necessary to *being* a rational agent in this sense? Two reasons might be advanced for thinking so.

The first concerns pure rationality. As Buchanan notes, although what is involved in revising one's ends may not be particularly taxing, denying 'one ought to maintain an attitude of critical revisability toward one's life plan' is. For it commits one to hold several 'exceedingly strong and implausible epistemological theses' about the basic infallibility of one's ends and about one's beliefs about those ends.[48] In short, denying that one's ends are potentially open to revision is a highly dubious, if not irrational, position to adopt. Be this as it may, *liberal* autonomy and rational agency can scarcely preclude the holding of erroneous or dubious beliefs. As liberals at least since Mill have been fond of emphasizing, individual freedoms, such as those of expression and association, are important precisely because we can be mistaken in our present beliefs and need opportunities to test them.[49] One might deny the revisability of one's ends with total conviction, even as one is testing them in the field.

A second reason, perhaps, for insisting on an 'attitude' of critical revisability towards one's ends concerns the split-level self. Critical reflection and adjustment of one's preferences just is the definition of autonomy. To be sure, it might be argued that rational revisability need only entail scrutinizing one's first-order preferences so that they accord with one's second-order preferences or ends, which are themselves held constant and beyond rational revision. Still, there is good reason for retaining the idea of autonomy as involving the scrutiny also of one's ends and yet thinking that self-consciousness is *in*essential to it. The process of reflective scrutiny need not be, and probably mostly is not, an explicit cognitive and linguistic exercise. 'If we think of the process of reflection and identification as being a conscious, fully articulated, and explicit process', Gerald Dworkin observes, 'then it will appear that it is mainly professors of philosophy who exercise autonomy'.[50] Susan Babbitt points out that 'nonpropositional understanding' forms the basis of much human activity, from 'feeling one's way' in a new culture to what is generally regarded as the most rational of all human endeavours, namely the scientific enterprise.[51] Thomas Kuhn's work on paradigm shifts in scientific theory is, in this sense, only a controversial formulation of the more general point that a good deal of scientific inquiry proceeds on less than strictly rational and systematic criteria. Intuition, inspiration and sociological factors all contribute to the shape, direction and results of the inquiry. A more realistic notion of autonomy would acknowledge 'the role of important kinds of nonpropositional understanding in rational deliberation'.[52]

The scrutiny and evaluation of our preferences is likely, then, to be undertaken through our entire being and experience rather than through simply conceptual examination. On this richer account of autonomy, one's self-understandings may well 'hover above' the main action of one's rational agency, rendering our expressed conceptions of ourselves, at times, perhaps not the best guide to who and what we actually are.

Rawls and Kymlicka allow that 'Some people may think of themselves as incapable of questioning or revising their ends', even where 'in fact "our conceptions of the good may and often do change over time, usually slowly but sometimes rather suddenly"'.[53] On their account, because such people deny that their ends are subject to revision, they violate the requisite conditions of being a ('good') liberal citizen. This position is a mistake, and has potentially illiberal consequences. Self-consciousness or understanding of one's agency is no measure of how one actually relates to one's ends. While this is particularly the case where the notion of autonomy is broadened to include nonpropositional understanding, it is also, I think, the case with the more conventional, propositional accounts. First, if, as Rawls and Kymlicka agree, some people do revise their ends, even where they might not think of their ends as subject to revision, this presumably must also include people who do revise their ends by standing back and assessing them. Furthermore, it is worth recalling that Kymlicka's argument against political liberalism is about people's *actual* relation to their ends, not their understanding of this relation. He thinks that, if people are capable of standing back and critically revising their social attachments and ends for public purposes, then they will also do this, and need to do this, in their nonpublic lives. The concern is about a capacity and its exercise, not about understanding of this capacity and its exercise.[54]

The preoccupation in modern liberal theory with people's self-understanding is, in some ways, ironic. Liberalism began life, and almost always has been a politics, designed to transcend the embattled realm of self-understandings. While liberal conceptions of the self are meant to embody just this transcendence through a capacity for critical self-detachment from one's deepest convictions, it is the capacity and not the understanding of it that is crucial to driving liberal politics. The allure of self-understanding nonetheless oddly persists. Kymlicka, for example, rejects certain justifications of national rights because 'this is not how most indigenous peoples themselves understand ... their national rights [or] the nature of their cultural identity', as if his own argument conceiving culture as a context of choice accords with, or is meant to accord with, or even should accord with, these groups' understanding. Margalit and Halbertal criticize Kymlicka's account of culture as a context of choice because it 'does not agree with the viewpoint of the culture-bearers themselves'. Yet it is unlikely that ultra-Orthodox culture bearers in Jerusalem would agree with Margalit and Halbertal's conception of their right to their way of life as an *individual* right grounded in a Razian notion of entitlement.[55]

Liberalism is politics from a third person perspective, not a first person or 'sense of self' perspective. Self-understandings, whether they are of indigenous people, ultra-Orthodox Jews, or autonomous liberal citizens should be of little concern to the justification and practice of liberal institutions. What *is* of the utmost concern is people's autonomy or *capacity* to assess and revise their ends. So people's self-understandings (or lack of self-understanding) rightly become a concern to liberals where they lead to self-harm, to jeopardizing others' life and liberties or, as in the case of the British Muslims wishing to deny a general education to their children, the denial of opportunities to develop a capacity for autonomy in the first place. Even here, however, the focus of the state's attention is properly on removing the interference rather than on reforming the self-understanding. Elsewhere, a capacity to assess and revise one's ends may, of course, involve the understanding of one's agency, and, in some cases, such self-understanding may be required. But, if so, this is particular to certain occupations, roles or assumed responsibilities, it is not part of liberal citizenship in *principle*. Liberal citizens, including our British Muslim authors, are entitled to wear a veil of ignorance also outside of the original position.[56]

Notes

1   Islamic Academy, *The Teaching of Islam in British Schools: An Agreed Statement*, Cambridge: Islamic Academy, 1985.

2 Charles Larmore, *Patterns of Moral Complexity*, New York: Cambridge University Press, 1987, pp.73–4.
3 Notable examples include Bhikhu Parekh, *Rethinking Multiculturalism: Cultural Diversity and Political Theory*, London: Macmillan, 2000; William A. Galston, *Liberal Pluralism: The Implications of Value Pluralism for Political Theory and Practice*, Cambridge: Cambridge University Press, 2002; Chandran Kukathas, 'Are There Any Cultural Rights?', *Political Theory*, vol.20 (1992); and Avishai Margalit and Moshe Halbertal, 'Liberalism and the Right to Culture', *Social Research*, vol.61 (1994).
4 See, for example, John Rawls, *Political Liberalism*, New York: Columbia University Press, 1993; Charles Larmore, *The Morals of Modernity*, Cambridge: Cambridge University Press, 1996; and J. Donald Moon, *Constructing Community: Moral Pluralism and Tragic Conflict*, Princeton: Princeton University Press, 1993.
5 Allen Buchanan, 'Revisability and Rational Choice', *Canadian Journal of Philosophy*, vol.5 (1975).
6 The *locus classicus* is Harry Frankfurt, 'Freedom of the Will and the Concept of the Person', *Journal of Philosophy*, vol.68 (1971).
7 Gerald Dworkin, *The Theory and Practice of Autonomy*, Cambridge: Cambridge University Press, 1988, p.16.
8 Joseph Raz, *The Morality of Freedom*, Oxford: Clarendon Press, 1986, p.372.
9 J.S. Mill, *On Liberty and Other Writings*, ed. Stefan Collini, Cambridge: Cambridge University Press, 1989, p.59.
10 Will Kymlicka, *Contemporary Political Philosophy: An Introduction*, New York: Oxford University Press, 1990, p.209.
11 See, for example, Raz, *Morality of Freedom*, p.381.
12 Ibid., pp.370–71.
13 Galston, *Liberal Pluralism*, p.26.
14 Ibid., p.23.
15 See, for example, David Johnston, *The Idea of a Liberal Theory: A Critique and Reconstruction*, Princeton: Princeton University Press, 1993, pp. 71–7. Such meanings of moral autonomy should be further distinguished from more demanding Kantian notions of subjecting oneself to the moral law. Galston's citizen virtues are elaborated in his *Liberal Purposes: Goods, Virtues, and Diversity in the Liberal State*, New York: Cambridge University Press, 1991, pp.224–7.
16 See, for example, Joshua Cohen and Joel Rogers, *On Democracy*, New York: Penguin, 1983; and Amy Gutmann, *Democratic Education*, Princeton: Princeton University Press, 1987.
17 Galston, *Liberal Purposes*, p.227.
18 William A. Galston, 'Two Concepts of Liberalism', *Ethics*, vol.105 (1994/5), p.529; Galston, *Liberal Purposes*, pp.23–4.
19 Bhikhu Parekh, 'Minority Practices and Principles of Toleration', *International Migration Review*, vol.30 (1996), p.254.
20 Ibid., pp.251, 259.
21 Ibid., p.259.
22 See, respectively, ibid., pp.268, 271 and 273.
23 See Margalit and Halbertal, 'Liberalism and the Right to Culture'; and Moshe Halbertal, 'Autonomy, Toleration, and Group Rights: A Response to Will Kymlicka', in David Heyd (ed.), *Toleration: An Elusive Virtue*, Princeton: Princeton University Press, 1996, p.109.
24 Halbertal, 'Autonomy, Toleration, and Group Rights', pp.111–12.

25 Margalit and Halbertal, 'Liberalism and the Right to Culture', p.493.

26 Ibid., p.508. Emphasis added.

27 Halbertal, 'Autonomy, Toleration, and Group Rights', p.107.

28 See, respectively, John Rawls, *A Theory of Justice*, Oxford: Oxford University Press, 1971, and Rawls, *Political Liberalism*.

29 Rawls, *Political Liberalism*, p.78. By 'full autonomy', Rawls means the two moral powers taken together: a capacity for a sense of justice; and the capacity to form, revise and rationally pursue a conception of the good. These mirror his distinction between 'the reasonable' and 'the rational' (*Political Liberalism*, pp.48–54).

30 Eamonn Callan, *Creating Citizens*, Oxford: Oxford University Press, 1997, pp.35–6.

31 Rawls, *Political Liberalism*, p.199.

32 Ibid., p.193.

33 Ibid., p.200, for this and the preceding quotation.

34 Will Kymlicka, *Multicultural Citizenship: A Liberal Theory of Minority Rights*, Oxford: Clarendon Press, 1995, p.232, n.9.

35 Ibid., p.160.

36 Brian Barry, 'How Not to Defend Liberal Institutions', in R. Bruce Douglass, Gerald Mara and Henry S. Richardson (eds), *Liberalism and the Good*, New York: Routledge, 1990, p.53.

37 Rawls, *Political Liberalism*, pp.30–34, 72.

38 Ibid., p.13. On political liberalism as a 'partially comprehensive' moral argument, see Lief Wenar, '*Political Liberalism*: An Internal Critique', *Ethics*, vol.106 (1995/6).

39 Kymlicka, *Multicultural Citizenship*, pp.160–62.

40 Moon, *Constructing Community*, pp.63–73.

41 On this line of argument, see John Tomasi, *Liberalism Beyond Justice: Citizens, Society, and the Boundaries of Political Theory*, Princeton: Princeton University Press, 2001.

42 Nancy L. Rosenblum, *Members and Morals: The Personal Uses of Pluralism in America*, Princeton: Princeton University Press, 1998, pp.36–41.

43 Sue Walpole, 'Women's Rights, Human Rights: Achievements and Aspirations', paper presented at WEL National Conference, Sydney, January 1996, p.12.

44 Another reading is that the scholars simply wished to protect their children from a liberal education at too early an age, giving them the benefit of a secure cultural environment until mature enough to make their own decision. While a possibility, this reasoning is not what the scholars convey in their agreed statement, which is fundamentally opposed to the values of liberal education. I thank Simon Keller for raising this suggestion.

45 See, respectively, Will Kymlicka, *Liberalism, Community, and Culture*, Oxford: Clarendon Press, 1989, p.52 (original emphasis); and Rawls, *Political Liberalism*, p.30.

46 Buchanan, 'Revisability and Rational Choice', p.399.

47 Ronald Dworkin, quoted in Kymlicka, *Multicultural Citizenship*, p.91.

48 Buchanan, 'Revisability and Rational Choice', p.400.

49 Kymlicka, *Multicultural Citizenship*, p.81; Kymlicka, *Liberalism, Community, and Culture*, pp.10–13.

50 Dworkin, *Theory and Practice of Autonomy*, p.17.

51 Susan E. Babbitt, *Impossible Dreams: Rationality, Integrity, and Moral Imagination*, Boulder: Westview Press, 1996, pp.50–58.

52 Ibid., p.59. A similar position is implicit in Martha C. Nussbaum's *Upheavals of Thought: The Intelligence of Emotions*, Cambridge and New York: Cambridge University Press, 2001. For an excellent discussion of the complexity of critical evaluation, see Owen Flanagan, 'Identity and Strong and Weak Evaluation', in Owen Flanagan and Amelie

Oksenberg Rorty (eds), *Identity, Character and Morality*, Cambridge, MA: MIT Press, 1990, pp.37–65.

53   Kymlicka, *Multicultural Citizenship*, p.91. Kymlicka's own quotation is from John Rawls, 'Justice as Fairness: Political not Metaphysical', *Philosophy and Public Affairs*, vol.14 (1985), p.242.

54   Indeed, there is a hint that Rawls may have hesitated on requiring that citizens *understand* their ends to be revisable as against simply relating to their ends in this manner. Whereas political liberalism requires that citizens view themselves as 'having the moral power to have a conception of the good', the need of revisability is addressed in the negative: '*This is not to say* that, as part of their political conception, they view themselves as inevitably tied to the pursuit of the particular conception of the good that they affirm at any given time.' So phrased, it is an open question whether it is to say that they *do not* view themselves as inevitably tied to their ends. Interestingly, Rawls's next sentence elaborating the point is framed from the third person, *impersonal* perspective: 'Rather, as citizens, *they are seen* as capable of revising and changing this conception on reasonable and rational grounds, and they may do this if they so desire.' See Rawls, *Political Liberalism*, p.30. Emphases added.

55   See, respectively, Kymlicka, *Multicultural Citizenship*, p.104; and Margalit and Halbertal, 'Liberalism and the Right to Culture', p.505.

56   I am grateful to Igor Primoratz and the participants at the workshop on 'Identity, Self-Determination and Secession', Centre for Applied Philosophy and Public Ethics, University of Melbourne, August 2003, and to Amy Gutmann, Jeff Spinner-Halev, Chandran Kukathas, Will Kymlicka, Bhikha Parekh, and Nancy Rosenblum for helpful comments on earlier drafts or sections of this chapter.

II
IDENTITY, COUNTRY AND NATION

Chapter 4

Nationalism and Identity

C.A.J. (Tony) Coady

Like Mark Antony my purpose here is interment not acclaim. But where Antony really thought the object of his address 'the noblest Roman' and regretted his passing, I think nationalism mostly deserves to go, though, as much slaughter and mayhem in trouble spots around the world indicate, it is sadly far from dead. Nonetheless, many others enthuse about it, so, in criticizing nationalism, I shall also try to understand their enthusiasm and give it what due it merits. Instead of cruelly burying it alive, we may have to put it in an isolation ward to await eventual death and burial.

On the face of it, my project would seem to involve charting a course that gives appropriate respect to the rocks of proper patriotism on the one side and the savage reefs of jingoism or even racism on the other. This means acknowledging what is valuable about the emotions and attachments that many people feel toward what they think of as their nation, but disentangling this from the darker side of national sentiment – the side that leads to hatred, persecution and simple misunderstanding. Of course, faces can deceive and there are many voices to tell us that patriotism should not even be taken at its face value. It is, Dr Samuel Johnson avers, the 'last refuge of a scoundrel' (Ambrose Bierce thought, to the contrary, that it was the first) and E.M. Forster famously said that if he had to choose between betraying a friend and betraying his country, he hoped he would have the guts to betray his country.

Forster's *bon mot* is worth a bit of attention because it encapsulates quite a lot of what is at stake morally in various debates about nationalism. Those supportive of Forster see him as nobly putting personal attachment ahead of devotion to an abstraction. His critics tend to see him as putting an attachment to one person ahead of an attachment to many, and as narrowing the range of ethical concern while ignoring the reciprocities required by the contributions a larger community has made to his own wellbeing. Forster himself talks of betrayal in both cases, however, and says that 'probably one will not be forced to make such an agonizing choice', though he thinks that whenever love and loyalty to an individual run counter to the claims of the state, then 'down with the State'.[1] This at least suggests that he is thinking of two legitimate attachments and offering a ranking of them. Construed this way, we might think (without having to endorse nationalism) that the major criticism to be made is that his judgment in favour of friendship is too global, too undiscriminating about contexts and variable circumstances.

In any case, we are in the domain of loyalty, a complex and often strange phenomenon, and a puzzling virtue, if a virtue at all. Forster believed above all in

61

personal relationships, hence the overriding attachment to friendship. But others extend the idea of loyalty to entities like nations, states, Churches, empires. We must see what there is in this extension in the case of nations, what it licenses and what it does not.

1   The Meaning of Nationalism

It is time to be a little more careful about our use of the terms 'nation' and 'nationalism'. The varied employments of these terms in the literature provide one reason for so much confusion and heat in exchanges on the topic. Much of the variation arises from conflicting interpretations of the term 'nation', which is certainly one of the messier political concepts in use. Other variations come from the different types of moral and political significance attributed to the attachments that nationalism is taken to denote. I shall begin with the concept of a nation, though it will be necessary to mention nationalism from time to time as we proceed.

I doubt that a coherent definition, capable of capturing all the common usages of 'nation' or 'nationalism', can be provided. It would have to capture the passionate commitments of modern Americans to their ethnically and culturally diverse nation as well as the fierce loyalties of native Maoris to theirs (and here I do not mean New Zealand), or the strong attachments some Scots feel to their country, and perhaps Highlanders to theirs. Historically, elucidations have been offered in terms of a shared language, a shared culture, a shared racial background, a shared territory or a shared history, or a combination of some of these. Taken individually, none of these marks looks very plausible; their very success in picking out some instances of nationhood seems to disqualify them from picking out others. At the very time that the United States asserted itself as a separate nation from Great Britain, their ethnic composition was virtually identical and they had a common language. Territory is clearly important, but whether it is really shared is precisely what is unclear when national secession is in question. The same applies to culture and history, as the case of the former Yugoslavia illustrates. Many of the people now called Bosnian Muslims and Bosnian Serbs thought they had the same history and culture until very recently, but this is precisely what the zealots on both sides now deny. Culture is itself such an opaque notion that recourse to it in this context looks like explaining the mysterious by the ineffable.

It is hard to resist the thought that what is real in all this is not the entity but the attachment. This thought is made more seductive by the wealth of evidence that nationalists in fact tend to define themselves and their national attachment by oppositions: opposition to the invader, to the distant imperial centre, to the dominant nearby power, to various forms of excluded 'other' who may be seen as internal representatives of the hated group. Several writers on nationalism have made this sort of point about the national reality being created by the attachment. Gellner says that one useful definition of a nation is that 'two men are of the same nation if and only if they recognize each other as belonging to the same nation ... nations are the artefacts of men's convictions and loyalties and solidarities'.[2] David Miller, a supporter of nationalism (or, at any rate, of nationality as a crucially important political value) admits that there is no objective basis for attributions of nationality and that 'a nationality exists when its members believe that it does'.[3] Many other commentators have noted the degree of error, confusion, contrivance and manipulation that often goes to make up the objects of nationalist attachment, whether they be items of history, ritual or character. Much of the Fijian nationalism, for instance, that has had such alarming and disruptive effects in recent years was a calculated creation of the British colonial administration earlier last century. It is symptomatic of all this confusion that writers on nationalism and nations disagree dramatically on the chronology of the phenomenon in question. Many believe that the nation is a very modern thing, dating it to the eighteenth or even nineteenth century. Others argue that it is as old as human societies themselves. So, William Pfaff sees it as basically a nineteenth-century phenomenon arising from European romanticism, whereas Conor Cruise O'Brien finds its powerful expression in the Bible.[4]

Although this subjectivity in the understanding of the key concept in nationalism is often noted with some enthusiasm, it should be more alarming to the supporters of nationalism than appears to be the case. David Miller, for instance, says that 'nations almost unavoidably depend on beliefs about themselves that do not stand up well to impartial scrutiny'.[5] These beliefs seem to include all or most of those that Miller himself takes to be constitutive of 'nationality', such as mutual belief in their belonging together, a shared history, common action, connection to a particular territory and shared, distinctive characteristics. That this cluster of beliefs may be, in whole or part, fantastic and delusional seems to be no barrier to the supposed value of the national identity that it sustains. Nor is this value threatened by the less-noted fact that very similar clusters of belief can exist within subnational groups, such as states within a federation, even where there is no suggestion that they have the moral standing of nations. Yet the only difference seems to reside in a failure to apply the word 'nation' in the expression of these beliefs. Whether one can be so sanguine about the moral and political structure built upon such foundations is something that will concern us in the next section of the chapter.

Given all these different conceptions and attendant confusions, there may be little point in providing a restrictive definition that ungenerously narrows, or a broad one that too permissively widens, the terms of discussion. A sketch of the conceptual geography of the debate should suffice for our purposes. Nonetheless, it is plausible to suppose that the present ambiguities of the concept have a certain genesis and development. My speculation is that the concept arose in the context of culturally and ethnically unified communities who either had or wanted to assert a political identity and sovereignty. As such groups became dispersed or diluted by invasion or migration their political aspirations became inhibited or implausible, for one reason or another, and a more pluralistic group formed with an overarching claim to political authority. To the degree that this claim became acknowledged, the national sentiment and attachment was transferred to this more complex group. Although the meaning of the term and the ontology of its referent had shifted dramatically, the sentiments and terminology remained constant, with the result that there is now a deep ambiguity in the idea of a nation that any discussion must register. This is between a nation understood as a political entity, rather than as a racial, religious, tribal or ethnic group. These two understandings of 'nation' are importantly different, though they are often confused, and it is worth seeing how different they are, while keeping in view certain underlying similarities. Let us call the ethnic sense 'NE' and the political sense 'NP'. In the NE sense, countries like Australia and the United States are not nations at all, and it is very hard to find a clear case of a country or state that is a palpable nation in this sense. In the NP sense, they are paradigm cases. The term 'culture' is sometimes used to explicate the NE sense of nation, but it might just as easily be cited in connection with the NP sense. Although the United States and Australia are, in a sense, multicultural states, there is also an equally clear sense in which they have overarching national cultures that strike foreign visitors with great force. When the British or Japanese or Australians lament the swamping of their societies by American culture, it is clear enough what they mean, and it has no direct reference to ethnic cultures within the USA. For this reason, the term 'culture' should be used with great care; as already noted, if any term is even more opaque than 'nation', it is 'culture'. Nor does language or religion help much, since different nations in either the NE or NP sense may have the same religion or the same language, just as the Filipinos and the Irish share English and the Brazilians and Poles share Catholicism.

As for the passion with which people are committed to nations, there is a tendency to think that the NE sense has a monopoly here, but this is far from the case. The nation (NP) can certainly give rise to powerful unifying emotions and commitments even where it is, as so often, a composite of many nations (NE). This was true of many of the unifying nationalist movements of the nineteenth century, such as the Italian, and it remains true today of ethnically diverse nations such as India, Australia and the United States, though all of these are also subject to certain disintegrating tendencies, as indeed is modern Italy. Gellner, and others, who see the basic principle of nationalism as demanding an identity of national and political units are wrong if they take this to mean that one cannot be an enthusiastic (NP) nationalist without advocating the political dominance of some (NE) nation. Clearly, one can parade as a committed Australian, American, Canadian or Italian nationalist without thereby promoting the internal political ambitions of any constituent national subgroup, such as Croats or Calabrians. Indeed, many have thought that promotion of the former requires suppression of the latter. Others have supposed that the value of the latter requires the elimination or diminution of the former. Lord Acton noted the tension between these different forms long ago and thought that a multinational state with little or no overarching nationality (NP) best preserved liberal values.[6] This is a matter to which we shall return, but Gellner's idea at least has the merit of calling attention to the way in which any form of nationalism seems to have a political drive of some sort built into it. I doubt that we should call anything a form of nationalism that did not seek or defend some form of institutional or political power for that group.

As for nationalism itself, it is an ideology or outlook that insists on some sort of moral priority for national attachment, a priority that has political implications. The extreme version of nationalism is encapsulated in the slogan 'my country right or wrong' but this is so morally absurd as not to require any refutation. Short of this, the nationalist claim must be that national ties provide some sort of presumptive claim to moral and political consideration. A common nationalist claim is that recognition of national status must involve the granting of full-blown political autonomy. Gellner, for instance, in recognition of this, actually defines nationalism as 'a political principle which holds that the political and the national unit should be congruent'.[7] Gellner then has little difficulty in showing that very few actual sovereign states are nations, at least if 'nation' is understood in NE terms involving ethnic or similarly tribal identifications (real or imaginary), and, moreover, that the consequences of granting political sovereignty to all who are, or who think of themselves as, nations, would be disastrous. This is a point to which we shall return, but it is important to note here the complementary fact about the nation/state connection that it is perfectly possible to have two states whose separate nationals, in one sense, belong, in another sense, to the same nation. As we noted earlier, at one point in history virtually all the citizens of the newly created United States of America had much the same ethnic composition as the Great Britain they had disowned.

2 National Ties and Morality

The nationalist case invokes a distinctive sort of moral underpinning for the status of national sentiment and attachment. This underpinning proceeds by way of a claim about morality and a related claim about personal identity. The claim about morality appeals to the importance of particularities for the moral life, and especially the particular attachments that go with a certain use of the personal pronouns 'my' and 'our'. This is clearest with relationships like friendship, kinship or love. And its significance is thought to be a major problem for utilitarianism and other forms of consequentialism. We might recall in this connection the furore created by the anarchistic rationalist William Godwin's insistence that, if the great theologian and sage Archbishop Fenelon and his no-account valet were trapped in a flaming building and only one of them could be rescued, the rescuer would be obliged to save Fenelon even if the valet were his own father, brother or benefactor. Even the valet, if thinking soundly in this fundamentally utilitarian way, should acquiesce, for he would be acting unjustly if he preferred his own life to the far worthier Fenelon. Actually, my version of the example is taken from later editions of Godwin's book, where it was toned down because of the outcry occasioned by the first edition. There, the competitor with Fenelon for rescue is a chambermaid who is imagined to be the rescuer's wife or mother. The utilitarian temper and its distance from the commonsense morality is well caught by Godwin's comment: 'What magic is there in the pronoun "my" to overturn the decisions of everlasting truth? My wife or mother may be a fool or a prostitute, malicious, lying or dishonest. If they be, of what consequence is it that they are mine?'[8]

Non-consequentialist moral thinking, by contrast, tends to emphasize the fact that ethics is concerned not only with impersonal outcomes but very centrally with the quality of actions by agents whose identities as moral beings are partly bound up with emotions and dispositions dependent to a high degree upon attachments of precisely the particularist kind that Godwin dismisses. The pronoun 'my' functions here not to register property rights (as certain views of the family, both conservative and radical, mistakenly assume) but as an indicator of identification. This is part of the point behind the commonsense attitude to the special moral obligations generated by friendship and kinship towards which utilitarian theory is either dismissive or (in its more complex forms) awkwardly accommodating. The claim, mentioned earlier, about personal identity is then offered partly as an explanation of these moral intuitions, and partly as an expansion of them. As explanation, it tries to show that the privileged moral status of these attachments stems from the way in which they serve to constitute, or help constitute, an individual's sense of him- or herself. They seem to me to have a certain amount of success in this explanatory enterprise (though they cannot be the whole story), but, emboldened by this partial success, they then tend to link up with an even grander enterprise, about which I am much more suspicious.[9]

The grander enterprise claims that an individual's identity is constituted, or partly constituted, not only by their intimate connection to family and friends but by their culture, their society, their tribe, their nation or (in some versions) their state. Without wanting to deny some influence to these factors in how a person lives and understands their life, I think that the talk of identity here (as in many other contexts in moral and political philosophy) is overblown, at least as a claim about how people must be in order to have significant self-understanding and a rich moral life. Someone altogether bereft of family and friends is not only unfortunate, but is likely to suffer the sort of deprivation that strikes directly at what seems to be meant by talk of identity, and their lack seems necessarily to involve an impoverishment of their moral resources. At least a case to this effect can be made with considerable plausibility, but as the circle covered by the pronoun 'my' widens to take in such entities as culture, ethnic community or the state, the plausibility of such strong claims diminishes. (This is one of the points that lies behind Forster's dictum about the relative weights of betrayal of friends and nations. Forster is not offering a universalist or utilitarian objection to nationalist or state claims but a more urgent particularist claim.) To take the NE sense of 'nation', some people do build their lives emphatically around racial or tribal or national identifications, but, at least in modern societies, this is not inevitable and I very much doubt that it is usually morally desirable.

It is a curious fact that the identification is often invested with greatest passion and significance where it no longer genuinely represents a reality of daily life, as in the case of expatriate groups who cling to myths, beliefs and symbols that frequently no longer resonate in their homelands and have merely artificial relevance in their present environment. There is a psychology at work here somewhat like that described by G.K. Chesterton with reference to those who 'long for the old feasts and formalities of the childhood of the world' yet have no relish for the living rituals of their own time, and who, had they lived 'in the time of the maypole would have thought the maypole vulgar'.[10] Sometimes a fair degree of this sort of attachment is harmless, as in a delight in the cuisine, geography, fauna, art or folk songs of one's ancestral homeland; often it is harmful, as, I think, it too frequently is in the political passions and activities of expatriate communities, and more alarmingly in the fracturing activities of various tribal affiliations in Africa, most notably of course the tragic divisions in Rwanda.

I do not of course deny that ethnic or nationalist feelings and sentiment are sometimes powerfully felt and have powerful effects; my view is rather that they do not have the close connection with basic moral thinking that is often claimed for them. In the case of familial and friendship or love relations, there is plausibility (I claim no more here) in the idea that such relations generate special duties and rights just because of what they are, no matter how independently worthy are the people they relate. It is difficult to explicate exactly where the moral significance of such ties is located, but part of what is involved is surely connected with the rich potentialities of such intimate relations and the close dependencies and ties they embody. There is nothing vague or mysterious about the reality of the sharing and the histories invoked here, and this contrasts markedly with my relations with my conationals, most of whom I do not know at all. Such intimate relations are not, of course, the whole moral story since there are many moral limits to what we can do on behalf of our children or our friends, but their desires and needs create some presumptive priorities in a way that the demands of wider communities need not. Of course, our choices and our loves and other attachments tend to create responsibilities and loyalties wherever they rest, but the moral force of the 'my' here is much less primitive and the moral question will usually turn heavily upon whether what is loved, chosen or pursued is independently valuable. It is surely pertinent that nationalist attachments have such a strong tendency to be harnessed, manipulated and often created in the cause of wreaking havoc on people and institutions perceived as 'outsiders'. (Families, by contrast, when they do damage, more often do it to those within.)

These points are relevant to the argument of those, such as the Israeli philosopher Yael Tamir, who try to distinguish between good and bad nationalisms. Tamir wants to endorse a good form that she calls 'liberal nationalism', but with this, as with other forms of 'good' nationalism, it is hard to avoid making the adjective do all the serious moral work.[11] That people are loyal and passionate about their liberal state or community is no doubt a good thing for them and for the stability and endurance of that sort of state, but it seems to be their commitment to liberal values as embodied in their particular polity that is the object of approbation and we can advance this point without recourse to the currency of nationalism.

In opposition to the demarcation I am trying to sketch are various philosophers, most notably Hegel, who subordinate individual wellbeing to that of the nation-state. Defenders of Hegel would no doubt prefer to speak of integration rather than of subordination, but the latter phrase seems appropriate given Hegel's glorification of the nation-state as a sort of mystical individual with moral demands on citizens that transcend the particular perspectives they may take to be morally decisive. The case of war brings this out nicely, for not only is Hegel contemptuous of Kant's more internationalist perspective and his argument for 'perpetual peace', but he insists that the idea that morality can serve to provide a critique of politics 'rests on superficial ideas about morality' since the 'welfare of a state has claims to recognition totally different from those of the welfare of the individual. The ethical substance, the state, has its determinate being, i.e., its right, directly embodied in something existent, something not abstract but concrete, and the principle of its conduct and behaviour can only be this concrete existent and not one of the many universal thoughts supposed to be moral commands.'[12] One does not have to be an anarchist to find Hegel's rhetorical exaltation of the nation-state overblown, unrealistic and repellent; nor does rejecting his picture require some sort of blinkered individualism. My claim, at any rate, is merely that, when we are talking of the individual's identity in ways that have some compelling moral force, there is a point in appealing to those familial and amicable relationships that pre-eminently and inevitably constitute the personal sphere, and that this point is far less evident in appeals to the nation, the race or the state.

I do not deny that some degree of special attachment to one's country and its political and cultural institutions can be harmless, and even a good thing, up to a point, as long as those institutions and attachments are in fact valuable (or at least not vicious). A sense of place is certainly a constituent of most people's make-up, and an attachment to the geographical and physical surroundings in which one grew up, and the social 'feel' that accompanies that growing up is natural to human beings, though it can be destroyed by circumstance (as with those German Jews who cannot bear the thought of returning to or visiting Germany) and it can be removed to other locales (as many migrants find). But nationalism goes well beyond this, for, as we have seen, it essentially involves a political commitment, and a privileging of certain forms of power. Any such attachment is likely to be most valuable when the nation or the group of whatever kind is actually suffering persecution or oppression precisely because it is (or is believed to be) a group of that kind. In the United States, it is not surprising that fantasies about 'the African nation' should take root, even though, by any account of 'nation', there is clearly no such thing.[13] In my country, proud identification by people of indigenous descent with 'the aboriginal nation', though somewhat absurd when one considers the diversities and hostilities of the original tribal inhabitants of Australia, is not only understandable in the light of historic and continuing injuries which presumed such a group identification, but clearly has some political, psychological and moral advantages. Where the oppressed band together under group labels, it is easy to sympathize with them, but, even here, the bonding carries the characteristic dangers, as is so evident in the American phenomenon entitled 'The Nation of Islam', where genuine identification with a tragic past and a legitimate attempt to repair present misfortune have sometimes been distorted by fantasy and hatred into alarming extremes of racism. We should recognize the inevitability of these invocations of national identity and sentiment, and countenance what positive aspects they may possess, without forgetting their delusional, destructive and harmful sides. The primary task is not to canonize these attachments, but to keep them from getting out of hand. Recent attempts by philosophers and other theorists to give a palatable face to nationalism may make this task of restraint more difficult to achieve.

3 A Positive Side to National Myths?

Against this, some philosophers argue that the moral case for nationalism rests upon the positive social function that such feelings and identifications fulfil. David Miller, for instance, argues that commitment to the nation is morally valuable partly because of the communal solidarity it creates, a solidarity that works against the atomistic and alienating effects of modern market economies and the outlooks that accompany them.[14] This is one way of giving some content to the supposed moral significance of the identity that nationality helps constitute. The first point to make about this claim is that solidarity built around confused and delusional beliefs is inherently prone to cause harm since it is already out of kilter with reality. No doubt a belief in Santa Claus is relatively harmless, but its focus is very narrow. It does not condition a whole social and political agenda, and shape momentous decisions to do with how one shall live and how one shall relate to other people, including those who live in other territories. By contrast, as Hobsbawm notes, 'nationalism requires too much belief in what is patently not so'.[15] Even in the case of persecuted groups, where one's sympathies with nationalist rhetoric and its role in building solidarity must, as noted earlier, be greatest, the degree to which this rhetoric and solidarity rest upon falsehood, misrepresentation and baseless beliefs must present a danger for the political actions they ground. 'Noble lying' has a long history in the practice of politics, and (witness Plato) in the philosophical theories that purport to explain and justify political behaviour, but its value for liberal democracy is surely low. The second point is that there are other and better ways of defeating social isolation and social selfishness than by invoking the fantasies of nationalism. Included in these are the commitments of a broad ethical consciousness, especially to human rights and sympathies, and an attempt to identify with suffering and deprivation wherever it occurs. The additional consideration must also be acknowledged here that the social bonding, under the banner of nationality, that people like Miller seek has historically a strong tendency, at the very least, to limit emotional sympathies and restrict generosity. At worst, it has often been an ingredient in xenophobia, racialism and group belligerence. Whether these attitudes are inherent in nationalism or merely contingent accompaniments of it is perhaps debatable, but, if contingent, they are certainly common enough to be morally alarming.

David Miller has an interesting objection to the sort of criticism I am making about the dangers of delusional beliefs. He argues that we need to distinguish between background and constitutive beliefs, and, where the background beliefs to some institution or practice are delusional, this may be no bad thing, and it may not be rational to want the delusion to be destroyed. He instances the case of a happy family in which, owing to a hospital mix-up, one of the children is not genetically related to the family. He thinks 'it will not be rational in these circumstances to want to have the false belief brought to light'.[16]

Miller's reaction to the example is understandable in view of the distress any such information is likely to cause, and it may well be impertinent and intrusive for any outsider to provide such information unasked. But it is curious that such a supporter of the moral significance of identity as Miller should treat genetic identity so lightly. It is reminiscent of older attitudes to the suppression of information about adoption when it was widely believed either that families could not survive an adoptee's knowing that he or she was adopted or that existing familial ties would be badly damaged by an adoptee's having access to their genetic parent or parents. I do not want to adjudicate upon the moral importance of any such entitlements, but, from Miller's own particularist perspective, it can hardly be negligible. In any case, one can hope that strong enough familial commitments would survive such revelations (though not unmodified), but it is less clear that nationalist sentiments will survive the dissipation of the nationality myth, which is presumably why Miller argues for the rationality of leaving falsehood undisturbed.

For Miller's argument to apply to nations, it is important that the various false beliefs are only background to, and not constitutive of, the reality of nationality. It is therefore curious that he builds his case on the analogy of individual genetic inheritance since it is surely plausible to view genetic identity as constitutive rather than mere background. The same seems true of the many false elements that he and others claim to be involved in the idea of a nation: for example, various false beliefs about shared history, common action, connection to a particular territory, and shared, distinctive characteristics.

As already remarked, the falsity of many such beliefs is frequently conceded by the fans of nationalism, but its apparent necessity for production of the various benefits claimed for it is pursued no further. Yet it seems unlikely that the elements of falsity and delusion are either necessary for all the good effects they are supposed to produce or beyond revision. A pride in genuine past achievements and openness about past faults is surely a better basis for a present sense of dignity and solidarity than reliance on illusion. In any case, some argument is required to show that illusion is a preferable base. Most Germans have learnt to reject the absurd fantasies of the Aryan master race without a massive decline in communal solidarity even if it took a military defeat to trigger the reappraisal of their history. If we are interested in understanding ourselves and our current circumstances, it is better to confront falsity and distortion rather than absorb it comfortably and uncritically into our identities.

A further problem for the Miller view, and others like it, is that a fully subjective account of nationalism basically erodes the existential import of the beliefs that unify the attitudes of nationalism. It is not simply that the beliefs are false or confused or based on illusions. We have already discussed the problems associated with this admission. Rather it is that the key concept 'nation' cannot achieve genuine reference merely by figuring in beliefs of this sort. Recall Miller's comment: 'a nationality exists when its members believe that it does'. Associated with his view that there is no objective basis for the attribution of 'nationality', this strongly suggests that a nation comes into existence when (and only when) a group of people jointly believe that they are all members of it. But this raises the question: what reality do they believe they are members of when they have this belief? The fact that they can all parrot the word 'nation' (or 'nationality') in response to this question advances us no distance at all. They do not believe that they are members of a word, and the word has no referent other than that given by their joint beliefs. Yet these joint beliefs point nowhere. They give no such referent. It is not merely that the supposed members cannot say precisely what the referent is, or cannot define it: that might be the outcome of inarticulateness on their part or complexity or extreme simplicity in the concept. By Miller's admission (and, it seems, that of Gellner) there is nothing that more articulation or more analysis could reveal. Imagine a group of people scattered across several lands who come to believe that they share the nationality Umpalan. They tell us that 'we Umpalans' have a proud history of literature, a record of military valour, a common ancestry, a common religion and a common language. They have always welcomed strangers into their land, 'their land' being the collection of geographical positions they occupy plus those bits occupied by their ancestors. Most of this turns out to be false. No matter, say the theorists of nationality, they exist as a nation because they believe that they do. But this is a much harder saying than its authors seem to think. The people calling themselves 'Umpalans' have a number of false beliefs about the group of people they associate with in this strange way, but these are not false beliefs about an existing nation (its existence established by the beliefs). We might as well say that Santa Claus exists, because a whole lot of children use the name and have false beliefs about someone who rides in the sky in a sleigh pulled by deer and comes down chimneys with presents. (There are indeed many differences between a belief in Santa Claus and a belief in nations, apart from the relative harmlessness of the former, but here it is the similarities I am concerned to highlight.) Of course, the nationalist could give up the strange idea that the beliefs create the existence of what they are about, and merely accept that a nation is a fiction somewhat like Santa Claus. But is it sane to live and die for a fiction?

Partly because of this difficulty, David Archard, who is sympathetic to Miller's outlook, is careful to deny that the nation to which nationalists are attached is a completely subjective idea. He admits the component of false belief that surrounds the nationalist allegiance, but claims that there must be a number of true beliefs central to the nationalist's thinking about her nation. As he puts it: '... inasmuch as the subjective criterion of nationhood is plausible *some* version of an objective criterion must be true to *some* degree'.[17] Archard is not forthcoming about what this objective criterion should encompass, but he seems to have in mind such facts as the following: there have been people living within this geographical area for a long time, relating to each other by way of trade, family ties and legal regulation, and I am related to some of them by descent. Facts of this kind will be available to anchor some of the beliefs that go into the nationalist mix, though it is worth remembering that immigrant nationals will not be able to make the last of the above claims in the first generation. Their offspring may, though this will depend on either intermarriage with non-immigrants or what 'a long time' is supposed to mean.

Yet if Archard's view is not exposed to the objections to the purely subjective account, it has problems of its own. For one thing, this set of facts may be objective but it dubiously grounds an objective criterion of nationhood. It seems to produce at once too few nations and too many. The set will be true of the whole of Europe for instance, or Africa, even possibly the whole world, but it may also apply to very small groups such as villages who presumably can have no entitlement or aspiration to nationhood. It seems likely that these difficulties can only be overcome by bringing in the subjective beliefs that give rise to the problems discussed earlier. These beliefs power the drive to strong political autonomy that is associated with nationalism, and to the (very considerable) extent that they are false this drive is dangerous. But, more to the present point, they will deprive the term 'nation' of determinate reference.

Like Miller, Archard also argues that the false beliefs commonly pertaining to nationalism can play a positive role in strengthening communal identity and encouraging good behaviour. In this respect they function like (and sometimes are) myths that support positive attitudes like courage in the face of adversity. He takes the Dunkirk myth as an example. In spite of the elements of falsehood in it, the story presents certain truths about national character and helps reinforce Britons' sense of themselves as embodying those characteristics. Indeed even where the story does not present truths about national character, it may help in the aspiration towards those valuable characteristics it depicts.[18] There are important differences between these two claims. The first requires that, despite distortions, the national myths present certain truths about the national character; the second admits that the myth presents no such truths about what the character is or has been, but provides encouragement to acquire the valuable characteristics embodied in the story. Allowing, what may well be disputed, that there is some meaning to the term 'national character', we might think of the Dunkirk myth as presenting Britons as especially resourceful, courageous and loyal to one another in order to reinforce these existing values. But if Britons do have these characteristics anyway, what is the point of producing or sustaining falsehoods about history in order to promote them? Why not cite true examples of the virtues in action? Falsehoods may produce good outcomes, but the nationalist needs to show us why they are not only sufficient but necessary for the outcomes. Here the first claim tends to fall back upon the second. If Britons are not particularly resourceful, courageous and loyal, then lies about their past may help remedy their deficiencies.

Quite apart from any inherent wrong in the lying and deception that promoters of such nationalist myths must countenance and advance, there are two other problems with the strategy. The first is that building virtues upon a web of falsity is essentially fragile since exposure of the false history may wreak havoc with the qualities that have been built upon it. This in turn encourages amongst the authorities and others dedicated to the myth defensive and censorious attitudes to the uncovering of truth about the relevant past. Hence the various attempts to suppress or condemn the work of those citizens who try to correct the record and show the crimes or follies of the national past. There is no need to recite the many examples of this, though the Smithsonian scandal about attempts to present some details of the moral enormity of the American bombing of Hiroshima in the Enola Gay exhibition provides a classic illustration.[19] Attempts by Australian authorities and conservative academics to sanitize the history of European treatment of the aboriginal population represents another.[20] This shows the nature of the second problem: the deceptive myth cannot be neatly quarantined and its implications are invariably damaging to the health of the civic community.

4   Further Issues

Most of the criticisms I have made of nationalism apply equally to the NP or NE forms of nationalism, but they have a particular relevance to the NE version, and here it is instructive to examine more closely a claim on behalf of the NE variety that is becoming more and more respectable. This is the claim that national attachments have a particular and positive role to play in the wider political order to which these groups belong. Sometimes this is an empirical claim about the best way to promote overall wellbeing, sometimes it is a more rights-based claim that need not be consistent with a thesis about the best overall consequences. The more rights-based version argues that the flourishing of the individual or (in a liberal account) the individual's adequate exercise of autonomy or freedom requires their involvement in the sort of NE communities that are their natural homes. The wellbeing thesis, by contrast, simply claims that the best outcomes for the wider society will flow from encouragement of intense commitments to the NE subgroups. Both of these versions attempt to defuse the tensions noted earlier that can arise between the NP and NE forms of national allegiance. In the context of the debate about nationalism, we need to distinguish the social and the political forms of these arguments. It may be that immersion in one's ethnic community has certain benefits for the individual or the wider community without this creating any case for the state to devolve political powers and privileges to that community. After all, many people gain much of their identity from their religious affiliations, their spiritual groups, their sporting associations or their workplace community without this providing any case for these organizations being granted some privileged political power within the wider community. Unless the organizations are vicious, the state should not stand in their way, and might even provide some impartial forms of support across the spectrum, but there seems no basis here for any form of devolved political sovereignty. As for the empirical claim that flourishing ethnic communities make for a healthier public life in the wider community, I doubt that we know the truth of this; indeed, I doubt that there is a perfectly general truth to know. Too much depends upon what forms this flourishing takes. The strong counterclaim that the flourishing of such subgroups is inevitably destructive of community life in the nation (NP) does, however, seem to be quite false, as the comparative success of multicultural societies like Australia, Canada and the USA shows. But we should, I think, be wary of the idea that responsibility for the protection of independently grounded human rights and liberties should be handed over to subgroups in the community, if only because the claims of their 'leaders' to represent their members are often even less well-grounded than the claims of the state's political leadership to represent citizens generally.

I should make it clear that I am not here taking a stance against devolved political powers. Nationalism is not the same as regionalism or a commitment to local forms of governance. There are things to be said in favour of some devolution of powers to local communities, but such considerations need have nothing to do with any national or ethnic homogeneity of such groups. Mostly, these considerations will be to do with the superiority of local knowledge and the virtues of self-help. These certainly have some force though they need balancing against the demands of wider obligations and attachments.

There is one other confusion that can obstruct discussion here. This is the confusion between national independence and popular sovereignty. The latter notion is basically that of a certain sort of involvement in political processes, and can be characterized as the idea that those who are ruled should have a significant say in how they are ruled; it goes very naturally with democracy, but is perhaps compatible with a benign, consultative autocracy, or even a benign consultative *imperium*. It has no need to invoke the nation, in either the NE or NP sense. There seems no reason why a group of 'rootless cosmopolitans' living together in a territory cannot engage in such self-rule without invoking a 'self' that has the thick emotional and moral connotations beloved of nationalists. Even such cosmopolitans may rightly want to resist invasions or interventions from those who want to destroy or degrade their political arrangements, and could resist them as attacks upon popular sovereignty. On the other hand, it is all too sadly clear that one can have what is called national independence in the absence of anything resembling popular sovereignty. The national independence achieved by decolonization processes is often nondemocratic, and often also represents the independence of a nation very much in the NP sense because the new nation, inheriting colonial boundaries of a sometimes capricious nature, will encompass diverse tribal and ethnic groups that can be hostile to one another. Often the struggle for independence will have forged bonds between individuals or groups for whom the NP nation is more important than their own NE nation, and who believe that the good of the whole community requires the dampening of the enthusiasm for ethnic nationalism. But even here such nationalists may (and sometimes do) have very little enthusiasm for popular sovereignty as I am using the term. Nor is the divorce between nationalism and popular sovereignty restricted to the third world. Hitler's national socialism drew deeply upon delusional nationalist myths and was undoubtedly popular at different times, but the Nazis maintained their rule by abolishing democracy.

Of course, the world of geographically demarcated sovereign states and its role in organizing people's lives is a current reality and unlikely to vanish in the near future. It leads to particular obligations, rights and even loyalties without which any such method of political organization cannot survive, and if it were a good way of so organizing lives this might be a sufficient moral justification of it, and hence perhaps of a weak NP attachment. (Though some might require it to be the best.) Robert Goodin, in a utilitarian spirit, has offered a justification of particularist duties to compatriots along these lines.[21] His idea is that nation-states restrict duties and impose burdens as the best way we have to satisfy perfectly general duties. An initial difficulty for this suggestion is that, on the face of it, it seems implausible that the present arrangement of nation-states is the best, or even a particularly good, way to achieve human duties to each other. The fantastic discrepancies of wealth, comfort and freedom from disease across the international order serve as a stumbling block to this line of justification, as do the damaging effects of the idea of national self-interest as an implement of international moral and political thinking. Even so, it might be argued that we are not talking of what is ideal, but of what is pragmatically possible. Perhaps the alternatives to the nation-state have their own stumbling blocks, many of them built by the passions and loyalties to which nationalists appeal, others provided by the circumstances of distance and the interpretive problems of cultures. If so, then we have a moral situation which is typically 'messy' in a way that I have discussed elsewhere.[22] We may have to continue with the apparatus of nation-states until we can develop better ways of satisfying the moral and political obligations and responsibilities that human beings have to one another. But this is no reason to exalt nationhood or endorse the spirit of nationalism. On the contrary, a cool attitude to the demands of nationalism may be the only way to advance beyond the nation-state. The last decades have seen some depressing manifestations of the national spirit, but they have also seen some interesting, if ambiguous, weakenings in the sovereign powers and pretensions of nation-states under infranational, supranational and international pressures. It is important to evaluate these changes and pressures for change in a critical spirit, but it may be that they presage the decline in importance of the nation-state and point to better ways of fulfilling general duties and achieving public goods, even where such means can only now be dimly imagined. If so, a revived enthusiasm for nationalism may be the last thing we need.

Notes

1 E.M. Forster, 'What I Believe', *Two Cheers for Democracy*, 2nd edn, London: Edward Arnold, 1972, p.66.
2 Ernest Gellner, *Nations and Nationalism*, Ithaca: Cornell University Press, 1983, p.7.
3 David Miller, 'In Defence of Nationality', *Journal of Applied Philosophy*, vol.10 (1993), p.6.
4 See O'Brien's review of Pfaff and Tamir in his essay 'The Wrath of Ages: Nationalism's Primordial Roots', *Foreign Affairs*, vol.72 (1993).
5 Miller, 'In Defence of Nationality', p.8.
6 Lord Acton, 'Nationality', *Essays on Freedom and Power*, ed. Gertrude Himmelfarb, Gloucester, MA: Peter Smith, 1972.
7 Gellner, *Nations and Nationalism*, p.1.
8 W. Godwin, *An Enquiry Concerning Political Justice*, ed. Raymond A. Preston, New York: Alfred A. Knopf, 1926, vol.1, p.42. (See Introduction, p.xxx for details of alterations in later editions.)
9 Someone who consciously makes the jump that concerns me here is David Miller in 'The Ethical Significance of Nationality', *Ethics*, vol.98 (1988/9). The target for his pro-nationalist attempt at persuasion is precisely someone with the position I am advancing, namely (as he puts it on p.659) 'someone who is willing to entertain particularist commitments but believes that there is something fishy about nationality'.
10 The quotations are from Chesterton's 'Christmas and Aesthetes', in *Heretics*, London: J. Lane, 1919; reprinted in *The Essential G.K. Chesterton*, Oxford: Oxford University Press, 1987, p.74.
11 Yael Tamir, *Liberal Nationalism*, Princeton, NJ: Princeton University Press, 1993.
12 *Hegel's Philosophy of Right*, trans. and ed. T.M. Knox, Oxford: Oxford University Press, 1967, para.337, p.215.

13 For an excellent discussion of Africa and its diverse cultural, political, religious and tribal loyalties, see Anthony Appiah, *In My Father's House: Africa in the Philosophy of Culture*, London: Methuen, 1992.

14 Miller, 'In Defence of Nationality', p.9. It is interesting to note that Miller is one of the several recent writers with a leftist orientation who are flying the banner of nationalism. It has never lacked supporters on the right.

15 Eric Hobsbawm, *Nations and Nationalism since 1780: Programme, Myth, Reality*, Cambridge: Cambridge University Press, 1990, p.12.

16 Miller, 'The Ethical Significance of Nationality', p.655.

17 David Archard, 'Myths, Lies and Historical Truth: A Defence of Nationalism', *Political Studies*, vol.43 (1995), p.474.

18 Ibid., p.475. Actually, a little later, Archard, in summarizing his argument to that point, moves from the claim that myths *may* have that estimable effect to the assertion that they do (see p.477). This is presumably just a slip. His general position is that he is not offering arguments for nationalism, merely rejecting one argument against it, but the slip suggests that he may find this stance a little uncomfortable.

19 See Michael J. Hogan, 'The Enola Gay Controversy: Hiroshima, Memory, and the Politics of Presentation', in Michael J. Hogan (ed.), *Hiroshima in History and Memory*, Cambridge: Cambridge University Press, 1996; and Martin J. Sherwin, 'Hiroshima as Politics and History', *The Journal of American History*, vol.82 (1995).

20 See Stuart MacIntyre and Anna Clark, *The History Wars*, Melbourne: Melbourne University Press, 2003.

21 Robert E. Goodin, 'What Is So Special about our Fellow Countrymen?', *Ethics*, vol.98 (1988/9).

22 'Messy Morality and the Art of the Possible', *Proceedings of the Aristotelian Society*, supplementary vol.64 (1990).

Chapter 5

Patriotism as Bad Faith*

Simon Keller

Patriotism, too, is an issue of identity, at least from the point of view of the patriot. Most people think that patriotism is a virtue. That, at least, is what is suggested by a quick glance at the political world and the popular media in the United States and similar countries. In everyday life, you are usually offering a compliment when you call someone a patriot, and patriotism is usually thought to be something that we should foster in ourselves and our children.

Much recent philosophical interest in patriotism is premised upon the thought that a philosopher's attitude to patriotism will correspond to her attitude to loyalty in general. This thought, if true, makes trouble for anyone who wants to say that patriotism is a bad thing. It seems obvious that some kinds of loyalties are desirable; few would want to disapprove of loyalties to parents, children, romantic partners and friends, to give some examples. But if it is wrong to favour someone just because she is your compatriot, is it not also wrong to favour someone just because she is your mother? If we cannot place patriotism on solid philosophical ground, then won't we have to regard loyalties to family, romantic partners and friends as equally problematic?

That is certainly what many philosophers seem to think. Alasdair MacIntyre treats patriotism as 'one of a class of loyalty-exhibiting virtues (that is, if it *is* a virtue at all), other members of which are marital fidelity, the love of one's own family and kin, friendship and loyalty to such institutions as schools and cricket or baseball clubs'.[1] Andrew Oldenquist invites us to think of ourselves as sitting at the centre of a number of concentric circles, each of which represents a domain of individuals to whom we feel a loyalty; close to us is a circle representing loyalty to family, much further out is a circle representing loyalty to species, and somewhere in between is a circle representing patriotic loyalty to country.[2] Marcia Baron's defence of (one kind of) patriotism is embedded in a general theory about how the liberal universalist approach that she favours can be squared with a person's favouritism for her own family and friends.[3] And so on.[4] While it is often admitted that there are more and less extreme forms of patriotism, it is generally accepted that patriotism is an attitude of essentially the same type as our loyalties to family, friends and the rest, just with a different object.

---

* First published as Simon Keller, 'Patriotism as Bad Faith', *Ethics*, vol.115, no.3 (April 2005), pp.563–92.

In the present chapter, I dispute that analogy. I try to show that there are differences between patriotism and other familiar kinds of loyalty, and that they are of ethical consequence. More precisely, I argue that patriotism, properly understood, involves a disposition to fall into a kind of bad faith, and that this is a reason to think that patriotism is certainly not a virtue and is probably a vice. If I am right, then it is possible to demonstrate the undesirability of patriotism without implying anything too implausible about the ethical status of other loyalties and allegiances.

What is Patriotism?

Choice

Understanding the nature of some kinds of loyalty involves understanding that the loyalty involved is given by choice, and could be transferred to some other object should the subject so decide. Consider, for example, the loyalty that you might have for a political candidate. Typically, in such a case you have a number of candidates to whom you could give your support, and you find a way of deciding between them. Should you judge that your candidate has changed or failed, or should there be a change in your own political opinions, then you have the option of shifting your loyalty to a different candidate.

Other forms of loyalty, like the loyalty that people characteristically have for their parents, are not in this respect subject to choice. You cannot choose who is to be the object of your filial loyalty, if anyone is. The only people to whom you can show filial loyalty are your parents (or those who play that institutional role), and you do not, exceptional cases aside, get to decide which people are your parents (or play that role).

In this regard, patriotism is similar to filial loyalty and different from loyalty to a political candidate, because you cannot, in standard cases, decide which country is your own. Exceptional cases aside, one who asks, 'Should I be a patriot?' does not typically face the further question, 'If so, then of which country?'

Loyalties Derived and Underived

Some loyalties are derived from different, more fundamental loyalties. Your loyalty to a political candidate might be derived from a more fundamental loyalty to certain values and principles, or from a more fundamental loyalty to the candidate's party. You might be loyal to a particular brand of toothpaste because of your deeper loyalty to your hometown, which is where the toothpaste is made.

Other loyalties are underived or 'first-level' loyalties, or loyalties 'in the first instance', meaning that there are no deeper loyalties of which they can informatively be regarded as manifestations. My love for the Geelong Football Club is not an expression of my deeper love for something else, and does not depend essentially on any value or principle that the club represents; I just find myself loving and caring about the club for its own sake. And filial loyalty, again, is an obvious case of a loyalty that tends to be nonderived. There is just no answer to the question, 'In virtue of which more fundamental loyalty do you love your mother?' So far as a hierarchy of loyalties is concerned, this is a place where explanation bottoms out.

Love of country could be derived. Your love of Switzerland may stem from your love of cheese, your love of Nepal from your love of climbing. As philosophers have often pointed out, however, something important about patriotism is missing from loves like these.[5] What is missing is the importance of the patriot's country's being *her* country. Anyone who loves cheese, whether a Swiss native or not, can love Switzerland for its cheese. And being Swiss, loving cheese and recognizing that Switzerland has great cheeses is not enough to make you a Swiss patriot. It is not as though the patriot has some pre-existing set of values – endorsed from a perspective that is free of allegiances to this country or that – and then determines that these values are, fortunately enough, manifested or represented by her own country. Patriotism – unlike some other forms of loyalty, including some forms of loyalty to your own country – is not just a manifestation of loyalty to an independently endorsed ideal. To some extent, the patriot's loyalty to her country is grounded in its being *her* country. A patriot is loyal to her country *in the first instance*, not in virtue of a deeper loyalty to something else.

Seriousness

There is a kind of seriousness that is involved in some loyalties but not others. If a loyalty of yours is *serious*, as I will use the word, then it can demand that you make significant sacrifices for the sake of its object; that you show its object a genuine, rather than ironic reverence; and that you allow that loyalty to have some force when making some morally weighty decisions.

My loyalty to the Geelong Football Club is passionate, but it is not serious, in the sense in question. I am not about to insist upon standing to attention during the playing of the club song, I am not going to compromise friendships for the sake of the club, and I do not think that my loyalty to the club could ever require me to commit acts of violence or enormous self-sacrifice.

Loyalty to a parent, on the other hand, is often serious. You might make enormous sacrifices for your parents, take your obligations to them to have a serious moral dimension (you might tell lies or break rules to keep them out of trouble) and show them a reverence that is neither ironic nor self-conscious. And this may be true even though your nonserious loyalty to a football club is in a sense more passionate and takes up more of your energy than your filial loyalty. The kind of seriousness of loyalties that I am trying to bring out here does not necessarily go along with intensity.

Patriotism characteristically presents itself as a serious loyalty. You can show your patriotism by standing during the national anthem, wearing your country's flag on your lapel or your backpack – in general, by showing an unironic reverence for your country. Patriotism is often cited (or appealed to) as a reason why you do (or should) make significant sacrifices for your country. It is difficult to imagine someone who is a genuine patriot, but takes her loyalty to country to generate no morally weighty reasons at all.[6] Patriotism is a serious matter, in a way in which some other loyalties – my loyalty to Geelong, for example – are not.

Patriotism and the Qualities of a Country

There is a conception of patriotism according to which it necessarily involves the belief that your country is, objectively, the best, or has features that make it superior to all others. Baron recommends a way of thinking about patriotism that, she says, 'certainly does not accord with the usual ways of thinking about it in our culture', because it does not require that the patriot see her own country as superior.[7] We should step back, though, from the idea that being a patriot means taking your own country to be the one that everyone has most reason to admire, or that looks most valuable from the neutral point of view. Someone who said, 'I don't think that my own country is by any means the best. There are others I could name that are better. But it is still, on the whole, a good country, and I'm proud to call it my own', could, surely, properly count himself a patriot.

Even the belief that your country is on the whole a good country, however, might not be a requirement of patriotism. There are dissidents who count themselves as patriotic, even while making broad condemnations of their own countries, and who indeed see themselves as expressing their patriotism through their very concern that their countries become better than they are. This is what we might call patriotic dissent, and it is not the same thing as just plain dissent. Distinctively patriotic dissent is made such by its appeal to qualities that the dissenter takes to be central to the identity of the country, but that she thinks it to be losing or ignoring or showing insufficient respect.

Where the (just plain) dissident might say, 'This policy needs to be changed, because it does not respect the rule of law, and the rule of law should be respected', the patriotic dissident might add, 'and what makes it especially important that we change the policy is that our country represents and is built upon respect for the rule of law. If we abandon that principle, then we abandon an aspect of our very identity; we cease to be the country that I recognize and love'. Cicero and the patriotic dissidents of late Roman times, for example, attacked their country for failing to live up to its glorious past. Patriotic American dissidents in the sixties complained that America was not being true to the values of freedom and equal rights that lie at its heart. In counting patriotic dissidents as patriots, we are counting those who say things like, 'There are some wonderful things about my country, but those things are being outweighed or overlooked in ways that make my country, on the whole, a pretty awful one at present. As one who understands what is truly valuable about this country, it is my patriotic duty to speak out against its present state.'

While the patriotic dissident might be reluctant to say that her country is on the whole a good one, her patriotism does make reference to characteristics of her country that she regards as genuinely, objectively valuable, and as playing an important role in making that country what it is. And this, I want to suggest, is a necessary condition for patriotism. Truly patriotic loyalty is entangled with a conception of the beloved country as having certain valuable characteristics, characteristics that make it, in some minimal way at least, *worthy* of patriotic loyalty. Patriotism always takes itself to be grounded in the relevant country's possession of certain specified, reasonably determinate qualities that the patriot takes to be genuinely valuable, and to make a nontrivial contribution to the country's identity.[8]

One way of grasping this point is to think about how a patriot would respond to the invitation, 'Describe your country for me. What is it like?' My suggestion is that when a patriot answers this question – when she expresses her characterization of her own country or her beliefs about what are its most central or defining characteristics – she must call upon some properties that she takes to be good properties for a country to possess. In this respect, patriotic love differs from the love that people characteristically have for their parents. It is missing the point to cite your parents' wonderful characteristics in explaining why you love them, because there are no particular features of your parents (of the type that count as having objective value) in which your love for them is essentially grounded. Not so, I claim, for patriotic love.

The claim is not that it is impossible to be loyal to your own country without taking it to be characterized by certain valuable qualities, just that such loyalty is not enough for patriotism. Rian Malan's book *My Traitor's Heart* is an account of the apartheid years in South Africa, told by a white Afrikaner who has come to believe that his country is cruel, paranoid and violent, and that its national project is rotten to the core.[9] While Malan regards South Africa with a distaste that sometimes seems very much like hatred, he displays a deep personal concern for his country – a concern that he does not hold towards any but his own South Africa. Malan might indeed *love* South Africa, but it would be an odd use of language to call him a South African *patriot*. His feelings for his country are not patriotic feelings. His book could not have been called *My Patriotic Heart*.

I want to harp on this point a little. The classic appeal to Athenian patriotism in Pericles's funeral oration moves seamlessly between claims that Athens is *ours* and claims that Athens is *great*.[10] If I tell you that a children's book called *America: A Patriotic Primer* has recently been published, I have said enough for you to confidently infer that it will focus upon good, not bad, things about America.[11] If I tell you that we are about to be treated to a patriotic discourse, or to attend a patriotic event, then you know that what is to come will involve some praise of our country's qualities. Patriotism is a kind of love for country that makes reference to, or latches onto, aspects of a country that are taken to merit pride or approval or affection or reverence. Without that, you don't have patriotism.

What is Patriotism?

Patriotism is not just a loyalty like any other. To be a patriot is to have a serious loyalty to country, one that is not characterized by the phenomenology of choice, is essentially grounded in the country's being yours, and involves reference to (what are taken to be) valuable defining qualities of the country. In one way or another, this sets patriotism apart from many other familiar forms of loyalty. This opens up the space for an argument against the desirability of patriotism that cannot be translated into an attack upon loyalty in general.

Against Patriotism

Confessions

When I am watching Geelong play football and the umpire makes a controversial decision, I very quickly form a judgment about whether it is right or wrong. If the decision goes the way of the other team, I will probably believe that it is the wrong decision. When I am talking about football with my friends, I will defend the sorts of views that you would expect a Geelong supporter to defend. If the discussion is about who is the greatest footballer in history, I will put the case for one of Geelong's great players. I will do my best to marshal facts in favour of my claim, and I will sometimes get them wrong; I might say that my favourite player kicked more goals than anyone else who has played in his position, and my sparring partner might produce evidence that this is not in fact the case. But this won't move me from my claim about which club is home to the greatest footballer. Perhaps I will say that the statistic in question is not so important after all, or perhaps I will dispute the evidence, or perhaps I will quickly decide that it is not really him but some other Geelong footballer that deserves the title of the greatest ever. One way or another, I will do my best to hang onto the beliefs that go along with being a supporter of my team.

Even as I express my disgust at the umpire's decision, and even as I defend the greatness of my own team's players, my companions and I are aware that my expressed opinions are not really what they present themselves to be. The purported facts to which I appeal in support of my opinions are not really what lead me to hold them. Really, I hold them because I am a Geelong supporter. It would spoil the fun for me or anyone else to point this out, but we nevertheless know it to be the case. That is why my football-related opinions are so easy to predict.

I do not know whether this way of behaving will be familiar to all or most supporters of football teams, but it really is the way things are for me. And my belief-forming habits as a football supporter make me guilty of a mild form of bad faith. 'The one who practices bad faith,' says Sartre, 'is hiding a displeasing truth or presenting as truth a pleasing falsehood.' 'I must know in my capacity as deceiver the truth which is hidden from me in my capacity as the one deceived. Better yet I must know the truth very exactly *in order* to conceal it more carefully – and this not at two different moments, which at a pinch would allow us to reestablish a semblance of duality – but in the unitary structure of a single project.'[12] My project is to hold Geelong-centric beliefs about the world of football; for these to be the sorts of beliefs that I can defend in conversation, I must take them to be supported by an interpretation of the evidence that is not influenced by the desire to reach one conclusion rather than another; but for them to be the beliefs that I want them to be I must actively interpret the evidence in a biased manner. I want to have certain beliefs, but to ensure that I have those beliefs I must deceive myself about my motivations, without acknowledging the deceit.

The use of Sartrean machinery to evaluate my attitudes towards the Geelong Football Club is more than a little overblown, and that is because my support of

Geelong is not a very serious matter. My being a supporter of Geelong, rather than some other team, does not influence any really important decisions of mine or result in any important change in my view of the world. But the point is not to confess to my own bad faith as a football fan, but to suggest that the same brand of bad faith is displayed by those with the much more serious bundle of attitudes that makes for patriotism.

Bad Faith and Patriotism

A patriot's loyalty makes reference to certain characteristics that she takes to be valuable and takes her country to possess. This amounts to the patriot's having beliefs, tied in with her patriotism, about her country's purely descriptive qualities. Some likely candidates are, 'My country is open and tolerant', 'My country is beautiful in a special and unusual way', 'In my country, great individuals are able to flourish' and 'Mine is a country of rolling green fields and friendly farmers'. Even a patriot, whose loyalty to country is entangled with a belief that her country has valuable qualities, has a somewhat independent conception of the sorts of descriptions that a country must meet, if it is to have valuable qualities.

Each of the beliefs just mentioned is one that the patriot could have about any country, not just her own, and is a belief that could conceivably turn out to be false. It is quite possible to encounter evidence that a country is not really so beautiful; in fact contains a preponderance of very grumpy farmers; or is not as open and tolerant as it seemed. When the patriot encounters such evidence with regard to a country that is not her own, she will, depending on what kind of evidence it is, in certain ways alter her beliefs. Perhaps she will change her mind about whether the country is as she imagined, perhaps she will suspend judgment until further evidence emerges – whatever. But what I want to claim is that she is constitutionally unlikely to respond in the same sorts of ways to evidence that *her* country lacks the valuable qualities that she thought it to have, and that it is here that her bad faith is to be found.

If the patriot is guilty of the brand of bad faith that I display as a football fan, then that is because she interprets evidence with the goal of sustaining her conception of her country as bearing particular, valuable characteristics. Out of patriotic loyalty, she is motivated to believe that her country has certain features, and she marshals the evidence in ways that support this belief; but she cannot maintain the belief in its full-blooded form if she admits to herself that it is not grounded in an unbiased assessment of the evidence; so she does not make this admission. A patriot might find herself confronted with evidence that her country is guilty of systematic wartime atrocities, or that the founders of her country were motivated by a racist ideology, where this is evidence that, were it to concern a different country, would lead her to conclude that the country does not merit affection in the way that she had thought. If she responds in such a way as to avoid drawing the same conclusion about her own country – if she denies the evidence, or starts believing that wartime atrocities and racist ideologies are not so bad after all, or immediately turns her efforts to believing that her country has some different qualities that she can convince herself to think valuable – then we have our instance of bad faith.

All of this presupposes not just that the patriot has certain sorts of beliefs, but also that she is motivated to maintain them, even in the face of countervailing evidence. Must the patriot be so motivated?

She will be if she sees her patriotism as a virtue. To see a character trait as a virtue is to see it as one that the ideal person would possess, and is hence, in standard cases, to desire to cultivate it in yourself. A society in which patriotism is regarded as a virtue will be one in which people, especially children, are given special encouragement to view their country with pride and reverence, and to have the associated descriptive beliefs, supported by the relevant evidence or not. It indeed seems quite plausible to think that this pressure, and the brand of bad faith to which it gives rise, is present in societies that value patriotism. We have all heard claims to the effect that teachers and leaders should present our country's history and political system in a positive light, for fear that people will otherwise fail to love the country in the ways that they should.

The deep source of patriotic bad faith, however, lies in the tension between patriotism's demanding certain sorts of beliefs and its failing to be grounded in or dependent upon those beliefs.[13] The patriot does not direct her patriotic love at her country *just because* she judges it to have particular valuable qualities, but the kind of loyalty that she has to her country involves an acceptance of that judgment. The patriot is motivated to maintain her belief that her country has valuable features of a certain sort because she has a commitment that is grounded in that country's being *her* country. To admit to any such motivation would be to undermine the credibility of the belief and the integrity of the loyalty that depends upon it – and so the motivation cannot be admitted.

The patriot's belief that her country has certain attractive features presents itself as having been formed through an unbiased set of opinions about the nature of her own country plus some neutrally endorsed criteria for what properties of countries count as valuable, but this is not really the full story. Driven by her loyalty to country, the patriot will hide from herself the true nature of the procedure through which she responds to evidence that bears upon the question of what her country is really like.

That is my basic case for the claim that patriotism is connected with bad faith. I need to say more about the exact content and status of the claim, and why it gives reason to think that patriotism is a vice.

Clarifying the Thesis

My picture of patriotic bad faith relies upon a scenario under which the patriot encounters evidence that challenges her patriotic beliefs, or her picture of her country as being characterized by particular valuable qualities. There will be cases, however, in which the patriot's conception of her own country is perfectly accurate, and in which she never faces any reason to think otherwise. The patriot might believe that her country is founded upon the values of freedom and equality, and it may indeed be founded upon those values; if so, then she may never need to interpret creatively any evidence to the contrary.

Such a fortunate patriot might never fall into bad faith, because she might never need to hide from herself the truth about how she responds to the evidence about her country that she actually confronts – but she will still be *disposed* to fall into bad faith, under circumstances that (as it happens) never actually arise. She may never need to hide from herself the truth about how she responds to certain types of evidence, but she would, if such evidence were encountered. So while it is overstating things to say that patriotism inevitably involves bad faith, it still seems true – and this is my official claim – that patriotism involves the *disposition* to fall into bad faith under some easily imaginable circumstances.

The Strength of the Thesis

My claim yields what are, I suppose, empirical predictions, like the prediction that patriotic people will be especially resistant to evidence that places their home countries in a poor light. But I am not positing just a contingent correlation between patriotism and bad faith, of the sort that I would be positing if I said that patriots are disposed to choose country music over folk. I am positing an internal connection between the disposition to bad faith and the structure of patriotic attitudes themselves. That said, I do not want to go quite so far as to say that the connection is one of absolute conceptual necessity. I do not think that it is *impossible* to be a patriot who is not disposed to fall into bad faith. Let me explain.

I have described a patriot who, when her conception of her own country is challenged, ignores or creatively reinterprets the evidence, or changes her views about what features it is good for a country to have, in ways that allow her to maintain a picture of her country consistent with patriotic loyalty. Can we imagine a genuine patriot with a different pattern of response? What might a patriot be disposed to do in such circumstances, if not to fall into bad faith?

A couple of cases need to be dismissed at the outset. The first is of the putative patriot who, in response to evidence against her country's having the valuable features she believes it to have, happily abandons those beliefs and ceases to love her country. 'I loved my country because I took it to stand for freedom and equality,' she might say, 'but now that I see that it doesn't, there is no reason to love it.' This person never was a true patriot. Her loyalty to country has been revealed to be a derived loyalty, dependent upon her regard for freedom and equality plus the judgment, now revised, that those are things for which her own country happens to stand.

The second case to be dismissed is of the person who changes her beliefs in light of the evidence – who ceases to think of her country as having the relevant valuable characteristics – but finds that this makes no difference to the way that she feels about her country. 'It mattered to me that my country stands, or so I thought, for freedom and equality,' she says, 'but now that I see that it doesn't, I realize that my thinking that it did was never a condition of my loyalty. It's enough that my country is mine.' What is uncovered here is a loyalty that never really was grounded in a conception of the country as being, in some central respects, a good one. So it – again – never really was an instance of genuine patriotism.

More relevant, and interesting, is the case of a patriot who seriously and honestly confronts evidence that his country is not as he thought, and takes such evidence as a reason to examine and rethink his patriotism. Rather than avoiding consideration of the possibility that his country lacks the characteristics to which his patriotism makes reference, such a patriot is prompted to wonder whether he really ought to have the kind of first-order loyalty to country that he does.

This kind of response requires that the patriot examine himself, not just his country. Most likely, it will lead to the loss of any distinctively patriotic outlook, through a process that I think might be familiar to many readers. It is a process of moving away from an instinctive attitude to your own country of the form, 'This is my great/beautiful/free/... country', and towards the recognition that your country, like any other, needs to be critically evaluated, and that the patriotic picture of it held by you and others could well be illusory. In coming to this realization, you come to take a perspective upon your country that is too detached to coexist with genuine patriotism. To be a patriot who comes to such a point of view is to throw into question, and revise, what is likely to be a deeply held element of your way of making sense of the world. It is likely to involve a change, to a greater or lesser extent, in your self-conception; you are likely to cease to take your belonging to your country as a part of your identity in the way that you did. It can be difficult, disillusioning and traumatic. As such, it is not a process upon which most patriots are likely to embark, and it is a process of reevaluation that patriotic loyalty positively discourages. But it is one way in which a patriot might respond to challenges to his patriotic beliefs, and it need not involve bad faith.

Here, then, is my claim about the nature of the connection between bad faith and patriotism. The patriot can encounter circumstances under which she would, were her patriotism not at stake, revise certain of her beliefs, but under which she feels loyal to her country in a way that requires her to keep them. Usually, that loyalty will hence provide her with a motive to find ways of keeping those beliefs whatever the evidence, and that motive leads to bad faith. It is possible, however, that other elements of a patriot's psychology or circumstances will be such as to outweigh, or prevent the emergence of, that motive – most likely, I think, by prompting the kind of change in perspective described in the previous paragraph.[14] Patriotism is by its nature such as to make the patriot likely to have the disposition to fall into bad faith, but there can be exceptions.

Let me make a brief comment about the strength of my claim in another dimension. Whether or not you are convinced by the somewhat restrictive construal of patriotism for which I argued in the first part of this chapter, I want it to be clear that my argument really is supposed to reveal something about a very broad class of loyalties to country, not just about the unthinking, jingoistic forms of patriotism that are so easy to belittle. The claim also applies to patriotic dissidents, and to those whose patriotism is not really political in nature. Among the patriots whom I think likely to be guilty of bad faith are American dissidents who say that flouting international treaties is not just wrong but un-American, American patriots who are viscerally resistant to suggestions that the defenders of the Alamo did not really go down fighting, Australians overseas who tell us that people are friendlier back home, Australian patriots who insist that inner-city Melbourne or outback Queensland is the *real* Australia, and so on and on. I am not, of course, saying that the beliefs mentioned in these examples are false, just that the patriots concerned are unlikely to consider the evidence on its merits.

What is so Bad about Bad Faith?

Assume that I am right in my claim that patriotism involves the disposition to fall into bad faith: where does this leave us with regard to our assessment of patriotism? Is bad faith necessarily a bad thing?

I think that the link between patriotism and bad faith yields a clear presumptive case against patriotism's being a virtue, and for its being a vice. The structure and role of patriotic attitudes are such that the patriot is likely to have biased, poorly supported beliefs that play an important role in determining her view of the world. Her resistance to certain sorts of beliefs is likely to lead her to have an inflated view of her own country's value and importance, and to dismiss without adequate consideration those who are putting forth reasons to doubt that her country is what she takes it to be. Depending upon what sorts of beliefs ground her patriotism, the patriot is likely to be drawn towards unrealistically rosy pictures of her country's people and history, the principles for which it stands, or the ways in which it operates. All of this could well turn out to be influential when it comes to her making morally significant decisions: decisions about whether to support or fight in a war, about who should get her vote, about whether to make certain significant sacrifices, and so on.

There are various ways in which theoretical perspectives might add additional concerns. Perhaps the patriot, in deceiving herself about the nature of her belief-forming mechanisms, is treating her rational agency as a means, rather than an end. Perhaps true belief is of intrinsic value to the believer, so that someone who is disposed to form false beliefs is disposed to be worse off than she would otherwise be. Perhaps patriotism is in conflict with fundamental virtues like honesty, and with the epistemic virtues associated with good belief-forming, and perhaps there is good reason to think a character trait a vice if it clashes at a deep level with such basic virtues as these.

The claim that patriotism involves a tendency towards bad faith establishes a pretty strong prejudice in favour of the conclusion that patriotism is a vice. If the conclusion is to be resisted, then some work must be done in patriotism's defence.

A Necessary Vice?

Consistent with all that I have said is a defence of patriotism as a character trait that has instrumental value, or is contingently such as to promote the existence of the fundamental virtues. Patriots, it could be argued, are more likely to feel a sense of identification and solidarity with those around them, and are hence more likely to be charitable, generous and unselfish. Patriots may be more likely to have a sense of belonging and identity that leads them to be happier, better adjusted individuals.

Perhaps such considerations will be strong enough to have us conclude that patriotism is a necessary vice, or that its negative features can be outweighed. I will not explore this question, except to point out that there are also reasons to suspect that patriotism leads to war, intolerance, bigotry and stupidity – and is hence of instrumental disvalue.

Conclusion

I have argued that there are reasons to think that patriotism, by virtue of its very nature, is undesirable. Patriotic loyalty is of a kind that requires certain beliefs about its object, without being premised upon an independent judgment that these beliefs are true. As a result, the patriot has a tendency to make judgments about the qualities of her own country in a way quite different from that in which she makes judgments about others, but she is unable within her patriotism to admit to this tendency. That is patriotic bad faith.

Sometimes, the disposition to patriotic bad faith is not something that we need be too concerned about. In some cases, it will never be expressed. In others, the motivations underlying it will be very weak. Given, however, the moral seriousness of patriotism and the importance that patriotism tends to hold for those who have it, there is good reason to think that the disposition to patriotic bad faith will usually be more than just an interesting psychological quirk or harmless indulgence. Patriotic bad faith is likely to play a central role in the patriot's construal of the world and of her own moral obligations, and it is likely to lead the patriot to make bad decisions of real consequence.

There are other issues, like the contingent connection between patriotism and other virtues, that have not been fully explored here but are relevant to the question of whether we should see patriotism as, all things considered, something to be encouraged. But if my argument succeeds, then we have seen a presumptive case for the conclusion that patriotism is not a virtue and is probably a vice.[15]

Notes

1   Alasdair MacIntyre, 'Is Patriotism a Virtue?', The E.H. Lindley Lecture, University of Kansas, 1984; reprinted in *Patriotism*, ed. Igor Primoratz, Amherst, NY: Humanity Books, 2002, p.44 (this and future page references are to the Primoratz edition).

2   Andrew Oldenquist, 'Loyalties', *Journal of Philosophy*, vol.79 (1982), pp.179–80.

3   Marcia Baron, 'Patriotism and "Liberal" Morality', in *Mind, Value and Culture: Essays in Honor of E.M. Adams*, ed. D. Weissbord, Atascadero, CA: Ridgeview, 1989; reprinted with modifications in *Patriotism*, p.70 (this and future page references are to the Primoratz collection).

4   See also the contributions of Sissela Bok and Michael W. McConnell to Martha C. Nussbaum (ed.), *For Love of Country?*, Boston: Beacon Press, 2002.

5   See, for example, MacIntyre, 'Is Patriotism a Virtue?', p.44; and Igor Primoratz's 'Introduction' to *Patriotism*, pp.10–12.

6 Stephen Nathanson says that patriotic loyalty generates 'a willingness to act on the country's behalf, even if this requires some sacrifice ... A person who merely professed these attitudes but was unwilling to act on them would be a hypocrite, not a patriot.' (Nathanson, *Patriotism, Morality and Peace*, Lanham, MD: Rowman and Littlefield, 1993, p.35).

7 'Patriotism and "Liberal" Morality', p.77.

8 For a summary and endorsement of this criterion as presented in the philosophical literature, see Primoratz's 'Introduction' to *Patriotism*, especially pp.10–12.

9 Rian Malan, *My Traitor's Heart*, New York: The Atlantic Monthly Press, 1990.

10 Thucydides, *The Peloponnesian War*, Book II.

11 Lynne Cheney, *America: A Patriotic Primer*, New York: Simon and Schuster, 2002.

12 Jean-Paul Sartre, *Being and Nothingness*, trans. Hazel E. Barnes, London: Routledge, 1969, p.49.

13 Some awareness of this tension is displayed in the evocative final section of MacIntyre's 'Is Patriotism a Virtue?'

14 I have not gone into questions about exactly which components of a patriot's psychology or circumstances might prevent him from falling into bad faith when his patriotic beliefs are challenged. Depending upon how that question is resolved, it may be that the right thing to say is in fact that *all* patriots, *necessarily*, are disposed to fall into bad faith, but that in some cases the disposition is masked or outweighed or disappears under the conditions of its manifestation. On such dispositions, see Mark Johnston, 'How to Speak of the Colors', *Philosophical Studies*, vol.68 (1992); David Lewis, 'Finkish Dispositions', *Philosophical Quarterly*, vol.47 (1997); and Michael Fara, 'Dispositions and Habituals', *Nous*, vol.39 (2005).

15 This is a shortened version of a paper published in *Ethics*. I owe special thanks for the help and generosity of Igor Primoratz, who provided penetrating criticisms of several drafts of the paper, along with support and encouragement. I also received valuable comments and suggestions from the *Ethics* editors, and from Ben Caplan, Aaron Garrett, Cody Gilmore, Joshua Greene, Caspar Hare, P.J. Ivanhoe, David Lyons, Jessica Moss, Mathias Risse and David Roochnik.

Chapter 6

Patriotism: Worldly and Ethical[*]

Igor Primoratz

I

When asked who and what one is, one of the things one typically mentions in reply is one's country. The fact that one stems from or lives in a certain country is normally a component of one's identity, something that needs to be mentioned if the answer to the question 'Who are you?' or 'What are you?' is not to be significantly incomplete.

While almost everyone thinks of some country as his or hers, not everyone is a patriot. But many are. In quite a few countries today, patriotism is quickly regaining some of the popularity and vigour it once had, even in social environments that only a couple of years ago would have been quite inhospitable to it. If one is a patriot, that is a fairly important part of that person's identity, of her sense of who and what she is. If this seems a moot point, think of someone who says, 'I'm an American patriot, but that doesn't matter much with regard to my identity, to who and what I am.' To say that would be quite odd.

Thus patriotism is one of the things worth considering when discussing issues of identity. Elsewhere I have looked into the moral standing of the kind of patriotism that philosophers have been discussing in recent years and that most patriots exhibit. For reasons to be spelled out later, I propose to term that type of patriotism 'worldly'. In this chapter I do two things. First, I highlight a series of distinctions regarding patriotism, including that between its worldly and distinctively ethical varieties. Then I focus on patriotism as a distinctively ethical stance. I argue that, while a certain kind of worldly patriotism is morally *permissible*, but devoid of positive moral significance, a distinctively ethical type of patriotism is, under certain fairly typical circumstances, a stance we *ought* to adopt.

Before attempting to sort out the varieties of patriotism, I need to distinguish patriotism from a related stance, that of nationalism (another important issue of identity). The two terms are often used interchangeably but that, of course, should be avoided. This may not be obvious as long as we are dealing with highly homogeneous nation-states, but becomes clear once we take into account multinational states as well. For, in such a state, the love of, identification with, concern for, country and nation no longer coincide, but rather part ways. Indeed, that is the case

* First published as Igor Primorac, 'Patriotism: Mundane and Ethical', *Croatian Journal of Philosophy*, vol.IV (2004), no.10, pp.83–100. Published by KruZak, Zagreb. Reprinted by permission.

in many nation-states too, namely those that are not entirely ethnically homogeneous. If you are a Croat living in Croatia, you may be a Croatian patriot and a Croat nationalist. However, if you happen to be a member of the Serb minority in Croatia, you can be a Croatian patriot, but cannot be a Croat nationalist.

On the other hand, it will not do to conflate country and nation and then distinguish between patriotism and nationalism in terms of the intensity of the love one feels for it, the degree of one's identification with it, the strength of one's concern for it. It will not do to say that, when these are exhibited in a reasonable degree and without ill thoughts of and unpleasant deeds towards others, that is patriotism; when they become unbridled and make one think ill of and act badly towards others, that is nationalism. This approach need not, but easily may, encourage the use of a double standard of the form 'us vs. them' that seems to have a foothold in common usage. When *we* love our country or nation and put it above others, that is patriotism, a perfectly natural and appropriate attitude to take; when *they* love theirs and act accordingly, they are in the grip of nationalism, and we all know where that sort of thing is liable to lead.[1]

If we hope to understand these phenomena and to subject them to discerning moral judgment, it is more helpful to distinguish between these loves, identifications and concerns in terms of their objects. A patriot loves her *patria*, her country, identifies with it, and shows special concern for its well-being and that of compatriots. A nationalist loves his *natio*, his nation (in the ethnic, rather than political sense of the term), identifies with it, and shows special concern for its well-being and that of conationals. Both these attitudes – like any love, identification and concern – admit of degrees. And, in these matters, the degree of a commitment is crucial for the assessment of its morality.

II

Patriotism, then, can be defined, at least provisionally, as love of one's country and special concern for it and for one's compatriots. In order to take a closer look at patriotism, we need to ask an array of questions. Just what does 'country' mean? Why does one love it? How strong is this love of country, and what is a patriot willing to do for the *patria*? Are there any *moral* limits to what he should – or may – do for his country? Patriotism tends to be expressed in pride of one's country; are there other vicarious feelings appropriate, or even possible, for a patriot? Finally, what is the moral standing of patriotism or, rather, of its main varieties?

Object

Just what is *patria*, the object of the patriot's love, identification, and special concern? Does the term refer solely to the land, its landscape and climate, and to those who live in it and their way of life? Or does it also, perhaps even primarily, refer to their laws and political institutions? Is it a geographic or a political term?

The history of its usage and of the usage of its cognates, 'patriot' and 'patriotism', makes for very interesting reading, but tracing it would require too long a detour.[2] In modern usage, 'patriotism' refers to love of and identification with one's *patria* in both prepolitical and political senses, and to special concern for one's compatriots both as people stemming from or living in one's own country, and as one's fellow citizens. A patriot is committed to his country and compatriots and to his polity and fellow citizens. The latter means that he takes interest and, at least on important occasions, participates in his country's political life. A person who does not – an apolitical person – would not be considered a patriot.

Yet we can surely imagine, and may have come across, a person who claims to love her country and its people, to identify with them and have a special concern for their well-being, but who will have no part in their politics, will not serve their state (nor indeed any state). She may be merely a spontaneously, but deeply and incorrigibly, apolitical person; or she may be an anarchist, and reject politics and the state for well-considered reasons to do with the moral status of power and coercion. She would not count as a patriot in the sense we normally ascribe to the word; but if her claims about her love of, identification with, and special concern for her country and compatriots were true, and if, on the basis of that, she claimed to be a patriot, might we concede that her stance, too, is patriotism of sorts? If so, what we have here is a distinction between two types of patriotism: a minimal, apolitical or prepolitical variety of patriotism, quite unusual in our time, and its usual, comprehensive, prepolitical-cum-political variety.

Some philosophers and political theorists have recently been urging a retreat from this dominant, comprehensive variety of patriotism into a thin, emphatically political type of love of one's country. One motivation for this proposal, emphasized by John H. Schaar, is the need to dissociate patriotism from nationalism, 'patriotism's bloody brother'.[3] The only kind of patriotism that can hope for respectability is the kind that has been disentangled from nationalism: a patriotism that binds us to our country and to one another 'not by blood or religion, not by tradition or territory, not by the walls and traditions of a city, but by a political idea ... by a covenant, by dedication to a set of principles and by an exchange of promises to uphold and advance certain commitments'.[4] This 'covenanted patriotism' is in any case the only type readily available to Americans and citizens of countries with a similar history and similarly heterogeneous in virtually all prepolitical terms.

Against the background of a different history, some German thinkers, too, have been promoting a purely political variety of patriotism they call constitutional patriotism (*Verfassungspatriotismus*). Most notably, Jürgen Habermas has argued against the view that free institutions and liberal political culture can be strong and effective only if they are securely rooted in a particular historical and cultural community, in a particular prepolitical form of life citizens can identify with. Multicultural societies such as the United States or Switzerland show that 'a political culture in which constitutional principles can take root need by no means depend on all citizens' sharing the same language or the same ethnic and cultural origins. A liberal political culture is only the common denominator for a *constitutional* patriotism ... that heightens an awareness of both the diversity and the integrity of the different forms of life coexisting in a multicultural society.'[5]

Others remind us that the history of patriotism itself suggests this move: patriotism was originally a political notion, love of country was first and foremost love of polity, of its laws and institutions, and of the common liberty they make possible. It is only much later that patriotic discourse and patriotic passion got conscripted into the service of the nation-state and became submerged in those of nationalism. Today we are much wiser about nationalism and much more wary of it. Accordingly, thinkers such as Mary G. Dietz and Maurizio Viroli invite us to revive patriotism in its original, political or republican variety, sometimes also called 'patriotism of liberty', in order to oppose nationalism on its own ground, and to provide solid foundations for a stable and vibrant liberal and democratic polity.[6]

The first distinction to make with regard to patriotism, then, is that between (a) prepolitical, (b) comprehensive, and (c) purely, or at least primarily, political patriotism.

Reasons

Why does a patriot love his country and show special concern for its well-being and that of compatriots? Is it because the country exhibits certain valuable traits, because it has special achievements in certain fields of human endeavour? Or is it simply because it is *his* country?

The former reply indicates what might be termed value-based patriotism, the latter what we might call its egocentric variety. Each has both advantages and disadvantages. The former appears reasonable: when asked why does he love his country, why is he more concerned for its well-being than for the well-being of the rest of humanity, the adherent of value-based patriotism will give his reasons. He will point out the values exhibited by his country, its impressive merits and achievements. In doing so, he will be assuming certain standards of value which others can acknowledge as valid. However, we may suspect that this is a somewhat superficial, if not merely apparent, type of patriotism. For a patriot of this kind will, in consistency, have to concede that he ought to be no less concerned for the well-being of any other country that satisfies the same standards of value. It turns out that these values, rather than his country, are the true object of his love and concern.

Here an adherent of egocentric patriotism might appear to be at an advantage. She loves her country simply as *her* country, rather than as *a* country that lives up to certain standards of value. Her patriotism is not derived from some general values and merely focused on her country. It is rather directed at her country in an immediate and stable way, because that country, and that country only, is *her* country. The problem here is that this may strike us as unreflective, indeed irrational. We may be tempted to quote the words of J.B. Zimmermann that 'the love of one's country ... is in many cases no more than the love of an ass for its stall'.[7]

Thus both replies are one-sided, and neither will do very well by itself. The best account of patriotism should include both these partial replies, together with the tension between them. Neither the fact of the merits and achievements of the country, nor the fact that it is *her* country, is in itself sufficient, but each is necessary. What is sufficient is their conjunction. Patriotism appears as irrational, if not unintelligible, if the *only* reason the patriot can cite for her love and concern for her country is the fact that it is *her* country. We feel we should be given more: we should be told about some valuable traits, some impressive achievements of the country. But these traits and achievements provide reasons for her patriotism because they are traits and achievements of *her* country, and not in themselves. If they happen to characterize a neighbouring country too, that will not, and cannot, generate the same special relationship to that country, since the country is not *hers*.[8]

The second distinction we can make, then, is that between the (a) egocentric, (b) value-based, and (c) full-fledged types of patriotism.

Motive

Patriotism is normally considered an altruistic attitude. It is celebrated in much of patriotic literature and art as one of the main expressions of altruism – as selfless, indeed self-effacing, self-sacrificial love of and loyalty to one's country and compatriots. *Dulce et decorum est pro patria mori*: the willingness to die for one's country has always been seen as the ultimate test of patriotism, and doing so as its noblest consummation. According to Machiavelli, the citizens of Florence went even further, and were willing to jeopardize even their immortal souls for the sake of their city.[9]

Occasionally, however, patriotism has been presented in a different light: as motivated by nothing but self-interest, as a purely rational love and a loyalty that is prudent in a very down-to-earth way. The fact that one was born in a certain country, was brought up in it and has lived much of one's life among its people, spoken its language and participated in its culture and its political life need not necessarily determine that that country, and that country only, is one's *patria*. As Voltaire sees it, any country should do, as long as it guarantees the individual his rights and liberties, and he finds it convenient to be its citizen. Any attachment the individual feels in return is but an expression of his well-understood self-interest.[10]

Others do not propose to reduce all patriotism to this. They point out that the modern world is very much unlike that of the ancients, which first gave rise to patriotism. Thinkers such as Montesquieu and Rousseau contrast the noble patriotism of the ancients, based on social unity and expressed in sacrifice for one's country, with the self-interested concern of the denizens of the modern, atomized society, for the country that provides them with personal security and makes possible economic prosperity.[11]

Yet one might be reluctant to grant that this 'patriotism of the moderns' is true patriotism. How can this attitude of *ubi bene, ibi patria* ever justify what is, after all, the supreme test of patriotism, the willingness to lay down one's life for one's country? Indeed, how can it ever justify *any* sacrifice for one's country – anything that it is not merely a prudent investment, but rather a sacrifice in the strict sense of the word? If we can overcome this reluctance, we can distinguish two types of patriotism in terms of its motive: (a) self-interested and (b) altruistic patriotism.[12]

Strength

Patriotism as we know it from history and from everyday experience is much too often an attitude that invites criticism. The patriot loves his country above all others, but finds it difficult to appreciate the same attitude in a foreigner. When confronted with a foreigner who is a patriot of *her* country, he finds her attachment overblown, if not altogether inappropriate. While his love of his country is patriotism, a natural and unobjectionable feeling, the foreigner's love for hers is nationalism, an unreasonable, antagonistic and dangerous passion. The patriot not only puts his country above all others, but actually does not have much time for others. Charity begins, but often also ends, at home. The patriot's love of the *patria* is so strong that no price, including *moral* price, seems too high to pay, no means too questionable to use, when its well-being is at stake. This love is also uncritical, unconditional. For his country either can do no wrong or, if it can, it is *his* country, right or wrong.

Understandably, patriotism has been subjected to severe moral criticism. Critics have argued that it is an arbitrarily exclusive and ultimately egocentric position, incompatible with universal justice and common human solidarity, and unrestrained by moral considerations. They have also pointed at the historical record of patriotism, which shows that it makes for international tension, conflict and war. For all these reasons, they have enjoined us to discard all patriotism, to think of ourselves as human beings first and last, and to act accordingly.[13]

In recent years, some philosophers have sought a middle ground between patriotic partiality and universalism or cosmopolitanism urged by the critics as the sole alternative. Thus Stephen Nathanson concedes that the dominant variety of patriotism is exposed to the objections that have been advanced against it, but argues that these objections need not apply to all patriotism. He goes on to construct a moderate version of patriotism, in which the attachment to one's country and compatriots is constrained by universal morality, and which accordingly steers clear of the pitfalls of both extreme patriotism and sweeping, uncompromising universalism. The conflict between impartiality and partiality, the universal and the particular, Nathanson argues, is not as deep as it may appear. Morality allows for both types of considerations, but at different levels. At one level, one is often justified in taking into account one's particular attachments and commitments, including those to one's country. At another, higher level, one can and should reflect on such attachments and commitments from a universal, impartial point of view, delineate their proper scope and determine their weight. It turns out that universal, impartial justice allows everyone to be partial to their own within appropriate limits; universal human concern is best promoted if everyone takes care first of their own. This holds in general and also, in particular, with regard to one's own country and compatriots.[14]

This new, moderate variety of patriotism is not exclusive. Its adherent acknowledges the fact that other people love and have special concern for *their* countries and compatriots, and accords their stand the same legitimacy she claims for her own. That is, she is willing to universalize the judgment that she is allowed to prefer her country and compatriots to other countries and their inhabitants, and to grant everyone the right to this type of partiality to their country. This shows her claim that she is allowed to be partial to her country to be a genuine moral judgment, for universalizability is a defining trait of such judgments. An extreme patriot does not universalize his stand and does not see that foreigners are equally entitled to be patriots of their countries; his is a stance of an arbitrary and morally indefensible exclusivity.

Moderate patriotism is compatible with a decent degree of humanitarianism. Its adherent shows special concern for her country and compatriots, but that does not prevent her from having a measure of concern for other countries and their inhabitants. Moreover, it allows for the possibility that the concern for human beings in general will sometimes override the concern for one's country and compatriots. Extreme patriotism, by contrast, gives greater weight to the interests of one's country and compatriots than to those of other countries and their inhabitants whenever the two come into conflict.

Moderate patriotism is not unbridled. It does not enjoin the patriot to promote her country's interests under any circumstances, by any means. It acknowledges the constraints morality imposes on our seeking to attain our individual and collective objectives. For instance, while it may require the patriot to fight for her country, it will do so only if the war is, and remains, just. An extreme patriot will not flinch from fighting for his country whether its cause be just or not, and in whatever way it takes to ensure its victory.

Finally, moderate patriotism is not uncritical, automatic, egocentric. For an adherent of this type of patriotism, it is not enough that the country is *her* country. She also expects it to live up to certain standards of value and thereby deserve her support, devotion and special concern for its welfare. When it fails to do so, she will support it no longer. An extreme patriot, on the other hand, loves his country uncritically. When questioned consistently enough, his patriotism turns out to be egocentric.

In terms of strength, then, we need to distinguish between (a) extreme and (b) moderate patriotism. While the latter is morally acceptable, the former is not.

Dominant Vicarious Feeling

Writing in 1943, and addressing major moral and political issues facing her country, Simone Weil discussed patriotism too. At the time, patriotism seemed an understandable position to take. Weil does not question that; but she warns that the kind of love of country the French are likely to exhibit may not be the right kind. She distinguishes between two types of patriotism in terms of the dominant vicarious feeling, patriotism of pride and patriotism of compassion, and enjoins her compatriots to eschew the former and embrace the latter.

Patriotism we know from both history and present experience is that bequeathed to posterity by ancient Romans: patriotism expressed in the identification with and pride in the power, greatness and glory of one's country. This pride tends to be exaggerated. It also makes the patriot uncritical, oblivious of those aspects of the country's past and present that are nothing to be proud of. To dwell on the country's failings and misdeeds, and even to concede them, is tantamount to betrayal.

Whereas both morality and good breeding keep a lid on pride and egoism in private life, collective pride and egoism of this sort know no bounds and no shame. This patriotism of pride is an idolatry of the collective self; if a virtue, it is a pagan one. It is exclusive in several related senses. It is defined by, and confined to, the country's boundaries. It is removed from everyday life, and comes to the fore only on special occasions. It is more readily accessible to the upper classes; common people are drawn to it only in times of upheaval, when anyone can hope for success and fame.

There is, however, a different type of patriotism, which the people too can embrace: that of compassion. A patriot of this type does not love her country solely, or even primarily, for its greatness that holds the promise of eternity, but rather 'as something which, being earthly, can be destroyed, and is all the more precious on that account'.[15] She is particularly alive both to her country's limitations and the hazards and misfortunes it is facing, and to its failings, lapses and misdeeds; and she responds to them with concern and compassion. While patriotism of pride is after the style of Richelieu, Louis xiv, Corneille or Maurras, patriotism of compassion is exemplified by Joan of Arc, who used to say she felt pity for her country. While patriotism of pride is pagan, patriotism of compassion is the only type of love of country possible for a true Christian. It is also the heritage of the French Revolution. Thus it is not exclusive, but rather universal. Unlike pride, compassion can 'cross frontiers [and] extend itself over all countries in misfortune ... for all peoples are subjected to the wretchedness of our human condition'.[16] Unlike patriotism of pride, that of compassion can easily permeate daily life with its inevitable trials and misfortunes. And it is not the preserve of the rich and powerful, but is readily accessible to the common people, who 'have a monopoly on a certain sort of knowledge, perhaps the most important of all, that of the reality of misfortune'.[17]

While patriotism of compassion neither ignores nor rejects what is truly great in the country's past and present, in contrast to patriotism of pride, it is not uncritical:

> Such a love can keep its eyes open on injustices, cruelties, mistakes, falsehoods, crimes and scandals contained in the country's past, its present and its ambitions in general, quite openly and fearlessly, and without being thereby diminished; the love only being rendered more painful. Where compassion is concerned, crime itself provides a reason, not for withdrawing oneself, but for approaching, not with the object of sharing the guilt, but the shame. [...] Thus compassion keeps both eyes open on both the good and the bad and finds in each sufficient reason for loving.[18]

Patriotism is very much a matter of vicarious feelings. In this respect, with Simone Weil, we can distinguish (a) patriotism of pride and (b) patriotism of compassion.

Moral Import

It might be thought that the relation of patriotism and morality has already been dealt with under the heading of 'Strength', where I explained the distinction between extreme and moderate patriotism. The latter position has been constructed in response to moral objections advanced against the former, as an attempt to show that one does not have to choose between the popular, extreme and therefore seriously morally flawed type of patriotism, and the rejection of all patriotism and adoption of a universalistic, cosmopolitan stance. There is a middle-of-the-road position, which maintains a degree of patriotic attachment and concern, but constrains it by universal, impartial moral considerations of justice and humanity. Stephen Nathanson, who advocates this position, defends patriotism by setting moral limits to its intensity, without changing its contents.

There is, however, another, more radical strategy of defending patriotism against moral criticism: one that does not merely rein in the pull of patriotism, but rather changes its contents. For both the extreme and moderate varieties of patriotism aim at defending and promoting the worldly – political, economic and cultural – interests of one's country and compatriots. The difference between them is the length to which this will be done: an extreme patriot will ultimately go to any length for the sake of the *patria*, whereas a moderate patriot will acknowledge that universal justice and common human solidarity set limits to what may be done for its sake. Marcia Baron who, like Nathanson, seeks a middle ground between universalism and extreme patriotism, also emphasizes the constraints universal, impartial morality imposes on the patriot's loyalty to his country. To that extent, her position is very similar to Nathanson's, but she also calls for an expanded understanding of patriotism as a special concern for the flourishing of one's own country, including its 'moral flourishing'. The concern for the moral flourishing of one's country, she suggests, should be seen as an additional manifestation of patriotism, and one that should make it even more acceptable to adherents of universal, liberal morality.[19]

Baron's position is thus half-way between the usual, worldly type of patriotism, and what I propose to term its distinctively ethical type. The latter would put to one side objectives such as the country's political power, riches or cultural vibrancy – things that constitute the country's well-being in a worldly, non-moral sense. It would be concerned instead with the country's distinctively moral well-being, its moral identity and integrity. A patriot of this sort would not express her love for the *patria* by seeking to husband her country's resources and preserve its natural beauty and its historical heritage, or make it rich, powerful, culturally preeminent, or influential on the world scene. Instead, she would want to see to it that her country lives up to moral requirements and promotes moral values, both at home and internationally. She would be investing time and effort into building and preserving a just and humane society at home, and making sure that her country also acts justly beyond its borders, and that it shows common human solidarity towards those in need, however distant and unfamiliar they might be.

In addition to these concerns for the moral integrity of her country at present, she would also be concerned for its past moral record and its implications for the present. She would support, and perhaps initiate, attempts at exploring the darker chapters of the country's history, acknowledging the wrongs perpetrated in decades or centuries past, and responding to that past in appropriate ways, whether by offering apologies or making amends, and by making sure such wrongs are not perpetrated yet again.[20]

To be sure, a patriot of this, distinctively ethical, type would want to see justice done, rights respected, basic human solidarity at work at any time and in any place. But her patriotism would be given expression in her special concern that her country be guided by these moral principles and values, a concern more sustained and more deeply felt than her concern that these principles and values should be put into effect generally. Indeed, she would feel that her own moral record and her own moral identity are inextricably interwoven with those of her country.

Like Weil's compassionate patriot, a patriot of this type would have occasion to feel compassion for her country; for every country has its share of misfortune of one sort or another. However, this compassion may well be felt less keenly when the misfortune is richly deserved, as it sometimes is. Unlike a patriot of the more worldly type, she would not feel great pride in her country's worldly merits and achievements. However, she would be proud of the country's moral record, when it is such that it can inspire pride. But her patriotism would be expressed, above all, in a critical approach to her country and compatriots. She would not deny, justify, excuse or belittle her country's unjust or inhumane practices, laws or policies, whether at home or abroad, as a patriot of the more popular type is much too prone to do. On the contrary, she would feel entitled, and indeed called, to submit them to critical moral scrutiny, and to speak out and act so that they may be identified, acknowledged and dismantled. She would not shirk her part in collective moral responsibility for wrongs present or past, but would rather willingly shoulder it. And she would act accordingly.

This, then, is the last distinction I want to make in this chapter: between (a) worldly and (b) distinctively ethical patriotism.

In terms of the preceding distinctions, the latter, ethical type of patriotism is, first, of the comprehensive sort: it is committed to the *patria* in both the prepolitical and political senses. For both the social and cultural practices that constitute a country's prepolitical foundations, and its political institutions and domestic and foreign policies, are proper subjects of moral assessment and concern. In terms of reasons, ethical patriotism is neither egocentric nor value-based. If it were the former, it would be asinine; if it were the latter, it might not be stable and persistent enough. Like all full-fledged patriotism, it contains both a particular and a general component. In terms of motive, ethical patriotism, just like any other moral commitment, is not self-interested. Its main thrust is other-regarding. Yet this type of patriotism is, in a sense, self-regarding too, in so far as one's country's moral identity and integrity is felt to be bound up with one's own. The distinction between extreme and moderate patriotism is not to the point, since it applies only to patriotism of the usual, worldly sort. Finally, ethical patriotism is not one of pride. It may or may not be Christian, but it is certainly not pagan. Nor is it quite the same as Simone Weil's patriotism of compassion, although there are points of convergence; for the latter is still concerned with a range of worldly matters which the former would rather put to one side.

III

Elsewhere I have discussed the moral standing of worldly patriotism. I have concurred with Stephen Nathanson, who finds its extreme version morally untenable, but defends its moderate version: a patriotism that is universalizable and constrained by considerations of impartial morality. But I have also pointed out a lack of clarity on his part about just what it is his arguments establish. For to show that moderate patriotism is not morally unacceptable is not, as Nathanson sometimes seems to assume, to demonstrate its positive moral import: to show that it is morally mandatory or, alternatively, that it is not obligatory, but is morally valuable or virtuous if freely adopted. I have discussed a series of arguments for the view that moderate patriotism is a moral duty and have found them all unconvincing. I have also taken a critical look into the claim that such patriotism is a supererogatory virtue and have found that line of argument, too, implausible. Thus I have been left with the conclusion that moderate patriotism lacks positive moral significance and that we have no moral reason for adopting it.[21]

Is there something to be said for the distinctively ethical type of patriotism I have just sketched? Do we have reasons for adopting it? I think we do have at least three such reasons.

Being Best Placed

Bringing to a close his essay on the concept of fatherland, Dolf Sternberger brings up, and rejects, the saying 'My country, right or wrong', as 'a barbaric regression ... that has become a general pardon for every crime committed in the name of the fatherland'. He then calls for its reversal: 'one should seek the Right, first and foremost, in one's own house, in particular because criticism is most likely to bear fruit there. [...] It is only natural and reasonable to promote the good ... in one's own land, rather than in a foreign one.'[22]

Here we have the first, rather obvious, argument for adopting the distinctively ethical type of patriotism. By and large, I am better placed to determine what is right and what is wrong, to judge it accordingly, to propose ways and means for setting it right, and to implement the solutions proposed, at home, among my own, than abroad, among foreigners.

I am more likely to be aware, and to have a lively appreciation, of the injustice or lack of compassion in a practice of my own society, than in a practice of another, more or less distant and different society. I am in a better position to identify unjust or inhuman laws and policies of my own polity, than such laws and policies of other, more or less distant and different countries. My moral judgment will be both better grounded and more discerning when exercised on a subject more familiar and better understood than when pronounced on matters about which I may know little and understand less.[23] My moral criticism stands a better chance of being heard, understood, and appreciated at home than abroad, by my own people than by foreigners. Last but not least, my efforts to find like-minded people and, together with them, to set right a wrong, to put an end to an unjust or inhumane practice, policy or law, are also more likely to succeed in my own country, among my compatriots, than in some other, far-away place, among strangers. And many, if not most, moral issues that need to be addressed and settled in a society or polity can in any case be addressed and settled only by members of that society, by citizens of that polity. Nobody else can really do it for them – or for us.

Benefits and Solidarity

Normally, when someone is wronged, someone else benefits from that wrong in some way. When a society maintains an unjust or inhumane practice, or when a polity enacts and enforces an unjust or inhumane law, or lays down and implements such a policy, at least some, and sometimes many, of its members reap benefits from it. Sometimes such a practice, legislation or policy relates to or affects people beyond the country's borders; in such cases, the whole society or polity may benefit from it.

In all these cases, the responsibility for the injustice or lack of basic human solidarity lies, in the first instance, with those who make the relevant decisions and those who implement them. It also lies, in the second instance, with those who give support to such decisions and their implementation. But some responsibility in this connection also devolves on those who have no part in the making of the decisions or in their implementation, nor even proffer their support, but accept, rather than merely receive, the benefits such a practice, law or policy generates.[24] These are fairly straightforward types of collective moral responsibility.

Such responsibility may also encompass those who have no part in designing or putting into effect immoral practices, laws or policies, do not support them or benefit from them, but do benefit in various significant ways from being members of the society or citizens of the polity at issue. These benefits may, but need not, be of the usual palpable sort. One may derive considerable psychological benefit merely from membership in and identification with a society or polity: from the sense of belonging, support and security such membership and identification afford. It seems to me that, if people accept, rather than merely receive, such benefits, while knowing about the immoral practices, laws or policies of their society or polity, or having no excuse for not knowing about them, that, too, generates collective moral responsibility.

It may be thought unduly harsh to talk of collective responsibility in relation to some wrongdoing accruing to individuals who make no causal contribution to that wrongdoing, have no control over its course and no way of putting an end to it. But, of course, I am not suggesting that they are responsible in the same way and to the same degree as those who make the relevant decisions, those who implement them or those whose support makes the decisions and their implementation possible, and that they are as blameworthy as those others. I am only saying that, in accepting benefits from those wrongs, or from their association with the wrongdoers, they underwrite those wrongs. In doing so, they accrue a degree of moral responsibility and join the class of those properly blamed. Their share of responsibility relating to the wrongs at issue is of course lesser and the blame to be laid at their door is lesser too – but they still bear *some* moral responsibility and deserve *some* moral blame on that account. They cannot say in good faith, 'Those wrongs have nothing to do with us! We are in no way implicated in them!'

Furthermore, it might be argued that, independently of any benefits, sheer solidarity with one's society or polity is enough to relate the individual to its immoral acts or practices about which she knows, or has no excuse for not knowing, even though she is otherwise not implicated in those acts or practices. The kind of solidarity I have in mind involves a community of interest, a common lot, and bonds of sentiment, and is usually indicated by vicarious pride and shame. To be sure, here the term 'responsibility' might be thought too strong; if so, we can talk of moral taint instead. Although one is in no way causally connected to the wrongdoing of which one's society or polity is guilty, or even implicated in it through the acceptance of some benefits, one may still be considered morally tainted by one's solidarity with those who are.[25]

Thus I have a reason to develop and exercise a special concern for the moral record, the moral identity and integrity of my country and compatriots. I ought to be concerned about immoral practices of my society, immoral laws and policies of my polity, since they tend to impose collective moral responsibility I, too, have to shoulder, or to taint, the moral record of many members or citizens, including myself. I ought to be concerned that such practices, laws and policies be identified, acknowledged and dismantled, and that their harmful effects be redressed. By doing so, I will also be concerned for an important aspect of my own moral identity and integrity.

Democracy

The preceding two arguments hold generally, irrespective of the system of government. In general, I am in a better position to attend to the moral record of my own country than to judge and amend unjust and inhumane practices, laws and policies of foreign countries, whether the system of government of my country is democratic or not. If my country has such practices, laws or policies in place, and I knowingly and willingly benefit from them, then I, too, may well share the collective responsibility for them, whether the system of government is democratic or not. I may share this responsibility even if I do not benefit from them, but do benefit from living in the country and being its citizen. I may be morally tainted by such practices, laws or policies, if I feel and show solidarity with my country and compatriots, whether the country is a democracy or not. But if I am a citizen of a democracy, I have an additional reason to adopt the distinctively ethical type of patriotism: to cultivate and exercise a special concern for the moral well-being of my country and compatriots.

In a democracy, sovereignty rests with the people. The government passes laws and decides on policies on behalf of the people. It is the people who are ultimately responsible for those laws and policies. When they are unjust or inhumane, the moral responsibility for the injustice or inhumanity lies with the people. That means that it lies with all full-fledged citizens of the polity, for it is on their behalf – on behalf of all of them, and thus of each one of them – that these laws are passed and enforced, these policies designed and implemented. If I am a full-fledged citizen of a democracy, I have a reason to show concern about such laws and policies different and, other things equal, stronger than my concern about immoral laws and policies of other countries. For they are laws and policies of my polity, designed and put into effect on my behalf too. They generate collective responsibility of all citizens, myself included.

It might be objected that this claim is too sweeping: that responsibility for laws and policies of a government can be ascribed only to those who voted for it, but not to those who voted for the opposition. If those latter had prevailed, the laws and policies would have been different. But although this counterfactual may well be true, it is not enough to get those who voted for the opposition off the hook. For taking part in democratic elections does not commit me to the outcome *if* my position prevails, *if* my party gets to govern the country; it commits me to whatever government gets elected and whatever laws and policies it puts in place. Democracy could not function in any other way. Therefore, even if I had voted for the opposition, the government that got elected is, in the relevant sense, my government. My vote, although cast for the party that lost, authorized the party that won to act on my behalf too. Accordingly I, too, have a share in collective responsibility for what it does. My own moral identity and integrity is bound up with that of my government, my polity.

Of course, I can refuse to share the responsibility for an unjust or inhumane law or policy of my government. I can dissociate myself from it. I can protest against it and work in various ways to change it. I can do so even if I voted for the current government in the last elections. But this does not show that the claim that citizens in a democracy are collectively responsible for the immoral laws and policies of their polity was indeed too sweeping and must be qualified. For those who take up this option are actually living up to their collective moral responsibility for their polity – they are acting as ethical patriots.

IV

None of the arguments I sketched in the preceding section severally, nor all of them jointly, succeed in establishing a duty to be a patriot in the pertinent, ethical sense that holds universally, admitting of no exceptions. An individual is normally particularly well placed to submit her own country and compatriots to sustained moral scrutiny and criticism, and to do something about the moral lapses and outright wrongdoings this scrutiny brings to the fore. Accordingly, she ought to make use of this opportunity. But she can also come to the conclusion that her country is, morally speaking, beyond the pale, and decide to dissociate herself from it. By disowning her country, she also casts off the duty of special concern for the country's moral well-being. An individual may well be benefiting from his country's unjust or inhumane practices, laws or policies, or at least from being its citizen. Acceptance of these benefits entangles him in collective responsibility concerning those practices, laws and policies. But there are also those who reap no benefits from the injustice or inhumanity with which their country treats others and, in general, receive much less than their fair share of the benefits the country produces and distributes. The disadvantaged and alienated, obviously, should not be expected to be patriots of any sort. As for the argument from democracy, individuals and whole sections of the population may refrain from taking a significant part in the political life of their country, and in particular from voting. Those who do refrain have no part in collective responsibility for the unjust or inhumane outcomes of the political process, and therefore need show no special concern about them.

There is thus no moral duty to be an ethical patriot binding all and sundry. Nor is there a moral duty to be a patriot of the other, worldly sort. On the other hand, this other, worldly sort of patriotism comes naturally to many of us. Or, at the very least, many of us are neither disadvantaged nor alienated, and find it natural and appropriate to think of our country as home and of its inhabitants as, in some significant sense, 'our own', to identify with our country and compatriots, to participate in the political life of our country, to accept various tangible and intangible benefits of being its citizens, and to understand who and what we are, in part, in terms of these thoughts, feelings and actions. What I hope the arguments for ethical patriotism I have sketched do establish is that *if* one as a matter of fact thinks and feels about one's country and compatriots in this way and acts accordingly, *then* one has the duty to show special concern for its moral well-being, its moral record – that is, to be an ethical patriot.[26]

Notes

1   See M. Billig, *Banal Nationalism*, London: SAGE Publications, 1995, pp.55–9.
2   See M.G. Dietz, 'Patriotism: A Brief History of the Term', in I. Primoratz (ed.), *Patriotism*, Amherst, NY: Humanity Books, 2002 (henceforth: *Patriotism*).
3   J.H. Schaar, 'A Plea for Covenanted Patriotism', in *Patriotism*, p.233.
4   Ibid., pp.238–9.
5   J. Habermas, 'Citizenship and National Identity', *Between Facts and Norms: Contributions to a Discourse Theory of Law and Democracy*, trans. by W. Rehg, Cambridge, MA: MIT Press, 1998, p.500.
6   See M.G. Dietz, 'Patriotism'; M. Viroli, *For Love of Country: An Essay on Patriotism and Nationalism*, Oxford: Oxford University Press, 1995. For a critical discussion of the main varieties of the 'new patriotism', see M. Canovan, 'Patriotism Is Not Enough', in *Patriotism*.
7   Quoted in S. Nathanson, *Patriotism, Morality, and Peace*, Lanham, MD: Rowman & Littlefield, 1993, p.3.

8   See A. MacIntyre, 'Is Patriotism a Virtue?', in *Patriotism*, pp.43–5. For an argument that patriotism is bound up with bad faith concerning the valuable traits of the *patria*, see S. Keller, 'Patriotism as Bad Faith', Chapter 5 in this book.

9   N. Machiavelli, *The Florentine History*, trans. by N.H. Thomson, London: Archibald Constable & Co., 1906, vol.I, p.175.

10 See M. Viroli, *For Love of Country*, pp.77–8.

11 Ibid., pp.75, 88.

12 I leave aside the complex relations between self-interest and altruism which patriotism may involve. Reinhold Niebuhr (who does not distinguish between country and nation, patriotism and nationalism) points out that 'there is an alloy of projected self-interest in patriotic altruism. The man in the street, with his lust for power and prestige thwarted by his own limitations and the necessities of social life, projects his *ego* upon his nation and indulges his anarchic lusts vicariously. So the nation is at one and the same time a check upon, and a final vent for, the expression of individual egoism'. This 'combination of unselfishness and vicarious selfishness in the individual … gives a tremendous force to national egoism' (R. Niebuhr, *Moral Man and Immoral Society*, New York: Charles Scribner's Sons, 1960, pp.93–4).

13 For a classic statement of this critique, see L. Tolstoy, 'On Patriotism' and 'Patriotism, or Peace?', *Writings on Civil Disobedience and Nonviolence*, Philadelphia: New Society Publishers, 1987.

14 See S. Nathanson, *Patriotism, Morality, and Peace*.

15 S. Weil, *The Need for Roots*, trans. by A.F. Wills, London: Routledge & Kegan Paul, 1952, p.164.

16 Ibid., p.166.

17 Ibid., p.169.

18 Ibid., p.165.

19 M. Baron, 'Patriotism and "Liberal" Morality', in *Patriotism*.

20 On some of the issues arising in this connection, see J. Thompson, *Taking Responsibility for the Past*, Cambridge: Polity, 2002.

21 See my 'Patriotism: A Deflationary View', *The Philosophical Forum*, vol.33 (2002).

22 D. Sternberger, 'Begriff des Vaterlands', *Schriften*, vol.IV, Frankfurt am Main: Insel Verlag, 1980, pp.32–3.

23 It is sometimes claimed that membership of a society or culture may have a stunting effect on an individual's ability to understand the immorality of certain acts, policies or practices characteristic of that society or culture. See, for example, N. Levy, 'Cultural Membership and Moral Responsibility', *The Monist*, vol.86 (2003). But even if that is true, surely such cases are exceptions, rather than the rule.

24 On the distinction between accepting and receiving benefits, see A.J. Simmons, *Moral Principles and Political Obligations*, Princeton, NJ: Princeton University Press, 1979, pp.125–32.

25 See J. Feinberg, 'Collective Responsibility', H. McGary, 'Morality and Collective Responsibility', and L. May, 'Metaphysical Guilt and Moral Taint', in L. May and S. Hoffman (eds), *Collective Responsibility*, Savage, MD: Rowman & Littlefield, 1991.

26 Thanks to Marcia Baron, Simon Keller and Stephen Nathanson for comments on an early draft of the chapter and to the participants at the workshop on 'Identity, Self-Determination and Secession', held at the Centre for Applied Philosophy and Public Ethics, University of Melbourne, in August 2003, for comments on a later version.

Chapter 7

Memory, Identity and Obligation

Janna Thompson

I

Memory plays an important role in the identity of members of communities and families. Families pass down narratives and mementos from generation to generation. The history of a people, presented in its stories, songs, history books and legends, is a source of collective pride, shame, congratulation or lamentation. Real or imagined, history explains to members of communities where they came from. It tells them what their ancestors and predecessors accomplished, gained, lost or left undone. It makes sense of their present circumstances and looms large in their relationships with other collectivities. Jeremy Waldron regards the relation between the history and identity of community members as a moral reason for paying proper attention to the historical record.

> To neglect the historical record is to do violence to this identity and thus to the community that it sustains. And since communities help generate a deeper sense of identity for the individuals they comprise, neglecting or expunging the historical record is a way of undermining and insulting individuals as well.[1]

I will describe as 'historical memory' the remembrance by members of real or imagined events in the history of their family or community, or of the intentions, values, wishes or deeds of their ancestors or predecessors. Because it generates an identity, historical memory is motivating. It makes members of communities or families want to live up to past glories, to right or revenge past wrongs and fight for causes that were once lost, to continue traditions, to do things for the sake of their dead. These motivations are not merely a matter of psychology. Members of communities often believe that they have moral obligations or entitlements that come from history. They believe that they *ought* to revenge a wrong done to their forebears, to maintain a tradition or to honour the dead; that they have a right to claim what was unjustly taken from their ancestors, or a duty to make reparations for a historical injustice committed by their society.

Demands, claims and beliefs about obligations and entitlements that arise from historical memory are problematic. Historical wrongs, real or imagined, have often been taken as licences to seek revenge, perpetuate hostilities or to commit atrocities.

But even when there is no doubt about the occurrence of a historical wrong and the demands are not excessive or used as an excuse to vent hatred, the idea that history creates entitlements or obligations remains problematic for reasons both conceptual and moral.

The injustices done to our dead ancestors or predecessors cannot be undone. Those who were persecuted, enslaved or dispossessed when they were alive cannot now be compensated or be restored to their possessions. The dead cannot be punished for the wrongs they did or made to pay reparations. The past is beyond the reach of our powers as agents and we have no responsibility for what past people did. It is therefore difficult to understand how we can have duties to the dead or obligations in respect to the deeds of our forebears. Joan Callahan insists that there is no rational basis for the desire to fulfil duties to the dead despite the belief of so many people that they have such duties.[2] She thinks that this 'irrationality' is prevalent because people tend to identify with the dead. Historical memory, in her opinion, encourages a false idea of obligation. For similar reasons, some people contend that it is irrational for members of communities to think that they have an obligation to apologize or make reparations for the deeds of their predecessors.[3] Those who regard themselves as having such obligations are presumably induced by historical memory – and feelings of guilt or shame derived from the identity created by this memory – into acquiring a mistaken sense of responsibility for the past.

It is sometimes said that we can make sense of, and even justify, responsibilities that people, under the influence of historical memories, believe that they have to the dead or for the past by interpreting them as duties to the living. Duties to the dead, so it is sometimes said, ought to be construed as duties to survivors – as showing proper respect and sympathy for their loss or a willingness to meet their justified claims as heirs. Waldron seems to take this view about apology for past injustices. He does not think that we have a historical obligation to make reparations for the misdeeds of our national predecessors. We are not obliged to give back what they took or to pay an equivalent amount in compensation. But he thinks that it is appropriate for us to apologize and make token compensation for historical injustices as a way of showing respect to present people whose identities are adversely affected by remembrance of the past.

There is a tension in Waldron's position between the respect that we are supposed to demonstrate for communal identities and a rejection of the obligations and entitlements that such identities give rise to. If historical memory encourages irrationality (not to mention resentment and hostility) then why does the identity it creates have to be respected? Rather than pandering to it, perhaps we should be trying to encourage people to forget the past of their family and community and concentrate on the present and future. But if we do respect an identity derived from history then it seems difficult to dismiss ideas about entitlement and obligation that it gives rise to. If the people to whom we offer an apology come to believe that we are only trying to assuage their feelings, they will probably not regard our behaviour toward them as respectful.

There is a further problem. Once we take the step of regarding duties ostensibly performed for the sake of the past or past people as really duties to the living, then it becomes difficult to regard 'historical' claims as being very important. Our concern to show respect for remembrance is liable to be outweighed in the interests of equity by more pressing needs and interests. Waldron, for example, thinks that making amends to people who demand historical justice should amount to token gestures because the more substantial claims that communities often make – for example, for return of ancestral lands – have to be dismissed in favour of the needs of people who now depend for their existence on the situation that has resulted from the injustice. The fact that the descendants of the dispossessed have a historical identity which predisposes them to believe that they are owed restitution or substantial compensation cannot be regarded as a weighty reason for letting them have it. Yearning for lost resources, organizing one's life around a campaign for restoration, does not, according to Waldron, give people an entitlement to get them back.[4]

Will Kymlicka's view on what should be done about broken treaties with Indian nations echoes the same preference for satisfying requirements of equity over catering to sensibilities concerning the past. 'Why should not governments do what principles of equity require now rather than what outdated and often unprincipled agreements require?'[5] But a position that so radically discounts intuitions about obligations and entitlements arising from history is difficult to maintain consistently, and Kymlicka does not do so. For he also thinks that states should keep their promises – including promises that were made in past generations. But if promise keeping is an obligation thrust upon us by our nation's history, then so too, surely, is the obligation to make reparation for historical failures to keep promises. If we accept a practice of promise making, then we also have to accept the obligations it entails, including the obligation to make appropriate amends for a culpable failure to do what was promised.

Nevertheless, any attempt to defend the idea that we have obligations and entitlements arising from the interests or deeds of past people must deal with a number of difficulties: first of all, the problem, already mentioned, of explaining how people can owe anything to, or in respect to, the dead or be held responsible for making amends for what past people did. If this can be satisfactorily explained, there remains the problem of determining the nature and extent of our obligations. Do we have more, or fewer, duties with respect to the past or past people than we generally believe? How, for example, do we adjudicate between conservative and liberal intuitions about our duties (if they exist at all) to preserve traditions and heritage or to honour the dead?

II

There are three common ways of justifying the belief that we have responsibilities with respect to the deeds and desires of past people. All of them encounter serious difficulties. The first is to take duties to the dead and historical entitlements and obligations as brute moral facts: we just do have responsibilities generated by the deeds or interests of past community or family members. If, for example, we take it for granted that states ought to keep their promises, then this gives us obligations with respect to the commitments of our national predecessors. The trouble is that, when ideas about historical responsibilities or duties to the dead are controversial, it is difficult to maintain that they are morally basic. And even if they are not especially controversial – like many of the obligations created by treaties of past governments or promises to those now dead – questions remain about how such responsibilities square with widely held views about collective responsibility or the rights and duties of individuals. Standard accounts of the responsibility of members for the deeds of officials or others in their collectivity insist that it depends on their ability to control or influence – which we do not have with respect to deeds of the past generations.[6] Standard accounts of why we have duties to other individuals do not explain how we can be beholden to those who are, apparently, beyond the reach of benefits or harms. Does membership in a political society, or a similar kind of collectivity, simply require that we take responsibility for the commitments and deeds of past generations? But debates about political obligations suggest that it is not at all clear what duties we incur by being members of a society. In any case, the idea that our collective or individual freedom of action is limited by responsibilities that come from the past is in tension with the democratic principle that people should be governed by their own decisions and not by the determinations of others. The dead, said Thomas Jefferson, have no powers or rights over the earth.

The second strategy is to insist that we *can* harm or benefit the dead, and therefore that respect for past generations, a desire to do well by them, to seek justice for the wrongs that were done to them, to benefit the people they would have desired to be benefited should become important considerations in our moral thought and action.[7] Some philosophers have attempted to make sense of the idea that we can harm (or benefit) the dead: harm them not as mouldering corpses but as the persons they were in some stage of their life.[8] This view is often contested (as by Callahan). But even if it is conceded that the dead do have interests that can be set back, these interests may not count for all that much when weighed against the palpable, pressing interests of the living.[9] Moreover, an account of how the dead can be harmed or benefited as individuals will not (always) explain why it is our relations to the dead which seem to generate responsibilities and not simply their interests as individuals. ('We have a duty to honour *our* dead.') Appealing to the interests of the dead is thus likely to prove an inadequate basis for defending the ethical intuitions of those with historical memories.

The third strategy for justifying ideas about historical responsibilities is to defend a theory of historic title and inheritance which implies that, if past people had rightful title to something which was unjustly taken from them, and if this title has been legitimately transferred by them to their heirs, then these heirs are now entitled to have it back (or at least to get back some part of it). This strategy for defending historical entitlements does not apply to many of the wrongs that have been done to past people or account for all of the duties we think that we have to the dead. But even within its limited scope it runs into well known problems of justification and application. Why should we accept the idea of historic title or allow that it can be inherited? Why should claims based on historic title prevail over demands of equity? And why, asks Waldron, should we believe that those who claim a possession would have received it if the injustice had not been done?[10]

More could be said about each of these strategies and other means that might be adopted for dealing with the problems, but this survey is sufficient to motivate the search for an alternative defence of intuitions about duty that arise from historical memory.

III

I will begin by defending some common and relatively uncontroversial views about responsibilities with respect to the past by explaining how the demands or deeds of members of one generation of a transgenerational society can morally bind their survivors or successors. A good place to start is with the obligation that most citizens take for granted: fulfilling the terms of agreements made by their state with other states or nations. Such agreements can be good things morally as well as pragmatically. But the problem remains of explaining why present citizens are morally justified in making commitments that impose obligations on their successors as well as themselves.

The answer seems to be this. Present members of a political society (or some similar collectivity) are entitled to make commitments that morally bind their successors if and only if they accept a practice which requires them to keep commitments of a similar kind made by their predecessors (all things being equal). This practice, as I suggested earlier, brings with it other requirements: to make amends for past failures to keep agreements, and also, as I argued in detail elsewhere, to make apologies and amends for past failures to demonstrate the respect which ought to exist between communities and which is intrinsic to the moral assumptions behind agreement making.[11] For communities like nations deserve respect, at least in so far as they represent their people, protect their collective endeavours or enable them to achieve important goods. But the appropriate demonstration of respect toward an intergenerational community with institutions and concerns that extend beyond the lifetime of present people is to reach a long-term understanding, formal or informal, about matters of common concern. Morally motivated citizens cannot avoid such commitments, at least with communities that they interact with. Since moral citizens do and should intend that their state establish and maintain respectful interactions with other collectivities, they must regard themselves as participants in a moral practice which commits themselves and their successors to maintaining these relations and, as a corollary, to making amends for past failures of respect.

This way of accounting for some ideas about obligations that arise from historical memory has several important implications. The first is that it gives this memory a moral significance (beyond that required by the duty of respecting what is important to members of a community). If citizens have an obligation to keep the agreements of their predecessors and make reparation for their injustices then they also have an obligation to remember these agreements and violations of them. They have an obligation to regard themselves as being responsible for apologizing and making amends for wrongs of the past and thus an obligation to construct their identity as citizens accordingly. The obligations do not merely belong to those who happen to care about their history and are predisposed to feel guilt or shame for injustices done by their forebears. The second implication is that these obligations arise from the role that citizens are supposed to play in transgenerational relationships, obligations that link them with the future and the past. The forward-looking aspect of this perspective is bound to influence ideas about what reparation requires. If citizens are supposed to be motivated (in part) by the desire to establish just and respectful continuing relations with others, then their reparative claims should be guided by this objective. Members of a wronged community may be entitled to more than a mere token, but the forward-looking framework in which a just settlement has to be made ought to encourage both parties to look for a result that everyone can regard as just, all things, including present conditions and needs, considered.

IV

Some ideas about obligation that arise out of historical memory have been given a justification, at least in outline. Citizens of intergenerational societies like states have responsibilities in regard to the past, but it remains to be seen whether they have duties to, or in regard to, the dead. If the dead do not have interests or their interests are not all that considerable then how can our intuitions about the existence and nature of these duties be justified? Once again, I think that this question can be best answered by an appeal to the role played by interests and relationships in a transgenerational society.[12]

Most people have what could be described as 'lifetime-transcending desires'. They want to be regarded in a particular way after their death; they want their projects to be continued, their efforts to be appreciated, their reputations protected, the organizations they are associated with to thrive. They want their children to be happy and prosperous; they may want them to live their lives in a particular way. They want their possessions and bodies to be disposed of according to their wishes; they want the unfinished business of their lives to be properly taken care of, and so on. Individuals will have many different lifetime-transcending desires and some may have none at all. But I will assume that most people will have some – at least at that point in their lives when they face their own mortality.

The fact that someone has a desire does not mean that anyone is obliged to fulfil it. This is particularly self-evident in a society which emphasizes the freedom of each individual to determine and pursue his or her idea of the good. But it does not follow that these lifetime-transcending desires can never be the source of reasonable moral demands. Indeed, it seems plausible that some of them are. For example, it seems reasonable that a person can demand that her successors respect her wishes about how her property or her body should be disposed of, that they should keep promises that they have made to her when she was alive, and that they should not tell slanderous lies about her after her death. But those who make such demands, or think that they would be entitled to do so, are committing themselves to maintaining and playing their proper role in a practice which requires successors to respect the bequests, promises and reputations of the dead (unless there is a good reason in a particular case for not doing so).

This argument might be judged unsound on the grounds that it is irrational for people to make demands of their successors, given that they will not care after their deaths about their property, their reputation or their promises (and irrational for their successors to think that they have to worry about such things). But the point is that they care now and have good reasons for doing so. If the fulfilment of a promise matters to a person; if it matters that her children be able to enjoy something she has treasured or has produced for their sake; if she has tried to be an honest, upright person, then it will undermine in a serious way her enjoyment of life or her ability to carry on activities that make her life meaningful if she believes that her promises and bequests might be ignored by her survivors or that her reputation might be subjected to slander. Since people generally do have lifetime-transcending concerns, and since these concerns are bound up with living a meaningful life, a moral outlook which requires respect for individuals, their interests and their ability to live good lives has to allow that they can be entitled to make moral demands of their survivors for the sake of these interests.

Not all demands made to survivors or successors have to be taken seriously. Parents who care very much about the state of their children's souls might be predisposed to demand that they adhere to a particular religious creed for the rest of their lives. But religious belief is something we think that grown individuals should be allowed to decide for themselves, and so parents' desire for religious conformity cannot create an obligation. Whether a demand should be regarded as creating an obligation depends on the reasons for making it and on other moral values. Even kinds of demands which are reasonable can be overridden by other moral considerations. Keeping a promise made to someone now dead may involve unreasonable sacrifice; considerations of equity may prevent us from permitting children to inherit all that their parents wanted to bequeath them. But given that the reasons for making demands are reasonable and there are no countervailing considerations, then they ought to be fulfilled.

If the above reasoning is sound, then at least some of the moral intuitions arising from historical memory are justified. We do have some obligations with respect to our dead (if not actually to them). The existence of these obligations does not depend on believing that the dead have interests; nor does it require a departure from the liberal idea that morality should focus on the interests and needs of individuals. But the existence of these duties gives individuals transgenerational entitlements and responsibilities which include in their scope duties in regard to the earlier generations. In accepting or demanding these entitlements individuals are also committed to the maintenance of institutions and practices which make carrying out their responsibilities possible – a further reason for respecting the intergenerational collectivities in which such practices can be maintained.

V

We have a duty to remember and acknowledge the wrongs done by our nation, an obligation to keep its promises and make reparation for its injustices. We have a duty to fulfil some of the requests made by people now dead. Widely held beliefs about responsibilities arising from historical memories can be defended. But other views about duties in respect to the past are much more controversial. Conservatives think that we have a duty to maintain our society's institutions and traditions, to honour our nation's dead and revere its past. Liberals, particularly those who have objections to present institutions and traditions or who insist on being forward-rather than backward-looking, think that we have no such duties. Some people think that a society ought to preserve its architectural, artistic or cultural heritage; others think that preservation gets in the way of developments which would better serve present interests. Some people value monuments, landmarks, customs which keep us in touch with our history and think that they ought to be preserved; others have no interests in these things. These differences of opinion about value and obligation suggest that our responsibilities in regard to the past are not always clear. Is there a way of adjudicating between opposing views about how we should value and treat our history and heritage?

The idea that we should honour the dead – at least, acknowledge and show respect for the sacrifices and contributions they have made – is not all that difficult to justify, up to a point. One reason for honouring those who made contributions or sacrifices during their lives is to encourage citizens now living to do likewise. But the belief that you will be honoured after your death is only motivating if you have certain lifetime-transcending interests: if you regard it as important that your survivors acknowledge and appreciate what you did (or tried to do) for their sake. Some people may desire this more than others; but the desire is not all that uncommon and indeed seems rational for the same sorts of reasons that it is rational to care about posthumous reputation. We want to have our accomplishments or sacrifices respected and acknowledged by the relevant people, and when we direct our efforts toward achieving long-term benefits for the people we love or regard as our fellows it is natural to want them to respect and appreciate what we have done. If you thought that they would not acknowledge your contribution, or not make an effort to appreciate it, this would undermine your pursuit of lifetime-transcending values and projects, and thus your ability to live a good life. Modesty or good manners may prevent people from making demands for posthumous appreciation but they will be predisposed to demand that people of their generation be properly appreciated for their contributions and sacrifices. And they have in consequence an obligation to acknowledge and appreciate the contributions of people of past generations.

However, this obligation comes with a number of conditions. We have no obligation to acknowledge or appreciate things that we do not regard as good or activities (however public spirited) which were misguided or based on false beliefs. We do not have to go along with official attempts to honour people when we think that they serve bad purposes. A pacifist does not have to honour those who died in war, though he or she may mourn the sacrifice of life. There is bound to be considerable debate in a society about what counts as a contribution worthy of honour, and later developments may change the ideas of people about the nature and value of contributions. This is something that has to be accepted by those who are now labouring to produce something of value for their survivors.

Do we have an obligation to maintain the traditions, customs, values and institutions that our predecessors valued and wanted to be preserved? The conditions imposed above suggest that the answer must be 'no'. We have no more of an obligation to maintain the traditions and uphold the values of our predecessors than we do to accept the faith or the politics of our parents. We are entitled to determine our own values. Nevertheless, the belief that we have duties of some kind in relation to the heritage handed down by our predecessors is common, even among people who endorse individual freedom. Annette Baier says that every generation has toward subsequent generations a duty to leave 'as much and as good' of the public goods previous generations have bequeathed them, an obligation, she thinks, which 'arises as much from a right of past persons to have their good intentions respected as it does from any right of future persons'.[13] If the present generation destroys or allows to deteriorate a good that its predecessors provided for the sake of future generations – if for example it does not maintain the universities which its predecessors founded for the good of posterity – it not only harms its successors, she says, but also commits a wrong in regard to these predecessors. A similar view is often expressed in public discourse. The present government of Victoria in Australia intends to use some of Melbourne's parkland for a Commonwealth Games village. After the Games are over, the houses will be sold as private dwellings. Some people have protested against this plan on the ground that it undermines the intentions and efforts of past citizens who set aside parklands for the future enjoyment of all Victorians.

However, this reasoning meets a number of serious objections. First of all, it is doubtful that citizens have a duty to pass on to their successors the public goods bequeathed to them by their predecessors, or even 'as much or as good' in the way of public goods. People of a nation might be better off if some public goods were transferred to private ownership. Second, and more important, it seems obvious that our motivation for preserving a public good ought to depend on its usefulness to present and future people. But if this is so then there seems no reason to bring the intentions of past people into an account of what is morally wrong with running down valuable public assets. In explaining why it would be wrong to allow universities to deteriorate, is it not sufficient to cite the harm likely to be done to present and future people?

When harm to present and future people is obvious no more needs to be said about why a policy is wrong. But it does not follow that there are no other reasons for condemning neglect of some public infrastructure. Let us consider a case where the harm to present and future people does not seem so obvious. Suppose (as in Victoria) that past generations have created a system of public parks for the enjoyment of future citizens. However tastes have changed. Most people no longer care for the recreation and scenery that parks provide. So the government of the day decides to use the land for other purposes: for housing, shopping centres, gymnasiums and other things that citizens now prefer. The trees planted by their predecessors are cut down, the ponds filled and the gardens that they so carefully constructed are destroyed.

Is there anything wrong about the decision to destroy the parks? Some people might argue that it is wrong because it destroys something of beauty and replaces it with an ugly commercial development. But the development may not be ugly, or people may not care all that much. Some may argue that generations further in the future might regret the loss of the parks. But it is not clear that present people have to take this possibility into account. Present generations indeed have a duty to be concerned about the needs of future people, but are they morally obliged to cater to tastes that may exist in the future? What is left as a possible reason for objecting to the destruction of the parks is an appeal to duties with respect to our predecessors: the duty to appreciate the goods that they provided for us (and perhaps the values they embody) and/or the duty to preserve and to pass on to the next generation what our predecessors meant as an inheritance for all future generations – and not just for us. How plausible are these ideas about duty?

We are not obliged to value what our predecessors valued; we do not have to appreciate things which we have reason to think useless or morally objectionable or just unaesthetic. We do not have to accept burdens that are contrary to our interests or get in the way of our pursuit of the good; nor do we have to maintain everything that our predecessors wanted us to have. But it does seem reasonable to think that we have a duty to appreciate the bequests of our predecessors, at least to try to understand why they regarded these things as good and wanted us to have them. Those who make sacrifices in order to pass on things they regard as good to their successors can, it seems, demand that their heirs make an effort to appreciate what they have received – for reasons similar to those discussed in the last section. The effort of appreciation will not be needed in those cases where their bequest is obviously valuable and when it is obviously lacking in value an effort is not required. But in cases where tastes have changed or the value of something is disputable, the duty would require that we make the effort.

The duty to appreciate cannot amount to a duty to preserve and maintain whatever our predecessors intended to give us. If we make the effort of appreciation and find no reason to value our inheritance (or value other things a lot more), then, as far as our own concerns go, the duty of appreciation gives us no reason to maintain it. But there is another consideration. Our predecessors did not bequeath the goods in question just to us. They wanted them to be available to posterity, including generations beyond ours. Future generations will not have a chance to appreciate their bequest if we do not allow them to experience it and this surely is another moral consideration in favour of preservation, one which may in some cases even override the failure of our efforts at appreciation.

The duty to preserve an inheritance for future citizens has to be regarded as an imperfect duty. We are not required to preserve and pass on everything that our predecessors regarded as good. Presumably we can pick and choose, leaving our successors some part of what they valued or a good example of a valued thing; or we can alter it in a way that reflects our values as well as theirs. A generation that no longer values the parks provided by their successors has no obligation to keep all of them, or to keep them exactly as they are. It could do its duty by its predecessors and successors, by preserving one of them – a particularly good example of what was once valued – or by changing some of their features to suit present preferences. But it also has the duty to preserve the records and documents which explain why our predecessors regarded such things as valuable. The duty of remembrance is inseparable from our responsibilities with respect to the past.

VI

In presenting justifications for some of the beliefs about duties or obligations arising from historical memory and the identity formed by this memory, I have also presented a way of reasoning about responsibilities in respect to the past. The approach I have adopted locates these duties in a framework of intergenerational relationships and requires that we see ourselves as having and bringing into existence moral obligations that transcend our own lives and deeds. On the other hand, it does not abandon the values fundamental to liberal philosophies: in particular, the importance attached to the ability of individuals to choose and pursue a life that they regard as good. On the contrary, it relies on these values in reasoning about the existence and nature of our responsibilities.

In this respect my approach differs from the perspective presented by most people who have been concerned with the relation between historical memory, identity and obligation. Consider, for example, Alasdair MacIntyre's view of how identity creates obligation:

> I am someone's son or daughter, someone else's cousin or uncle ... I belong to this clan, that tribe, this nation. Hence what is good for me has to be good for one who inhabits these roles. As such I inherit from the past of my family, my city, my tribe, my nation, a variety of debts, inheritances, rightful expectations and obligations. These constitute the given of my life, my moral starting point.

The self, he says, has a history that stretches back before an individual's birth. And he contrasts this 'narrative view of the self' with the viewpoint of modern individualism, promulgated by liberal moral and political thought, which detaches the self from social relationships and denies that a person can be held responsible for 'what his father did or what his country does or has done'.[14]

An individualism that does not allow that individuals as citizens or members of families can have responsibilities with respect to the past is inadequate. But one of the problems with MacIntyre's account of the responsibilities of the narrative self is that it does not seem to allow doubts about what this self must take as its 'moral starting point'. Those whose ideas of duty come from their role and tradition may think that they are obliged to take revenge for injustices done to their forebears; they could think that they have to sacrifice themselves or others for the sake of family honour; or that they are cursed by the sins of their ancestors. We want to be able to insist that individuals are not guilty of the crimes of their forebears and are not entitled to punish the descendants of those who committed injustices; that they are not required to sacrifice their lives and well-being for the sake of family duty or accept without question the traditions of their society; that is, we want to be able to counter some conceptions of duty by appealing to the 'individualist' ideas about responsibility that MacIntyre rejects.

My aim in this chapter is to show that a proper appreciation of lifetime-transcending interests of individuals and a view about collective responsibility which takes into account relationships of individuals in transgenerational communities enables us to justify some ideas about duty that arise from historical identity and memory while at the same time taking into account the value of individual autonomy and allowing that individual responsibility has its limits.

Notes

1   J. Waldron, 'Superseding Historical Injustice', *Ethics*, vol.103 (1992/3), p.6.

2   J. Callahan, 'On Harming the Dead', *Ethics*, vol.97 (1985/6).

3   For example, the Australian Prime Minister refuses to make an official apology for injustices done in the past to Aborigines because he believes that present generations should not be expected to take responsibility for the deeds of past generations. A lot of people seem to agree with him.

4   Waldron, 'Superseding Historical Injustice', p.19.

5   Will Kymlicka, *Multicultural Citizenship*, Oxford: Oxford University Press, 1995, p.116.

6   For example, see Joel Feinberg, 'Collective Responsibility', *Journal of Philosophy*, vol.65 (1968), p.687. He briefly discusses, but seems to dismiss, a way in which individuals might have responsibility without control (pp.687–8).

7   Michael Ridge argues this in 'Giving the Dead Their Due', *Ethics*, vol.114 (2003/4).

8   See, for example, Joel Feinberg, *Harm to Others*, Oxford: Oxford University Press, 1984, ch.2.

9   Aristotle thought that the effect of our actions on the dead must be 'faint and slight' (*Nicomachean Ethics*, Book I, Chapter xi), a description which suggests that harming their interests is not as serious a matter as harming the interests of living people. For further arguments, see my chapter, 'Intergenerational Responsibilities and the Interests of the Dead', in H. Dyke (ed.), *Time and Ethics: Essays at the Intersection*, Dordrecht: Kluwer Academic Publishers, 2003.

10 Waldron, 'Superseding Historical Injustice', argues that the problem of determining what would have happened if an injustice had not been done is not epistemological but ontological. There is no fact of the matter when choice is involved. See also his criticisms of historical title in Waldron, *The Right to Private Property*, Oxford: Oxford University Press, 1988, ch.6.

11 I have discussed what follows at much greater length in *Taking Responsibility for the Past*, Cambridge: Polity, 2002, chs 1 and 2.

12 The arguments in this section are presented in more detail in 'Intergenerational Responsibilities and the Interests of the Dead'.

13 Annette Baier, 'The Rights of Past and Future Persons', in E. Partridge (ed.), *Responsibilities to Future Generations*, Buffalo, NY: Prometheus Books, 1980, p.176.
14 Alasdair MacIntyre, *After Virtue: A Study in Moral Theory*, 2nd edn, London: Duckworth, 1981, p.220.

III
SELF-DETERMINATION AND SECESSION

Chapter 8

Self-Determination, National Minorities and the Liberal Principle of Equality

Aleksandar Pavković

Self-Determination: A Diversity of Normative Arguments

National minority movements in modern liberal democratic states usually claim the right to political self-determination for their group, which does not always imply the right to secession. But, while avoiding the demand for secession and thus claiming only a restricted right to self-determination, these movements still claim the right to establish state-like institutions within which their group would have a dominant majority or over which their group would have unchallenged control. The institutions demanded are only state-like because they perform only some but not all the functions of state institutions; most importantly the state-like institutions usually do not have complete or constitutionally entrenched monopoly over the use of force on that territory. Instead of the relatively (and often intentionally) vague term, 'self-determination', I shall use the term 'self-government' to refer to state-like institutions which are to be controlled by members of the culturally distinct group. Within the rhetoric of national[1] minority movements in support of their claim to such institutions, one can discern at least the following five strands of argument:

1   **The diversity argument**: that the diversity of culturally distinct groups is of intrinsic (moral) worth and that, since this diversity is most effectively preserved or supported by granting self-government to culturally distinct groups (at least to those whose preservation is desirable), self-government should be granted to culturally distinct groups.
2   **The historic rights argument**: that a culturally distinct and territorially concentrated group enjoyed some form of political self-government in the past and that, therefore, that group should be able to exercise that degree of modern self-government that its leaders now consider appropriate.
3   **The injustice argument**: that a group of this kind has been subject to political and/or social injustice of the kind which can be removed or prevented only through state-like institutions over which the group would have unchallenged control.
4   **The liberal equality argument**: that the majority national group is, through its control of the state, able to promote and protect its culture and associated

123

national identity and that the principle of equality of all citizens, so dear to the liberals, demands that any group, defined by culture and identity of a similar kind, should be able to do the same for its members.

5   **The 'pure' nationalist argument:** that national groups have a cultural and political life of their own and that, therefore, each national group, in virtue of being a national group, deserves a separate state or separate state-like institutions in order to protect and promote its distinct cultural and political life.

The principal thesis of the fifth, 'pure' nationalist, strand is that national groups, *qua* national groups, deserve states or state-like institutions of their own. Since states or state-like institutions are the primary conduits of political self-determination, the principal nationalist thesis is an assertion of the right to *national* self-determination: each nation, according to this thesis; has a right to its own self-determination. Often the first four strands of argument are, in some combination or another, deployed to support the principal thesis; that is, in support of the right to national self-determination. This chapter is not, however, concerned with the truth (or otherwise) of the thesis but only with its relation to the fourth strand of the argument, the argument from the principle of liberal equality.

It is far from clear whether those strands of argument are compatible one with another. For example, it is far from clear that the liberal equality argument is in fact compatible with the historic rights argument. The property or characteristics of belonging to a group with a 'self-government' past appears to be on a par with the colour of one's skin or with gender – it is an accidental or 'morally arbitrary' property of a person. If historical rights are to govern the distribution of the right to self-determination, then contingent or 'morally arbitrary' characteristics of groups determine what political rights these groups and their members have. The right to self-government would accordingly be unequally distributed according to accidental and historical properties of the groups. But the liberal principle of equality requires that citizens be treated equally, regardless of their accidental properties such as gender, skin colour or the past of their cultural group. If so, distributing rights on the basis of these 'historical' properties contradicts the principle of equality which requires that, in the distribution of political rights to citizens, accidental properties such as these be disregarded. No attempt will be made, in this chapter, to resolve the apparent incompatibility of the two arguments. Within the political rhetoric of self-determination, different arguments are presented to different audiences and, partly as a result of this, incompatibilities such as these are rarely noticed, let alone resolved.[2]

Apart from the question of their incompatibility, there is the question of whether the first four strands of argument are independent of the principal thesis of the fifth strand, namely, that each national group, in virtue of being a national group, deserves a separate state or separate state-like institutions. If it turns out that these four strands of argument presuppose, in one way or the other, the principal thesis, then the attempts to deploy these arguments in support of the right to national self-determination beg the question and may indeed be deceptive. In particular, if the argument from the liberal principle of equality presupposes that each national group deserves state-like institutions of its own, then this argument cannot plausibly be advanced in support of the right to national self-determination because the argument already presupposes that each national group has that right.

The question of dependence of the four strands of argument on the principal nationalist thesis is primarily of theoretical interest. Most advocates of political self-determination, in the propaganda directed towards their preferred stateless national groups, *assume* that these national groups have the right to self-determination; that is, they assume that the principal nationalist thesis holds at least for these national groups. For the purposes of mobilization of support outside their preferred group, they would welcome any argument in support of the self-determination of that group which appears persuasive to the unconverted. They would not find any such argument wanting if it turns out to presuppose a general corollary – the principal nationalist thesis – which they assume in any case.

However, a few advocates of the right to self-determination of national minorities believe that liberal and democratic principles should be sufficient to establish the right to political self-determination of stateless national groups without any reference to the principal nationalist thesis or any of its corollaries. In particular, they argue that the principle of liberal equality, as shown in the fourth strand of argument above, should be sufficient to establish that stateless national groups have at least a restricted right to self-determination. This chapter questions this belief only and thus concerns only the fourth strand of argument.

If a national group has a restricted right to self-determination, then it follows that the state within which it resides is obliged to allow the group to establish, unhindered, state-like institutions over which the group has an unchallengeable control; in short, it is obliged to guarantee at least the group's liberty to establish state-like institutions. In practice, the state would be obliged to pass legislation recognizing new state-like institutions and their jurisdiction and ensuring the required cooperation between the new and the already established state institutions. Thus the restricted right to self-determination of national groups has a correlate in the obligation of the state in which they reside to guarantee, at least, its free exercise. If so, the question of whether a national group has a restricted right to self-determination is equivalent to the question of whether the state within which it resides has an obligation to guarantee a free exercise of that right. The present chapter will then address the question: does the liberal principle of equality, in a variety of its interpretations, 'generate' the *obligation* of a state within which national minority groups reside to guarantee (at least) that these groups are free to establish state-like institutions over which they have unchallengeable control?

Liberal Equality as a Source of the Right to National Self-Determination: Five Arguments

Why is Culture Necessary? The Argument from the Equality of Citizens and of Cultures

A minority group which shares a culture distinct from the majority has a right to state-like institutions through which this culture is to be protected, promoted and, of course, expressed. Having a distinct culture is not, by itself, sufficient to claim the right to state-like institutions, but, according to the argument to be examined, is necessary for such a claim. If a minority group only shared a distinct lifestyle or a series of hobbies but not a whole culture, it would have no rights of this kind.

Why is having a distinct culture a basis for the claim to separate political institutions? The explanation, very crudely, is that one's culture is necessary for one's understanding of one's own self or for establishing one's own identity. One's culture provides a context for and shapes one's own identity: without it one would literally not know who one is. There are two further inferences which are usually drawn from the statements about the links of culture and personal identity. First, as one's culture provides the context within which one's own identity is determined, the culture also provides a context necessary for one's political choice and thus for the exercise of one's political liberty. Second, since one's culture is acquired through one's membership in a group which maintains the culture, one's membership of a cultural group is equally necessary for the individual's exercise of political liberties.[3] In short, if our cultures bestow our identities on us, then being members of the group which maintains our culture is necessary both for our identities and for the exercise of our political liberties. Not only is a culture necessary for all this but we must also feel that it is necessary: we feel 'deep bonds' to our culture and to our cultural groups and this type of feeling illustrates how important membership of a cultural group may be for many individuals.[4]

However important and deep the bonds that tie a person to the cultural group into which he or she is born, that culture and that group are not, necessarily, the *only one* which could provide him or her with a context for the exercise of his political choice.[5] Using philosophical jargon, one can say that, while in our world, such as it is divided into national and ethnic groups, for a person to exercise his political liberty it may be conceptually necessary that she or he belong to a national or ethnic group. Nevertheless, it is not conceptually necessary to belong to the group in which he or she was born or educated, however deeply he or she may feel attached to that group and its culture at any particular time.

This conclusion about conceptual necessity may appear quite trivial, but, if we accept it, it pre-empts the following type of argument for the right of self-determination for national minorities: a majority is obliged to support the preservation of minority cultures and groups since the latter provide the *only* context within which members of minority groups can exercise their political liberty. The above should show that this argument is untenable.

The preservation of minority cultures may be the matter not of conceptual necessities but of upholding the equality of the conditions for the exercise of political liberty. This, I take it, is the main point of the argument from liberal political equality. The argument runs very roughly as follows. In a modern nation-state, through the use of a chosen common language and through legislative acts, public and political (or state) institutions protect and promote a particular language and the culture which that language expresses, which is usually the language and culture of the majority population. But, according to the principle of equality of cultures, all cultures compatible with liberal–democratic principles are equal. This principle generates the obligation for a liberal democratic to protect and promote the minority languages and cultures in the same way that the majority language and culture is promoted. Therefore, a liberal–democratic state should (is obliged to) establish specific state-like institutions which would protect and promote the minority languages and cultures in the same way that majority language and culture are promoted and protected.

Arguments from Disability and Disadvantage of Minorities

The principle of equality of cultures, which constitutes the key premise of the above argument, does not, however, appear to be a fundamental political or normative principle of liberalism. If this is so, one would need to find out from which other liberal principle it may be derived. Since cultures are, as we have seen, necessary for the exercise of individual political liberty, perhaps one can attempt to derive it from the liberal principle of political equality of citizens or from the equality of political liberty of citizens. This principle demands that in the exercise of their political liberty all citizens be treated as equals. In its negative version, the principle requires that various differences in age (from adulthood onward), gender, ethnicity or nationality, wealth and education, amongst others, do not (and should not) affect the equal status of citizens as political actors. In its positive version, the same principle demands that those who are not able, through no fault of their own, to exercise their political rights or liberties in the same way as others, be enabled to do so. Therefore, disabled or ill people, those who are illiterate or those who are not proficient in the principal language of politics, are offered special state-provided assistance to enable them to exercise their political rights in the same way as others do. The positive implementation of the equality principle aims at removing specific obstacles or conditions which impair the exercise of political rights and thus restrict citizens' liberties.

Note that the principle as interpreted here does not demand that the state equalize the effectiveness of every political actor or equalize the cost that political participation incurs for everyone. A liberal democratic state assumes that its citizens will vary in their desire and their ability for political participation and is aiming to equalize neither their desires nor their abilities, but only their opportunities.[6] However, it is often difficult to distinguish the high cost of political participation from the lack of opportunity for political participation: costs that are too high may indeed lead to a lack of opportunity. But, while a liberal democratic state endeavours to avoid making political participation prohibitively costly, it does not aim to make it uniformly costly either. Both the very poor and the very wealthy may find, from their different points of view, that it is too costly to spend much time on politics. A modern republican doctrine would probably hold that the cause of liberty is in some sense priceless and thus should not to be measured in terms of personal costs of this kind. Some deliberative democracy theorists would regard the lack of desire to participate among a large and varied section of the population (for whatever reason) to be equally unacceptable. But the liberal conception of liberty also includes the freedom not to participate in politics if one is not inclined to it, however detrimental the consequences of such disinclination may be to one's own liberty or one's own interests. If this is so, the liberal principle of equality of liberty does not require that the costs of political participation be equalized.

In order to implement the positive version of the principle in cultural minority groups, one can argue that members of minority groups are, in comparison to the majority group citizens, somehow disabled from exercising their political rights. The 'disablement' version of this argument would run as follows: in order to be free to decide on matters political, it is necessary to share a culture. If a minority culture is unprotected and unpromoted, it is likely that its members would be left without a viable culture for that purpose; and they, like other disabled individuals, would be denied an opportunity to exercise their political rights and liberties in the same way that the majority individuals do.

Against this version of the argument, one could point out that, apart from the threatened minority culture, other cultures, such as the majority one, could provide the necessary context for minority group members to exercise their political liberties. In some cases, citizens from a minority culture have no choice but to do so: if the core of their minority culture is either non-political or non-liberal, it provides them with no sufficient or adequate cultural context to participate in liberal–democratic politics. Some minority (as well as majority) cultures focus on religious, family or household rituals: for example, the Rusin (Ukrainian) and Vlach cultures in the former Yugoslavia. As they do not relate to the matters outside family and religious realms, they leave wider political matters, in particular those relating to representative political institutions, out of their realm. Strongly patriarchal cultures, in which the elders control the younger members of the group (and women), offer a cultural context which is not conducive to the free exercise of political rights: in those cultures the dependent or lower-ranking members of the group are expected to follow the political choices of the elders and not to decide for themselves. If a minority culture falls in either of these two categories – non-political or non-liberal – its members need to share or understand another culture which would provide them with a context for their participation in liberal–democratic politics. The majority culture or at least some of its aspects may provide such a context.

Minority cultures which are losing their adherents may, like some non-political cultures, leave little if any context for the remaining adherents' exercise of political liberties.[7] If those who lack an appropriate cultural context for their participation in liberal–democratic politics are like other disabled people, they could be assisted, as the disabled people are, by being provided with precisely what they lack: an appropriate cultural context. This, as we have seen above, need not be their own 'native' culture but any culture with which they would be sufficiently familiar and which would enable them to participate or to exercise their free choice within a liberal–democratic state. Through public education, public political rituals as well as the media, liberal–democratic states attempt, often quite successfully, to familiarize their citizens with an overarching political culture which then provides all, independent of their belonging to other groups within the state, with a sufficient context for their political participation. This may be of assistance to those whose 'native' cultures do not provide them with a sufficient context for their political participation.

The 'disablement' analogy in the above argument offers no grounds for the premise in the above argument that the majority-ruled state is *obliged* to promote or protect all minority cultures. However, the disablement analogy may be used to argue that in some cases protecting and preserving minority cultures may be the *most effective way* of providing the required context for the exercise of their political rights. In some cases of indigenous cultures, the loss of their culture, and of the associated identity, results in personal disorientation of many of its members who cannot easily, or at all, adapt to the majority culture; in such cases, the most effective way of preventing this undesirable consequence is to protect the threatened culture and so enable its members to retain the identity they are in danger of losing. In such cases, the majority-ruled state may be obliged to do so for reasons of justice; that is, the obligation may arise from the need to redress the past and present injustices. In such cases, its obligation does not arise from the equality of cultures.

Let us now consider another kind of analogy, that of disadvantage and not of disablement: in a majority-ruled state the members of minority groups are simply disadvantaged relative to those of the majority group. The disadvantage consists in having to participate in politics within the framework of a culture which is alien to them, using a language which is foreign to them. This puts them at a disadvantage in two complementary ways: first, in a foreign language they are not as able to put their message across and to engage in political dialogue as the members of the majority group; second, in order to participate in politics, they need to invest significantly more energy and time to master the culture and language of politics than the members of a majority group. Moreover, the need to master the majority culture may suggest that theirs is an inferior culture, not worthy of promoting and developing. Suppose that one agrees that the first two are two aspects of a relative disadvantage of minority group members. From this admission and the liberal principle of political equality, it still does not follow that the state is obliged to protect and promote the minority language and culture. In so far as the lack of required language and cultural context is a barrier or obstacle to the participation of minority members, a liberal state is, by the principle of equality, obliged to remove it. But this does not mean that it is obliged to remove it *by promoting and protecting* the minority language and culture. The most effective way of removing this obstacle may be to provide the minority group members with an early education in the majority language and culture of politics. Sometimes the result of this type of policy is effective bilingualism in the majority and minority languages. If the minority population is bilingual, the costs of political participation in the majority language are at least equalized in this respect. In other cases a more effective way of doing this would be to protect and promote the minority language and culture and to transfer some of the political competencies of the state, regarding the protection and promotion of the minority language and cultures, to the minority group representatives. But, once again on this disadvantage analogy, the principle of liberal equality does not appear to generate an *obligation* on the part of the state to protect and promote all minority cultures.

An Argument from the Equal Treatment of Deserving Cultures/Cultural Groups

In the above two versions, the equality principle is supposed to apply to all citizens, as political actors, and to the conditions under which they exercise their political liberties. Instead, let us apply the equality principle directly to the cultures and cultural groups: all cultures and cultural groups (compatible with liberal–democratic principles) should be treated equally. The application of the principle of equality of cultures is often restricted to non-immigrant groups – to those whose group has been resident in the state for some time – and/or to those groups who want to establish self-governing political institutions.[8] I shall use the term 'deserving cultural groups' to highlight this restriction on the application of the principle.

The argument from the equal treatment of cultures would thus run as follows. If the state protects and promotes the majority culture, and all cultures should be treated equally, then it should also protect and promote the minority cultures in the same way as it does the majority culture. Since political institutions of the majority-ruled state protect and promote the majority culture, the equal treatment of cultures and cultural groups would require that minorities acquire similar political institutions which would protect and promote their cultures.

But why should a liberal–democratic state treat different cultures equally? One obvious reason would be in order to ensure that its citizens, who belong to different cultural groups, be treated equally. But in order to treat its own citizens equally, it is not necessary for the state to promote or support their different cultures equally: as we have seen, the principle of equal treatment of citizens, in its negative and positive versions, does not require that minority and majority cultures be promoted or supported equally, but only that the culture to which the citizens belong does not present obstacles to their participation in politics and to their receipt of services and protection from the state.

Another reason for this is found in the liberal rejection of any domination and subjugation: the equal treatment of cultures is necessary in order to prevent the domination of one culture over another, that is, the imposition of a 'stronger' culture on those citizens who do not share it. Equal treatment is thus necessary to prevent the involuntary acceptance of cultures by those belonging to minority or weaker cultures. But, in order to prevent this, it is sufficient to ensure that citizens have the right to equal political participation, protection and services from the state, without being in any way compelled to adopt a culture which they do not share. One way of ensuring this is to implement the negative version of the principle of equality of citizens: that is, to treat all citizens equally without regard to the culture to which they belong. Making the state a culture-blind state would, of course, deny any privileged treatment to the majority culture citizens and would prevent the imposition of a culture on those who do not share it.

But, some advocates of minority rights of self-determination argue,[9] in the present world of nation-states it is virtually impossible for a state not to 'privilege' its majority culture; that is, it is virtually impossible to make the state culture-blind. They argue that the business of the state and of political participation has to be delivered in a language – usually the language of the majority – and that the choice of public holidays is also culture-based. Therefore, in order for a minority group to participate in politics, its members have to adopt at least some aspects of a culture foreign to them. Since the majority of citizens do not have to do that, because they are native speakers, the minority citizens are not treated equally, and the state is not culture-blind. In order to treat minority citizens equally, these advocates propose, the minority language and culture should be treated equally to the majority one: in practice, the minority language(s) should also be official languages of the state, the knowledge of which would be required both by public servants and by politicians.

Against this, one can point out that the issue of the official language is not, necessarily, an issue of equal *political* treatment. The choice of the official language is a choice of an instrument of communication, and such instruments may be chosen on the basis of their cost and effectiveness.[10] If the official language is chosen on those grounds, then in some cases the choice of a majority language would be less costly and more effective for the purposes of communication among citizens. If the number of minority citizens is quite small relative to the number of majority citizens – say, less than 10 per cent of the majority citizens – it may be less costly to all citizens and more effective overall to provide training and early education in the majority language to all minority citizens so as to enable them to participate in politics via that language, rather than to make their language the second official language. If both the majority and minority groups regard the question of the choice of language as an instrumental one, they or their representatives may agree on a measure of this kind.

However, the above argument for the equal treatment of minority languages and cultures assumes or asserts that a choice of the official language of politics is not, or not primarily, a choice of instruments of communication. An official language is a source of political power and of status. If the use of the majority language, as the only official language in which politics is conducted, gives the majority citizens more political power and higher status than the minority citizens, then the principle of equality of citizens is breached. This is, indeed, a matter of unequal political treatment of citizens.

But, to avoid such an inequality of power and status arising from the use of the majority language, a liberal–democratic state may attempt to 'decouple' language, in particular the majority language, from political power. Here are only a few examples of policies which would have this aim. First, political mobilization of the population on the basis of their language identity could be ruled out, preferably through established political practice, and not through legal prohibitions. For example, candidates for political office would thus be bilingual and would studiously aim to appeal to the speakers of both languages. In such a situation, politicians' access to power would not be tied to the language of those who vote for them and the language one speaks would thus be 'decoupled' from the political support politicians enjoy. Further, discrimination against non-native speakers on the basis of their alleged inferior mastery of the language of politics would be ruled out, again through accepted convention rather than through legal prohibition. Last but not least, minority speakers and their culture should be present and celebrated within the mainstream cultural institutions, including the media, and not confined to separate cultural ghettos. This will indicate that the minority language and culture are, in their status ranking, equal to the majority one. These practices may not always succeed in decoupling political power and status from language, but at least they show that the use of a majority language does not, necessarily, lead to an inequality in the distribution of power and status. If this is so, using the language of the majority as the official language in a state does not, necessarily, imply a breach of the principle of equal treatment of citizens.

Nonetheless, some advocates of minority rights argue that all these attempts to decouple political power from the use of a language cannot change the fundamental inequality of power between a language majority and a language minority (or minorities), but may only hide it behind egalitarian and well-intentioned policies. However hard one tries to equalize the arena of, and the quest for, political power, the language citizens speak will remain a salient identification of minorities which is bound to have an impact on their access to political power. In short, a group that does not speak the majority language will remain a cultural/language *minority* within any system based on *majority* rule and thus end up with less political power and status than the majority. But the inequality in political power in such a case would result, not from an unequal treatment of cultures and languages, but from the system of political decision making in which a majority within a representative body can make decisions disregarding the views of the remaining, minority, representatives. The three versions of the argument from the liberal principle of equality discussed above assume that the argument is an attempt to redress the inequalities arising from the potential or actual unequal treatment of languages and cultures and not from a majoritarian decision-making system. We now turn to the inequalities of the latter kind.

An Argument from a Just Distribution of Power

Another possible source of the equality of cultures principle may perhaps be found in the principle of just distribution of political power and state resources. In its minimalist version, the principle demands that political power and state resources should not be distributed in a morally or politically arbitrary way. Being a majority cultural group is a morally (if not politically) arbitrary characteristic of groups. If so, this characteristic does not entitle a group to more resources for the protection and promotion of its culture than any other group.

An argument based on this principle would run as follows: in a liberal–democratic state in which a majority rules through its representatives, the majority population would have the command of the instruments of the state and would use these instruments to protect and promote its own culture but not that of the minorities who lack the command of the same instruments. This breaches the principle of just distribution (and its corollary, the equality of cultures principle) because it distributes the resources of the state unequally in a morally arbitrary manner: sharing the majority culture does not entitle the group which shares it to more state resources for its protection and promotion than those groups which do not share it. Since any majority-rule system yields this unequal and morally arbitrary distribution, in order to avoid this kind of injustice it is necessary to grant to the deserving minorities the command of the instruments of state (state-like institutions) sufficient for the protection of their cultures. In other words, the principle of just distribution of state resources and of the equality of cultures obliges the state to recognize the right to self-determination of every deserving cultural group in matters regarding its culture. In practice, this means that the state-wide majority-rule system should be fragmented, in regard to the matters of culture, into a majority-rule system for each deserving cultural group. A majority in each such group would be able to determine, without any superior arbiter, how to protect and promote its own culture. This is then an argument for the 'cultural' sovereignty of each deserving cultural group, a sovereignty limited to the matters of promotion and protection of its culture.

But why is it *necessary* to grant to the deserving minorities (national groups) the command of the instruments of the state (state-like institutions) with which they can protect their cultures? This alleged necessity does not arise because, as a matter of fact, cultural/national majorities cannot be expected or trusted to treat minorities as equals in the matters of the protection of their culture. If it is the question only of trust or expectation, one could design appropriate institutions which would protect and promote minority cultures even when such a trust or expectation is absent. These institutions, while not state-like or political self-governing institutions, would be independent of the majority group control and would enable minorities to promote and protect their cultures independently of the majority-controlled political/legislative institutions. In fact, the devolution of funding of minority cultures in some states with diverse cultures and cultural groups such as the Commonwealth of Australia, already ensures, at least to some extent, the minority control over the funding for the promotion and protection of cultures and thus a degree of independence from the control of the majority-ruled political institutions.

It appears that the alleged necessity arises, not from the defects of the majority rule, but from the deserts of minority cultures or cultural groups: minority cultural groups, in virtue of the need to protect their culture and not in virtue of their being a minority, *deserve* state-like institutions to protect and promote their culture. The distribution of power and status, we noted above, cannot be effected in a morally arbitrary manner. If a group has a distinct culture and a desire to promote and protect it, it is assumed here, it has a morally valid claim to the instruments for its protection, equal to the claim of a majority group. Therefore, if the majority group is protecting its culture via state-like institutions, the minority cultural groups have an equally valid claim to the same type of instrument or institution. It is in this way that one avoids the morally arbitrary way of distributing power and status which is based purely on the relative numbers of members of the group.

But on what grounds does any national/cultural group (be that a majority or a minority group) have a *morally valid* claim to the state-like instruments for protection of its culture? The question I am raising is not: is such a claim to state-like institutions morally valid? I am asking only on what grounds it may be morally valid. The principle of equality of cultures or cultural groups is of no help in answering this question. For the question here is not a comparative one, for example: if the majority has a valid claim to the instruments of protection of its culture, on which grounds does a minority make its claim to the same a valid one? The question applies to any group, whether a majority or a minority one. Therefore, the fourth strand of argument is of no help in this case.

The second and the third – the historic rights and the injustice – strands of argument are limited to the cases of historic rights and of special kinds of injustice and, therefore, are not applicable to *any* national or cultural groups but only to those which had exercised rights of self-governance in the past and/or suffered special kinds of injustice. The first (diversity) strand of argument asserts the moral worth of the diversity of cultures but it does not attempt to establish the (relative) moral worth of specific instruments for its protection. It assumes that, for the purpose of protecting this diversity, any instrument for the protection of that diversity is acceptable (provided that it is compatible with liberal principles). The first strand of argument, therefore, establishes neither what kind of instruments are *necessary* for the protection of particular cultures nor what *kind* of cultures (whether they have to be national as opposed to, for example, tribal cultures) have to be protected. None of the first four strands of argument appears to provide grounds for the above claim of right to state-like institutions.

The 'Pure' Nationalist Argument

The fifth 'pure' nationalist strand of argument does provide such grounds. It runs as follows: as national groups have a cultural and political life of their own, they are, as groups, capable of protecting and promoting their culture. The members of such a group are well aware of their cultural (and political) needs, and they are in a position to direct the promotion and protection of their culture in the most effective and satisfying way. For that purpose they not only need no help or direction from outsiders but also would find such direction and help both inappropriate and patronizing. Therefore, if they claim that their own state-like institutions are the appropriate instruments to that end, it is difficult to find any grounds to reject their authority to claim this. Thus, according to the fifth strand of argument, being a national group with a political and cultural life of its own provides grounds for a morally valid claim to state-like institutions for the promotion and protection of its culture. Whether these are good or plausible grounds for this claim is not at the moment in question.

To return now to the argument from the just distribution of power. On the above interpretation, the principal nationalist thesis provides some grounds for the premise of that argument, viz. that minority cultural groups have an equally valid moral claim to the instruments of protection of their culture as the majority group. If the argument from the just distribution of power is the preferred version of the argument from the liberal principle of equality, then the latter argument is, in part, grounded or dependent on the endorsement of the principal nationalist thesis as well. But if so, the fourth strand of argument is not independent of the fifth strand. Consequently, deploying the former in support of the latter begs the question. In short, if minority groups have valid claims to state-like institutions on the ground of being national groups, then it is question-begging (if not circular) to advance this assertion about grounds for state-like institutions in support of the thesis that national groups have the right to state-like institutions. On this interpretation of the fourth strand of argument, this strand of argument does not, on its own, establish the right to political self-determination of national/cultural groups or minorities.

Liberalizing the Nationalist Project?

The above rather lengthy examination of the argument from liberal equality can perhaps yield at least one positive result: it suggests that liberal and democratic principles alone may not be sufficient to generate the right to self-determination of national minorities and that for this purpose one may need to appeal to the principles or norms which are not, necessarily, of liberal or democratic provenance. The argument from the just distribution of power appears to presuppose the principal nationalist thesis, according to which each nation has the right to self-determination or deserves, as of right, its own state-like institutions or a state. As national groups are, in the above argument, defined by their distinct cultures, this thesis distributes the right to self-determination to groups according to their distinct, national/cultural characteristics which have no evident relation to the liberal or to the majoritarian principles. For example, in the above argument this right is equally or justly allocated to national groups regardless of whether or not such an allocation protects the rights and liberties of individuals/citizens.

In this case, the allocation of the right to self-determination to national groups, following the (allegedly) liberal principle of equal rights, may lead to an unequal protection of the same right to individuals: those individuals who do not belong to any (deserving) national group within the state simply have no group through which they can exercise their right to self-determination and so they would end up with no state-like institutions of 'their own'. In multinational states there may be a large number of individuals who do not feel that they belong to any of the 'deserving' national groups to whom this right is granted. Such was the case in 1981, with over one million Yugoslavs in the socialist federal Yugoslavia, whose group, labelled 'Yugoslavs', was not officially recognized as a deserving national group. As a consequence, the Yugoslav constitution did not grant this group the right of self-determination granted to the deserving or recognized national groups and no candidate for any political office at the level of federal units and the Yugoslav federation belonged (or could belong) to this group. Some Quebec secessionists deny the status of deserving national group to the indigenous populations in Quebec and in consequence deny these groups the right to self-determination as national groups.

It is thus not clear that the application of the principle of equality to national/ cultural groups yields an equal distribution of the rights and liberties of individual citizens, such as liberals desire. If this is so, it is equally unclear that the former principle, in its application to national groups, is a liberal principle at all.

Unlike liberals, nationalists would not necessarily be worried about the inequality of rights and liberties of a *few* individuals, in particular those who willingly opt out of their deserving national groups. Yet nationalists of liberal–democratic orientation should be worried if large groups of people are denied the right to self-determination and political representation on the grounds that they do not belong to a deserving national group. In such a case their concept of a (deserving) national group is used to exclude large groups of individuals from political participation. As this clearly breaches the liberal principle of equality, to appeal to this principle in an argument in support of self-determination of deserving national groups would be hypocritical and/or inconsistent. In order to avoid this kind of inconsistency, nationalists often insist that every individual within a state has to have a distinct and 'deserving' national identity so that his or her individual right to self-determination can be allocated on the basis of his or her membership in a deserving national group.

Unlike nationalists, liberals, at least theoretically, do not assign rights or liberties to citizens on the basis of their membership of any groups within a state. Individuals are supposed to exercise their liberties *qua* citizens of a particular state (or, according to some, as human beings), not *qua* members of a particular national/cultural group within that state. There are some obvious advantages to this liberal procedure. Some people may prefer to stay out of the cultural or social groups to which birth has assigned them and others may end up in or even choose groups which are too small to wield any effective political power or which are too politically inactive. If the liberties and rights of those citizens were allocated according to their group membership, they would end up with unequal or restricted rights or liberties. If, in order to make all citizens members of equal cultural/national groups, nationalists were to force citizens to join a particular cultural group which otherwise they would not join, they would end up breaching the liberal principle of the equality of citizens and/or severely restricting individual liberties of these citizens. Forcing individuals to belong to groups to which they do not want to belong obviously restricts their liberty and introduces further inequalities between those who are forced and those who are not. This suggests that an appeal to the liberal principle of equality in support of a nationalist political agenda fails to liberalize the agenda of nationalism and of national self-determination.

Mobilizing for Self-Determination: the Uses of Equality

There are good reasons why liberals would want to reject an argument for the allocation of rights which appeals both to nationalist and liberal principles. But however problematic an argument appealing to a nationalist principle may appear to liberals, it often reflects a rhetorical pattern successfully used in mobilizing populations to support nationalist or separatist programmes. Thus a culturally distinct population is often unaware of its need for state-like institutions until exposed, first, to cultural revivalist propaganda, instilling in them the pride in their cultural distinctness, and then, to a political movement which insists on its right to self-determination.[11] The standard nationalist platform, at least in European and North American nationalist movements, links the right to self-determination to the cultural distinctness of the target national group: it is in virtue of its being culturally different and having a distinct history that the group is held to have a right to self-determination. The distinctness is further linked to group equality: in its cultural distinctness the target group (a stateless nation) is equal to the majority group (the state-possessing nation) and, in virtue of its equality as a national group, the target national group deserves an equal right to self-determination as well. As noted above, this is an appeal to equality of collective and not of individual rights. But for the purposes of a political campaign such a distinction may appear quite irrelevant.

The mobilization of the target group, if successful, yields an electoral majority to the mobilizing movement or party. Political might of this kind attracts the attention of other political parties in the state in a way in which the mere rhetoric of equality and of national rights may not. In response to a display of this kind of might, some political parties with an electoral base in the majority population may seek to obtain the minority movement's support by establishing the very institutions of self-governance which the minority politicians demand. The latter would normally present this political concession as a belated recognition of their group's (equal) right to self-determination – the presentation which the majority parties may endorse for reasons of political expediency and/or of high principles. But behind the rhetoric of recognition of equality and of rights may lie the recognition of the electoral might of those who demand these rights, the might resulting from a systematic national mobilization of the minority population.

In this context, the appeal to the principle of equalization of political power of national groups may be regarded primarily as an instrument for equalization of the political power of the representatives of the minority group: if the minority group gets its own state-like institutions, its representatives will command political power within their group almost as great as the representatives of the majority group command in the state. The demand for national self-determination, in this context, is a demand for granting the parity of political power to the representatives of a minority, in spite of their being a minority. The demand for parity, as we have seen, may be based on the claim of the equality of cultures. Within the national self-determination discourse, a distinct culture entitles a group possessing that culture to political power, irrespective of its relative numerical size. The rhetoric of the right to national self-determination is in this context an instrument through which culture becomes transformed into political power, an instrument which defies the relative numerical strength of the cultural group. Thus culture comes to trump majority rule, and, if necessary, may trump individual liberty as well.[12]

Notes

1 'National movement' is here used in the widest possible sense of any movement of culturally distinct groups aiming at any degree of self-government or self-determination.

2 Coherence and consistency are not essential for the success of political rhetoric of any kind, let alone the national self-determination rhetoric. These arguments have, after all, other functions apart from that of establishing the truth of the rights claims of national minorities. As with other rights-based political arguments, these may tend to induce the feeling of shame – and even of guilt – among the members of those groups which are accused of breaching the rights (in this case the right to self-government) of others. Moreover, these arguments may also induce the members of the groups whose rights are thus alleged to be breached to believe that they are a wronged party which is morally justified in demanding that these wrongs be removed. To achieve either or both, these arguments do not need to be mutually or individually coherent or consistent.

3 Several authors have argued for this, at some length. See Will Kymlicka, *Multicultural Citizenship: A Liberal Theory of Minority Rights*, Oxford: Clarendon Press, 1995, in particular pp.80–94; and David Miller, *On Nationality*, Oxford: Clarendon Press, 1995, pp.85–6.

4 Kymlicka, *Multicultural Citizenship*, pp.84–94, deploys an argument from the 'deep bonds' to the importance of cultural groups and cultural identity.

5 For an elaborate argument on a similar conclusion, see Allen Buchanan, *Secession: The Morality of Political Divorce from Fort Sumner to Lithuania and Quebec*, Boulder, CO: Westview Press, 1991, pp.52–61.

6 In claiming this, I follow Brian Barry, 'The Limits of Cultural Politics', *Review of International Studies*, vol.23 (1998), p.314.

7 For this argument, see Buchanan, *Secession*.

8 For these restrictions, see Kymlicka, *Multicultural Citizenship*, pp.30–31, 95–8; and M. Keating, *Plurinational Democracy*, Oxford: Oxford University Press, 2001, pp.19–21.

9 Notably, Kymlicka, *Multicultural Citizenship*, pp.114–15.

10 See Barry, 'Limits of Cultural Politics', pp.314–16.

11 For a persuasive account of this process, see M. Hroch, 'National Self-Determination from a Historical Perspective', in Sukimar Periwal (ed.), *Notions of Nationalism*, Budapest: Central European Press, 1995.

12 I am grateful to Ruth Abbey and Igor Primoratz for their comments on an earlier draft of this chapter.

Chapter 9

A Principled International Legal Response to Demands for Self-Determination

Allen Buchanan

Secession and Self-Determination

The Need for a Principled View

Existing international law regarding secession is dangerously flawed. Lacking principled basis for responding to various groups' claims to self-determination beyond the narrow case of classic decolonization, the international legal community has tended to react only when demands for self-determination escalate to attempts to secede and attempts to suppress secession lead to massive violations of human rights. Since the NATO intervention in Kosovo in 1999, attention has shifted away from secession to the question of whether international law regarding humanitarian intervention needs reforming. In my view this is a mistake, if the assumption is that the task is simply to forge new criteria and procedures that allow the use of military force across borders for the sake of preventing massive human rights violations. Instead, what is needed is to develop a morally defensible and practicable international legal response to self-determination issues, and then to build a regime for intervention upon this.

Simply to focus on developing a better process for intervention after self-determination conflicts have exploded into human rights disasters does not go to the root of the problem. In addition, a principled account of when claims for self-determination are valid is needed to know whether and when to intervene and what to try to accomplish by intervening.

In this chapter I sketch in broad strokes a proposal for reforming the international legal response to self-determination issues.[1] The core idea of my approach is an 'isolate and proliferate' strategy. The suggestion is to isolate a limited right to unilateral secession understood as a remedial right only – to uncouple the unilateral right to the most extreme form of self-determination from the question of intrastate autonomy – and then proliferate the options for intrastate autonomy arrangements.

A unilateral right to secede is a claim right that a group has independently of any constitutional provision for secession or any right conferred by consent of the state. As a claim right, it includes two elements: the permissibility of the group attempting to establish its own state in a portion of the territory of the state in which it currently exists, and an obligation on the part of others, including the state, not to interfere with its attempt to do so. For obvious reasons, the unilateral right to secede is the subject of greatest controversy.

Elsewhere I have argued that the international legal order should include a unilateral right to secede, but only as a remedial right, a right which a group comes to have when it has been subjected to persistent rights violations and independence is the remedy of last resort against these injustices. Here I will not repeat the detailed critiques I have advanced against rival understandings of the unilateral right to secede. Instead, I will simply summarize my view of the unilateral right to secede as a remedial right and then use it as the basis for exploring the 'isolate and proliferate' strategy.

It should be emphasized that Remedial Right Only Theories only concern the conditions under which there is a *unilateral* right to secede. They are compatible with a very permissive stance on negotiated or constitutional secession. In that sense, Remedial Right Only Theories are not as conservative as they might first appear.

The Remedial Right Only View

This approach to unilateral secession recognizes at least two ways a group can have the requisite valid claim to territory: (a) by reclaiming territory over which they were sovereign but which was unjustly taken from them (as with the Baltic Republics' secession from the Soviet Union in 1991) or (b) by claiming sovereignty over the territory as a last resort remedy against serious and persistent injustices, understood as violations of basic human rights. A more expansive reading of (b) would include not only the violation of basic human rights, but also the state's major violations of, or unilateral revocation of, intrastate autonomy agreements (as with Milošević's extinction of Kosovo's autonomy in 1989). In the next section I argue for the more expansive reading.

The Isolate and Proliferate Strategy

Combining a rather constrained, justice-based view of the right to unilateral secession (the Remedial Right Only Theory) with a more supportive posture toward forms of autonomy within the state has several important advantages. First, uncoupling the right to secede from the legitimate interests that groups may have in various forms of intrastate autonomy is liberating: it allows groups to get what they need without the risks involved in secession. Second, states will be more receptive to legitimate claims for autonomy if they are assured that they can respond to these without implicitly recognizing the group's right to secede. Third, the justice-based account of the unilateral right to secede focuses attention where it belongs: on the need to provide better protection for human rights. States can avoid secession – or at least avoid international legal support for secession – if they do a creditable job of respecting the basic human rights of all their citizens.

This last point merits elaboration. The Remedial Right Only view of the unilateral right to secede allows the international community to acknowledge that in some cases groups have a valid claim to independence, but it does so without subscribing to the dangerous rhetoric of national self-determination. On the Remedial Right Only account, nations as such (or distinct peoples, and so on) should not be recognized in international law as having a right to independence or to autonomy of any kind. So, unlike theories that link self-determination with nationalism, the Remedial Right Only view is not vulnerable to the objection that implementing it would encourage forced removals or genocide, given the fact that virtually every state contains more than one nation and that nations are not generally concentrated in particular regions. Second, to know whether a group has the right to secede one need not be able to determine what counts as a nation or people, a matter on which there is not even theoretical agreement; nor need one determine which nations' claims that a certain region is their 'homeland' should take precedence. All that is necessary is to know whether a group has suffered a persistent pattern of violations of its members' basic human rights.

In the remainder of this chapter I elaborate the second prong of the 'isolate and proliferate' strategy by clarifying what it means to say that the international legal order should support intrastate autonomy. The chief question I seek to answer is this: under what conditions should the international community involve itself in the creation, maintenance or restoration of intrastate autonomy regimes?

Intrastate Autonomy

International Legal Recognition of a Right to Intrastate Autonomy

There are four circumstances in which international law should recognize groups as having a right to some form of intrastate autonomy. The first and most obvious is where a group has the right to unilateral secession but chooses to opt instead for a limited form of self-government within the existing state. If, for example, the Baltic States had chosen a new form of autonomy in association with Russia and other components of the Soviet Union in 1991, rather than full independence, they would have had a right to do so, according to the Remedial Right theory.

Second, the international legal order should support a right to intrastate autonomy for groups that have been granted significant forms of intrastate autonomy but then suffered serious and persistent violations of that autonomy through actions of the state. Because this scenario occurs frequently (and usually with horrific results), it makes sense to require that, where the state has granted intrastate autonomy to a group, the terms of the autonomy arrangement are to be upheld and the state may not unilaterally revoke the agreement or substantially modify its terms. Especially in cases where the group's reason for seeking the autonomy arrangement in the first place was because it had suffered serious human rights violations, but also in any case in which there is reason to expect that the state's violation of an autonomy agreement is likely to result in serious human rights violations, unilateral revocation of the autonomy of the group by the state should be regarded as violation of international law.

It would clearly be inappropriate for international legal bodies to condemn a state for unilaterally violating an autonomy agreement, much less use force against that state to reinstate the arrangement, without compelling evidence. For this reason it is crucial that the international legal community not only facilitate the creation of intrastate autonomy as a less destabilizing alternative to secession, but also monitor both parties' compliance with the terms of such arrangements.

A third circumstance in which the international legal order should recognize a right to intrastate autonomy arrangements is where the granting of autonomy to a group offers the best prospect for stopping a persistent pattern of rights violations by the state. In an imperfect international legal system in which more direct attempts to end discrimination against a minority group have failed, it may be justifiable for the international legal order to demand that the state grant the group autonomy, even if the rights violations have not reached a level of severity sufficient to justify the group's seceding. Thus, for example, international recognition of and support for a right to autonomy within the state might be an appropriate response to systematic and persisting failure on the part of the state to uphold certain national minority rights, such as constitutionally recognized rights to education in their own language.

Distinguishing the Grounds for a Right to Autonomy from Those for a Right to Secede

From the perspective of institutional design that takes incentives seriously, there is much to be said for making the remedial grounds for international legal recognition of a group's right to autonomy somewhat less demanding than those for international recognition of a unilateral right to secede. For one thing, if the standards were the same, discontented minorities might simply opt for secession. This would be unfortunate, given the international legal order's legitimate interest in stability and the greater risk of violence that secession usually entails. For another, as Donald Horowitz and others have rightly emphasized, secession often simply creates a new problem of minority oppression, as the dominant group among the secessionists now have their own state within which to oppress minorities within it.[2]

In contrast, where a minority achieves autonomy rather than full independence, the state will still be able to exert some control over the way the autonomous region treats its minorities, and the majority in the autonomous region will have incentives not to oppress its minorities. For both of these reasons, it makes sense for the international community to require a lower level of minority rights violations for the recognition of a right to autonomy than for a right to secede.

In the next section of this chapter I take up a fourth condition under which a group should be recognized as having a right to intrastate autonomy under international law: the special case of indigenous peoples. I will argue that they are entitled to international support for autonomy on several distinct grounds. But at this point I simply wish to stress that, so far as the international legal system should recognize a right to self-determination short of secession, it should do so because intrastate autonomy arrangements can either serve as a superior alternative to secession for those groups that have the right to secede on remedial grounds or because self-government for groups within the state can better protect the human rights of minorities, when the state has failed to protect them.

It is disappointing that the growing literature on autonomy regimes is not clear as to whether such arrangements are needed only because current political structures do not effectively protect minorities against violations of their individual human rights, especially their rights against discrimination on ethnic or religions grounds.[3] There are, in fact, two quite different ways to regard intrastate autonomy and to justify support for it by the international legal order.

On the one hand, they could be seen as remedial devices, needed only as back-ups for failures to protect minorities from various forms of discrimination and violations of other human rights. On the other hand, they could be regarded as being required even in the absence of human rights violations, as something to which groups are entitled simply because they are nations or partake of a distinct culture. The view I wish to defend is the former.[4]

It is important to understand that there are many things that states can do which would largely obviate the need for autonomy regimes or at least undercut the claim that groups have a claim of justice to such arrangements.[5] First and most important, states can provide better protection of individual human rights against discrimination, especially in employment and education, but also in access to political participation. Second, it will be necessary to undertake measures for some groups to counteract the continuing effects of past violations of individual human rights, for example through special subsidies for education or employment, various types of affirmative action programmes, and so on. Third, states can and should do much more to jettison the cultural baggage that they have tended to attach to public ceremonies, holidays and other items in the public space and that minority cultural group members find alienating, if not insulting. Even if it proves impossible for the state to be completely 'culturally neutral', the more egregious instances of favouring one culture or religion over others can be eliminated (and in some states already have been).[6]

I am not denying that in some cases the individual rights of members of minority groups can best be protected by some form of autonomy for the group. I shall argue below that this may often be the case for indigenous peoples. But if the case for autonomy is based on the fact that the minority group is oppressed, it would be a mistake to *begin* by promoting autonomy. Instead, the presumption should be that more must be done to protect minorities by respecting their individual rights, including the right to religion, to wear their distinctive cultural dress and to engage in their cultural rituals and ceremonies, as well as freedom from discrimination and exclusion.

There are several weighty reasons for focusing first and foremost on the protection of individual human rights. First, respect for rights generally is not likely to be enhanced by proliferating rights unnecessarily. If conscientious efforts to strengthen protections of individual human rights will do the job, there is no reason to create new autonomy rights. There is also the risk that, by shifting our attention to the problem of choosing from a large and complex menu of alternative autonomy regimes, we will be distracted from the crucial task of holding states accountable for their primary task of protecting the individual human rights of all their citizens. Furthermore, the creation of autonomy regimes does not itself guarantee that human rights will be respected; in some cases it simply shifts the locus of political power so that those who were the oppressed can become the oppressors. (Recall that, in the century between the end of the American Civil War and the passing of key Federal Civil Rights legislation in 1964 and 1965, the autonomy of Southern States legitimized the creation of a regime of institutionalized racism.) Finally, there is the additional risk that if autonomous units within the state have considerable control over revenues and other resources within their boundaries, they will act in ways that impede state efforts to implement distributive justice. In a world in which the state is the only entity approaching an effective agent for distributive justice, this is a serious consideration.[7]

The Many Forms of Intrastate Autonomy

A rich and burgeoning literature catalogues the varieties of extant as well as feasible but as yet untried intrastate autonomy regimes.[8] These range from consociation to various forms of symmetrical and asymmetrical federalism to forms of 'personal' rather than territorially based rights of self-government. There is an infinitely broad range of what might be called rights of collectivities, in which rights range from self-administration to genuine rights of self-government or from rights to participate in decision making regarding economic development in a group's region to state-like jurisdictional rights to create rules defining property rights within a territory.

Nothing general can be said about which sort of autonomy regime may be appropriate in a specific case. Understood as remedies for failures to protect human rights of minorities, autonomy regimes must be shaped to provide an appropriate remedy for the particular violations that have occurred, given the social and cultural context and the resources available. However, a brief examination of the case for intrastate autonomy rights for indigenous peoples will clarify the attractions of a remedial approach to international legal recognition of self-government short of full independence.

Indigenous Peoples' Rights

Group Rights and Individual Human Rights

Some advocates for indigenous peoples' rights understand them as including *group* rights that challenge the fundamental framework of the dominant individualist conception of human rights. I will argue, however, that, although a proper protection of the rights of indigenous peoples will require changes in international law, it is an exaggeration to say that achieving this protection requires a radical revision of the conceptual framework of human rights theory and practice. More specifically, there is no reason to conclude that taking indigenous peoples' rights seriously requires abandoning the idea that the international legal order should be grounded in the idea of individual human rights or embracing the view that a new conception of group rights must be incorporated in it.

Indigenous Peoples' Rights as Group Rights

Throughout the UN Draft Declaration on the Rights of Indigenous Peoples, various rights are ascribed to indigenous *peoples*, not to individual indigenous persons.[9] This choice of words signals the assumption that at least some of the rights set forth in the document are *group* rights. Because it interpreted the Draft's reference to the rights of peoples as signalling the assertion of group rights, the United States government has argued for revising the wording of the declaration so that only individual rights are recognized.[10]

The putative group rights of indigenous people are of at least two sorts: rights of self-government, usually understood as rights to autonomy rather than as rights to independent statehood, and rights to 'cultural integrity', understood to include not merely rights against interference with cultural activities, but also rights to positive actions by states to enable indigenous peoples not only to preserve but to 'strengthen' their cultures and to determine the direction of their cultural development.[11]

My concern in this chapter is primarily with rights of self-government, since the goal is to understand the role that support for intrastate autonomy regimes should play in the international legal system. However, since the justice-based, remedial approach to self-determination I am advancing rests on an individualistic conception of human rights, it will be necessary to clarify and evaluate the charge that such a normative framework cannot accommodate the legitimate claims of indigenous peoples.

Group Rights in International Law[12]

During the League of Nations period, between the two World Wars, international law provided what might be regarded as group rights, chiefly in the form of cultural rights for certain national minorities. Partly because the concept of minority rights was discredited by Hitler's appeal to alleged violations of the rights of ethnic Germans in Czechoslovakia and Poland as a pretext for invasion, minority rights were at first accorded almost no role in the new international legal order forged by the United Nations in 1945.[13] There is some indication, however, that greater attention to the rights of minorities is now emerging, especially in the area of indigenous peoples' rights.

The chief issue is whether the post-1945 era's near exclusive focus on individual rights is defensible or whether, in addition to the rights of states and the limited right of self-determination of colonized peoples, it ought to be supplemented with a richer menu of group rights. More specifically, if new group rights are to be included in international law, should they be understood as basic rights, coordinate with the most fundamental individual human rights, or as being in some way derivative? And if group rights and individual human rights conflict, which should be accorded priority?

Different Senses of 'Group Rights'

Before these questions can be answered, we must clarify what is meant by group rights. Unfortunately there is no fixed definition of the term. For purposes of the present discussion, the following quite different meanings may be distinguished.

(1) Group rights are those that can only be wielded (that is, exercised, waived or alienated) by a collectivity, not by individuals as such. The paradigm example of a group right in this sense is a right of self-government enjoyed by a state or a federal unit or municipality or some other collective entity within the state. These rights cannot be wielded by individuals as individuals on their own behalf; they can only be wielded by the whole collectivity, in the case of a direct participatory democracy, or by authorized representatives of a collectivity.

(2) Group rights are those that are ascribed primarily to groups, rather than to individuals – group rights are rights possessed by groups. Thus, if a group right in this sense is violated, it is to the group as such, not to its members as individuals, that apology, restitution or compensation is owed. The first concept of group rights distinguishes them from individual rights according to who or what *wields* the right; the second distinguishes them from individual rights according to who the *possessor* of the right is.

(3) A group right is one whose *justification* appeals to the interests of all or most of the members of a group, not just to the interests of an individual. For example, a right to vote might be ascribed to each individual in a polity (individuals are possessors of the right and wielders of this right), but the justification for this ascription might appeal to the interests that all members of the polity have in having broadly based participation in government. Note that, for a right to be a group right in this sense, one need not assume that groups have interests that are not reducible to the interests of their members. The point of meaning (3) is that the justification for the right appeals to the interests of all or most members of the group. Furthermore, it leaves open the question of whether the right is a group right in sense (1); that is, whether it is to be wielded by collectivities or by individuals as such.

It is important to see that international law, like all domestic legal systems, already includes group rights in sense (1). All rights of self-government, including the rights of states, are group rights in the sense of rights that can only be wielded collectively. No individual, as an individual, can exercise the sovereignty-constituting rights of the United States, or the rights of the state of North Carolina, or those of the City of Durham. So it is preposterous to say that the recognition of group rights in sense (1) for indigenous peoples or any other collectivities challenges the framework of international law. Indeed, until this century international law consisted almost exclusively of group rights in sense (1) – namely, the rights of states.

So, if what indigenous peoples are asking for when they demand group rights is only rights of self-government, there is nothing conceptually radical about this. They are simply demanding that some of the rights traditionally wielded by states should be wielded by their collectivities as well.

As noted above, advocates of indigenous peoples' rights typically call for recognition not only of rights of self-government but also of cultural integrity, and they regard the latter as a 'group' or 'collective' right. If this means that the right to cultural integrity is a group right in sense (3), then, as with sense (1), no radical revision in the individualist framework of the justice-based conception of international law is required.

The ascription of group rights to indigenous peoples could only challenge the conceptual framework of an individualistic moral theory of international law if group rights are understood in sense (2): if groups are understood to be the *bearers* of the rights in question, where the reference to groups is not simply shorthand for saying that the right is a right of each member of the group. To understand why this is so, it is important to emphasize that the so-called individualist conceptual framework is only individualistic in a *justificatory* sense: according to moral individualism in the justificatory sense, all justifications for ascriptions of moral and legal rights (and duties) must be grounded *ultimately* on consideration of the wellbeing and freedom of individuals.

Justificatory individualism is compatible with the view that groups are 'real', that not all the properties of groups can be reduced to the properties of individuals who are members of the groups.[14] It is a justificatory, not an ontological view. In addition, individualism as a view about justification of rights assertions is also obviously compatible with the ascription of rights in both senses (1) and (3): having institutions that allow certain rights to be wielded only by collectivities can be justified by appeals to the wellbeing and freedom of individuals, and justifications for rights that appeal to the interests of all or most members of a group also rest on considerations of the freedom and wellbeing of individuals.

The only remaining question is whether individualism in the justificatory sense is compatible with group rights in sense (2). It clearly is, if the sense (2) group rights are *legal* rights, but *not* if they are *moral* rights. There are sound individualistic justifications for having laws that designate certain collectivities as possessors of rights. For example, business corporations are possessors of rights in all western-style domestic legal systems, but this does not mean that corporations are moral entities in their own right and hence proper subjects for the ascription of moral rights. In contrast, to assert that a collectivity, as opposed to an individual, is a possessor of a moral right is incompatible with justificatory individualism because regarding a collectivity as a possessor of moral rights assumes that collectivities are moral subjects, and hence the kinds of things that have interests that can serve as the ultimate ground for moral justifications.

There are, then, two quite different ways to understand the assertion that the rights of indigenous peoples include group rights in sense (2). It can be understood as an assertion that international (and domestic) law should designate indigenous collectivities as possessors of legal rights, or it can be understood as claiming something further and much more problematic: that indigenous collectivities ought to be designated as the possessors of legal rights because they are the possessors of corresponding moral rights. Only the second assertion, not the first, is incompatible with the justificatory individualism that underlies the justice-based approach of this chapter.

Justificatory individualism rightly rejects as nonsensical the notion that groups are possessors of moral rights and hence on a par with persons. When the justificatory individualist speaks of the interests of groups he maintains that this is a shorthand for the interests of the members of the group. This is quite compatible, however, with understanding that individuals can have certain interests only by virtue of being members of a group.

To assert that indigenous collectivities, or any collectivities, are the possessors of moral rights is not only implausible, it is also *entirely unnecessary* from the standpoint of devising institutions for protecting the distinctive interests of indigenous peoples. To see why this is so, in the next section I sketch the main arguments for according indigenous peoples rights of intrastate autonomy.

Justifications for Intrastate Autonomy for Indigenous Peoples

There are four distinct and mutually compatible justifications for developing international legal support for intrastate autonomy for indigenous peoples. First, the creation of autonomy regimes for indigenous peoples can be required as a matter of rectificatory justice, in order to restore the self-governance of which these peoples were deprived by colonization and conquest. Second, autonomy can provide a non-paternalistic mechanism for protecting indigenous individuals from violations of their individual human rights and for counteracting the continuing detrimental effects of past violations of their individual human rights or those of their ancestors. Third, it may be necessary to establish or augment institutions of self-governance for indigenous groups in order to implement settlements of land claims in cases where lands that were held in common were lost owing to treaty violations. Fourth, rectificatory justice requires measures to protect indigenous peoples from the detrimental effects of the disruption of the indigenous customary law that defined and supported their way of life. Equipping indigenous peoples with powers of self-government that include the right to make new laws for themselves better accords with the fact that their cultures are dynamic and should not be frozen by attempts to restore customary law that no longer best serves their interests.[15]

These four arguments all fall under the category of remedial justifications. None of them assumes that nations or 'distinct societies' or cultural groups per se, whether indigenous or otherwise, have rights to autonomy. And none implies that there is a special category of indigenous peoples' rights; in each case, the argument could in principle apply to groups that are not classified as indigenous. It just so happens that the circumstances that make the arguments applicable most often obtain in the case of indigenous peoples.

All four justifications for indigenous autonomy appeal to the need to remedy violations of individual human rights, including the rights to communal property and to restore self-governance that was unjustly destroyed. It follows that the case for international legal recognition of autonomy for indigenous peoples does not require anything approaching a fundamental revision of the basic conceptual framework of the international legal order. Instead of being seen as a radical challenge to that framework, the struggle for self-government for indigenous groups should be seen as a reformist movement aimed at achieving a more consistent and impartial application of the existing international legal system's most normatively appealing principles.

Restoration of Self-government

In some cases the destruction of indigenous self-governance by colonial incursions is both relatively recent and well documented. Here the case for intrastate autonomy is, in principle, no more problematic than the case for restoring sovereignty to states that have been unjustly annexed. Although it may be true that the sort of self-governance enjoyed by indigenous peoples was not statehood in the sense defined by international law, rectificatory justice requires that they be restored to some form of self-government. And, to the extent that previous indigenous self-government was territorially based, rectification requires indigenous autonomy within a portion of the state's territory. As Margaret Moore has noted, the wrong done to indigenous peoples is the same as that perpetrated against colonized peoples generally: they were forcibly incorporated into a polity controlled by another group, even though they already enjoyed their own governance institutions.[16] In the case of classic colonization, the appropriate remedy may be independent statehood; in the case of indigenous peoples, it is more likely to be intrastate autonomy.[17]

However, the problem of reconciling the rectification of injustices to indigenous peoples with the demands of distributive justice regarding the larger society in which indigenous peoples find themselves is especially daunting. It seems unreasonable to hold that vast lands upon which millions of people who had nothing to do with the destruction of indigenous self-government now depend should be returned to the exclusive control of a relatively small group of indigenous persons, even if it is true that the indigenous group previously exercised some sort of control over all of that territory and were victims of the unjust conquest. But this is not to say that the claims of indigenous peoples to restoration of some sort of territorially based self-government can simply be dismissed. The problem is how to reconcile the competing claims of rectificatory and distributive justice. It should be emphasized that moral limitations on claims of restoration are not unique to the case of indigenous peoples. They apply equally to cases where states recover their sovereignty having been unjustly annexed. Neither the reasonable expectations of persons who had nothing to do with the annexation nor the requirements of distributive justice can be ignored in the process of restoring sovereignty.

Self-government as a Nonpaternalistic Mechanism for Preventing Human Rights Violations and for Combating the Continuing Effects of Past Human Rights Violations

Indigenous individuals often suffer human rights violations, especially in the form of economic discrimination and exclusion from political participation. In some cases the state is the violator of their rights, but perhaps more frequently the state allows private entities and individuals within the state to perpetrate violations against indigenous persons. In addition, indigenous individuals frequently complain that they are not accorded equality before the law, suffer discrimination at the hands of the police and face special difficulties in using legal processes to defend their rights and interests. At least for the foreseeable future, according indigenous groups rights of self-government may be the most effective way, or the only practicable way, to reduce violations of individual human rights and guarantee effective access to legal processes.

Like African-Americans and members of other groups that have suffered centuries of human rights violations, indigenous individuals frequently suffer from the effects of past injustices. The most cogent rationale for affirmative action policies in employment and in admission to institutions of higher education is that these measures are needed to counteract the continuing effects of past injustices. The same basic rationale can support the establishment or strengthening of autonomy for indigenous peoples, in cases where the groups in question (unlike African-Americans) are territorially concentrated on lands whose occupation and use is a part of their continuing efforts to throw off the burden of a history of injustices.

Establishing or strengthening indigenous self-governance, including tribal courts, in order to reduce current human rights violations and counteract the effects of past violations has the added virtue that it responds to the problem in a *non-paternalistic* fashion, by equipping indigenous peoples themselves with the institutional resources to ensure that their rights are protected and to overcome the disadvantages resulting from historical injustices. Too often in the past even the better-intentioned efforts of others have been ineffective or counterproductive because of a failure to understand the needs of indigenous peoples or to identify feasible measures for preventing violations of their rights, given their distinctive cultural beliefs and practices. Thus the case for intrastate autonomy as a mechanism for preventing human rights violations and counteracting the continuing effects of past violations rests both on the severity of the continuing discrimination and on the demonstrated inability of non-indigenous governments to respond adequately to it.

Self-government to Facilitate the Implementation of Land Claim Settlements

When indigenous peoples succeed in their struggles to regain lands that were taken from them in violation of treaties, institutions of self-government may be needed to determine the ultimate disposition of the lands. Since the lands were typically held in common, they cannot be simply returned to individual members of the group, even if it were possible to trace lines of inheritance. It would be a mistake, however, to assume that if the lands were once held in common, they must continue to be held in common once they are returned. Instead, it may be in the best interests of the group as a whole and of all or most of its individual members if the land is allocated in a system that includes both some common property and some individual ownership. The group's customary rules of common ownership (assuming they are known or can be recovered) may not be a suitable guide for making these crucial decisions about how the hard-won resource is to be used.

If the group currently lacks the institutions of self-government needed to make fair and effective decisions about how to dispose of land returned as a rectification of treaty violations, it may be necessary to create them. For these institutions to function effectively, they must receive legal recognition by the state.

Self-government as a Superior Alternative to the Incorporation of Indigenous Customary Law in the State's Legal System

The fourth and final justification for international legal support for indigenous autonomy flows naturally from the third. Generally speaking, self-government appears to be a more suitable device for indigenous peoples to protect their legitimate interests, including protecting their cultures, than incorporating indigenous customary law into the state's legal system. In traditional societies, customary legal systems change over time through the cumulative actions of the members of those societies. But when such societies have suffered severe disruption and the ordinary processes by which custom evolves have been destroyed or damaged, to attempt to incorporate into the state's law what is taken to be customary rules at a particular time is to treat indigenous culture as frozen and fixed. Autonomy regimes that include significant powers to create new laws are more consonant with the fact that indigenous cultures, like all cultures, can and must change in response to new situations.

Moreover, attempting to incorporate indigenous customary rules into the state's legal system often underestimates the degree of disagreement that can exist in traditional societies about what the customary norms are. If state actors rely on some sources within the indigenous culture to determine what the existing customary rules are, without ensuring that the opinion they glean is representative and in some way authoritative, they may unwittingly support one subgroup (a self-styled elite or the self-proclaimed interpreters of the authentic culture) and fix within the state's legal system a conception of indigenous life that does not serve the interests of all members of the group. But if they rely upon some institution within the group in order to determine authoritatively what the customary rules are that are to be incorporated in the state's legal system, then they can be accused of undercutting the ability of the group to continue to make and revise its rules. This uncomfortable dilemma can be avoided if the group is accorded the rights of self-government needed to make and revise laws as the culture develops.

Basic Individual Human Rights as Limits on Autonomy

When the case can be made that autonomy for indigenous groups or minorities is necessary to protect their members' human rights or to counteract the continuing effects of past violations of those rights, international law also should support intra-state autonomy for the same reason that it should support more direct protections for human rights. However, some have worried that granting intrastate autonomy might lead to the exercise of political power within indigenous communities that violate individual members' human rights, particular those of women.[18] It would be disingenuous to claim that autonomy will never be exercised in ways that violate basic individual human rights. However, this is a problem of government in general, not only of indigenous or minority self-government. Furthermore, it is inaccurate to say that indigenous cultures are especially prone to gender discrimination. Virtually every culture contains elements that support or can be manipulated to support gender discrimination, but virtually every culture also contains elements that can be marshalled in support of gender equality. Wherever there is political power, there is the risk that it may be exercised in such a way that the rights of individuals within the political community may be violated. But there is no special problem of a con-flict between individual rights and indigenous self-government.

I have argued that, in cases where effective protection of the individual human rights of indigenous persons requires it, international law should support indige-nous self-government. The same rationale that provides the strongest case for autonomy for indigenous peoples, the protection of individual human rights, also imposes limits on the ways in which the powers of self-government may be exer-cised. The state is responsible, and ought to be held accountable by international law, for ensuring that the exercise of powers of self-government by indigenous peoples or other groups within the states is compatible with its responsibility for ensuring that all its citizens enjoy basic individual human rights.

Thus the nature of the justification for intrastate autonomy for indigenous peoples makes a difference as to how to respond to possible conflicts between the exercise of powers of self-government and respect for individual human rights. If the ration-ale for intrastate autonomy is remedial, as I have suggested, then at least in princi-ple the limits of intrastate autonomy are clear. If, in contrast, one argues – as I have not – that international law ought to support intrastate autonomy for indigenous peoples because doing so is necessary to preserve their cultures, there is a funda-mental conflict of values between respect for cultural preservation and respect for individual human rights, with no indication of how it might be resolved even in principle.

Conclusion

In the aftermath of NATO's intervention in Kosovo, preoccupation with the problem of secession seems to have given way to concern over humanitarian intervention. However, the two issues are intimately connected. Reforming the international law of humanitarian intervention will require the development of an adequate international legal response to secession, for two reasons. First, the massive human rights violations that call for humanitarian intervention often arise because of conflicts over secession; if international law were reformed in such a way as to help reduce the risk of violent secession, this would alleviate the need for intervention. Second, when violent conflicts over secession do occur, the international community needs guidance not only as to whether to intervene but also on whose behalf the intervention should take place. There is a broad consensus that existing international law is inadequate to both these tasks, but much controversy as to how it should be reformed.

Two rival approaches to reform can be distinguished. The first would be to recognize a broad (and, in my view, potentially dangerous) right of self-determination for all nations or distinct peoples; the other is to frame a highly constrained remedial right to unilateral secession, combined with a much more supportive stance on intrastate autonomy short of full statehood. The advantage of the latter approach, which uncouples secession both from intrastate autonomy and from nationalism, is that it builds on the firmest foundation of existing international law, the commitment to human rights, while avoiding the vagaries and risks of a more expansive right of self-determination.

Notes

1   This proposal is developed in greater detail in my book *Justice, Legitimacy, and Self-Determination: Moral Foundations for International Law*, Oxford: Oxford University Press, 2003, ch.8.

2   Donald Horowitz, 'A Right to Secede?', in Stephen Macedo and Allen Buchanan (eds), *Secession and Self-Determination*, Nomos, vol. XLV, New York: New York University Press, 2003.

3   Donald Horowitz, *Ethnic Groups in Conflict*, Berkeley: University of California Press, 1985; Timothy Sisk, *Power-Sharing and International Mediation in Ethnic Conflicts*, Washington, DC: United States Institute of Peace Press, 1996; Arend Lijphart, *Democracy in Plural Societies: A Comparative Exploration*, New Haven: Yale University Press, 1977; Ruth Lapidoth, *Autonomy*, Washington, DC: United States Institute of Peace, 1966.

4   In *Justice, Legitimacy, and Self-Determination: Moral Foundations for International Law*, ch.8, I criticize in detail the assertion that nations or distinct peoples as such have a right to self-determination.

5   Hurst Hannum, *Autonomy, Sovereignty, and Self-Determination: The Accommodation of Conflicting Rights*, Philadelphia: University of Pennsylvania Press, 1996.

6   See Jacob Levy, *The Multiculturalism of Fear*, New York: Oxford University Press, 2000.

7   Allen Buchanan, 'Federalism, Secession, and the Morality of Inclusion', *Arizona Law Review*, vol.37 (1995).

8   Hannum, *Autonomy, Sovereignty, and Self-Determination*; Lapidoth, *Autonomy*; Sisk, *Power-Sharing and International Mediation in Ethnic Conflicts*.

9   *Draft United Nations Declaration on the Rights of Indigenous Peoples*, E/CN.4/1995/2.

10 *Report of the Working Group Established in Accordance with the Commission on Human Rights Resolution 1995/32*, U.N. Doc. E/CN.4/1999/82 at 40. See also Cindy Holder, 'Cultural Rights in the U.N. Draft Declaration on the Rights of Indigenous Peoples', unpublished manuscript (University of Victoria, British Columbia).

11 Articles 15, 29, 33 and 34 of the U.N. Draft Declaration on the Rights of Indigenous Peoples relate to intrastate autonomy and articles 9, 10, 12, 13, 14 and 16, 17, 24, 25 and 26 relate to cultural integrity.

12 This subsection is drawn from Allen Buchanan and David Golove, 'The Philosophy of International Law', in Jules Coleman, Scott Shapiro and Kenneth Himma (eds), *The Oxford Handbook of Jurisprudence and Philosophy of Law*, New York: Oxford University Press, 2002, pp.892–7.

13 Ibid., p.892.

14 Allen Buchanan, 'Assessing the Communitarian Critique of Liberalism', *Ethics*, vol.99 (1988/9); 'Liberalism and Group Rights', in Jules Coleman and Allen Buchanan (eds), *In Harm's Way*, Oxford: Oxford University Press, 1994.

15 See Levy, *Multiculturalism of Fear*, ch.6.

16 Margaret Moore, 'The Right of Indigenous Peoples to Collective Self-Determination', in Stephen Macedo and Allen Buchanan (eds), *Secession and Self-Determination*.

17 As Jeremy Waldron and others have argued, it is one thing to say that rectificatory justice requires the restoration of some forms of territorially based autonomy, but quite another to say that the right to control a portion of territory trumps all considerations of distributive justice and is impervious to all claims based on long-standing expectations under the principle of adverse possession. See Jeremy Waldron, 'Superseding Historic Injustice', *Ethics*, vol.103 (1992/3), and Jacob Levy, *Multiculturalism of Fear*.

18 Susan Moller Okin with respondents, *Is Multiculturalism Bad For Women?*, ed. Joshua Cohen, Matthew Howard and Martha C. Nussbaum, Princeton: Princeton University Press, 1999.

Chapter 10

Secession: Can it be a Legal Act?

Peter Radan

In what Allen Buchanan described as an 'age of secession',[1] the post-Cold War period has witnessed a plethora of learned writings about secession. However, relatively few of them have focused on the issue of whether an act of secession can be legal. It is the aim of this chapter to address that very question from the perspective of a state's domestic constitutional law.

The right of secession pursuant to the domestic constitutional law of a state has rarely arisen in case law. When it has, it has been in the context of federal states where a subunit of such a state has sought to secede. Accordingly, the analysis below is confined to the context of secession from federal states.

Few state constitutions, past or present, have had, or have, express provisions dealing with secession. Past illustrations include the constitutions of the former Soviet Union, Burma and Yugoslavia. Present illustrations include Saint Christopher and Nevis and Ethiopia.[2] In the case of Saint Christopher and Nevis, an attempt by Nevis to secede in 1998 failed to meet the necessary constitutional requirements.

In analysing domestic constitutional law and the right of secession the cases of the United States of America, the former Yugoslavia and Canada shall be explored. In each case the relevant state's supreme judicial body has given a ruling or rulings examining the right of secession pursuant to that state's constitutional law.

The United States

Professor Cass Sunstein has summed up the question of secession of an American state from the United States by asserting that 'no serious scholar or politician now argues that a right to secede exists under American constitutional law'.[3] Sunstein's assertion is based upon the American Supreme Court decision of *Texas* v. *White*. This case was decided in the wake of the Civil War, and concerned the sale by the Confederate state government of Texas of a number of United States bonds that had been in the Texas state treasury at the time Texas seceded from the United States in February 1861. Following the end of the war, the new reconstruction government of Texas sued for the recovery of the bonds on the basis that the sale by the Confederate state government was invalid. The Supreme Court, in a majority decision, upheld the claim.

Speaking for the majority of the Supreme Court, Chase CJ ruled in favour of Texas on the ground that the Confederate state government in Texas had no legal existence because the secession of Texas from the United States was illegal. As the Confederate state government was illegal, its act of selling the bonds was also illegal and of no effect. Thus Texas was entitled to the recovery of the bonds. The critical finding underpinning the ruling that Texas could not secede from the United States was that, following its admission to the United States in 1845, Texas became part of 'an indestructible Union, composed of indestructible States'.[4] In practical terms this meant that Texas had never seceded from the United States.

In the opinion of Chase CJ, the nature of the United States as 'an indestructible Union' is established by reference to the provisions of two documents. First, there is Article XIII of the *Articles of Confederation and Perpetual Union* of 1777, which declared that the United States union was to be 'perpetual'. Second, there is the Preamble to the *Constitution of the United States* of 1787, which states that the Constitution was proclaimed in order to 'form a more perfect union'. After referring to these two provisions, Chase CJ concluded: 'It is difficult to convey the idea of indissoluble unity more clearly than by these words. What can be indissoluble if a perpetual Union, made more perfect, is not?'[5]

In analysing the decision in *Texas* v. *White* it is important to understand what Chase CJ meant by the expression 'an indestructible Union'. Taken literally it meant that an American state could never in any circumstances secede from the Union. However, this interpretation can easily be rejected because Chase CJ recognized that a state could cease to be part of the union 'through revolution, or through consent of the States'.[6] The consequence of this statement is that the decision in *Texas* v. *White* is authority for the proposition that a *unilateral* secession of a state from the United States is illegal and unconstitutional. As Herman Belz has put it, for Chase CJ the secession of the Confederate States of America was 'unconstitutional because its proponents wrongly claimed for individual states a power rightly possessed by the states in union or collectively'.[7]

The recognition of revolution by Chase CJ was not novel, especially given that the union itself had arisen as the result of revolution. Eight years after *Texas* v. *White*, in the case of *Williams* v. *Bruffy*, the Supreme Court discussed the validity of acts 'where a portion of the inhabitants of a country have separated themselves from the parent State and established an independent government'. Speaking for a unanimous Court, Field J said:

> The validity of its acts, both against the parent State and its citizens or subjects, depends entirely upon its ultimate success. If it fail to establish itself permanently, all such acts perish with it. If it succeed, and become recognized, its acts from the commencement of its existence are upheld as those of an independent nation.[8]

The second way in which secession could occur was if a state's departure from the Union met with the 'consent of the States'. The critical question that arises is what is meant by the words 'consent of the States'.

Taken literally, the 'consent of the States' requirement would mean the unanimous consent of all of the states of the United States. However, such a requirement would be virtually impossible to achieve, as indeed was recognized at the Constitutional Convention of 1787 in relation to the identical requirement of Article XIII of the *Articles of Confederation*. Such a requirement would only encourage the revolutionary means of achieving secession. Because revolutions have a tendency towards violence, the requirement of consent from all of the states has little appeal.

The 'consent of the States' requirement could, however, be taken to mean their consent to a constitutional amendment approved by three-quarters of the states as set out in Article V of the Constitution. This approach is the one suggested by President Abraham Lincoln in his First Inaugural Address.[9] There is much to be said in favour of processing secession as a constitutional amendment, given the seriousness of the act of secession. However, Article V stipulates that a constitutional amendment needs to be proposed by a resolution passed by a two-thirds majority of both houses of Congress or by the legislatures of two-thirds of the number of states. This represents an almost impossible political hurdle to be overcome for any state wishing to secede.

I would suggest that in this context there is much to be gained from adopting the approach of the Canadian Supreme Court set out in its 1998 decision in *Reference re: Secession of Quebec (Secession Reference)*.[10] This case will be discussed in detail below. However, at this point it can be noted that it stands for the proposition that, following a referendum in which a clear majority of the population of a Canadian province voted in favour of a clearly worded question on secession, there arises an obligation for negotiations to be entered into with a view to reaching agreement on a constitutional amendment to facilitate the secession of the relevant province. In the context of the United States, if such negotiations were successful, Article V of the Constitution would necessitate that the proposed amendment be approved by three-quarters of the states for the secession to be legal.

On the question of whether, in the American context, a referendum on secession could trigger a lawful secession, Akhil Reed Amar has suggested that Lincoln may well have had no alternative but to accept the legality of secession supported by the people as evidenced by a (legally non-binding) *national* referendum. This was because, 'in a regime based upon the people's ultimate sovereignty', such a referendum would have carried 'great moral weight with those government actors … ordinarily involved in the amendment process'.[11] According to Amar, 'Conceivably, both Article V amendments and national referenda might have aimed to authorize a wholly lawful and peaceful secession'.[12] However, Amar's speculation does not countenance any possible legitimacy flowing from a referendum within a single state in favour of secession.

Former Yugoslavia

Unlike the United States and Canada, the former Yugoslavia's Constitution of 1974 contained an explicit reference to the right of secession, albeit in its Preamble. Section I of the Basic Principles of the Constitution stipulated as follows:

> The peoples of Yugoslavia, proceeding from the right of every people to self-determination, including the right of secession, ... have united in a federal republic of free and equal nations and nationalities and created a socialist federative community of working people.

Judicial consideration of the right to secession in former Yugoslavia occurred at a time when secessionist demands by some of its republics were being made in the late 1980s and early 1990s. Starting in January 1990, Yugoslavia's Constitutional Court considered a number of cases in which the central issue was the claim of a republic to the right of self-determination, including the right of secession. In all these cases the Court ruled against a right of *unilateral* secession from the Yugoslav federation.

The first of these cases was brought before the Court in the wake of the 1989 amendments to Slovenia's republic constitution: the *Slovenian Constitutional Amendments Case*.[13] One of the amendments asserted that Slovenia had the right of unilateral secession pursuant to the right of self-determination. In rejecting this assertion, the Constitutional Court ruled that secession from the federation was permitted only if there was the unanimous agreement of Yugoslavia's republics and autonomous provinces. In coming to this conclusion, the Court ruled that the right of self-determination, including the right of secession, flowed from the references to these matters in Section I of the Basic Principles of the 1974 Constitution, together with the provisions of the Constitution which determined the nature and composition of Yugoslavia and the rights and obligations of the federation. According to the Court, the rights of self-determination and secession belonged to 'the peoples of Yugoslavia and their socialist republics'. Whether the right of self-determination and secession was vested in the peoples and their republics was put in doubt by the later *Kosovo Declaration Case* of May 1991, in which the Court ruled that 'only peoples of Yugoslavia' had the right of self-determination.[14]

On the question of implementing the secession of a republic from Yugoslavia, in the *Croatian Independence Declaration Case*,[15] the Constitutional Court ruled that the fact that the procedure for the realization of the right to self-determination was not dealt with in Yugoslavia's federal constitution did not mean that the right could be realized by the unilateral acts of one republic. In the *Slovenian Constitutional Amendments Case* the Court was clear that this was a matter for the federal Constitution of Yugoslavia and not the constitution of any single republic. The Court did not elaborate much further on this matter, except to indicate that the approval of all of Yugoslavia's republics and autonomous provinces was necessary. In the later *Slovenian Referendum on Independence Case*,[16] the Court was more explicit in ruling that secession of a republic required a constitutional amendment.

A preliminary to such an amendment was agreement on a settled procedure pursuant to which negotiations on the future relationships between the republics would take place.

It is clear from all the cases considered by the Constitutional Court that the unanimous consent of all the republics and autonomous provinces was necessary for such a constitutional amendment. In the *Slovenian Constitutional Amendments Case* the Court ruled that such unanimous consent was needed because an act of secession by one people and its republic was relevant not only to that people and republic, but to all the peoples and republics that were part of the common state of Yugoslavia, in that secession of one people and republic affected the composition of the federation, its international borders, internal relations within Yugoslavia and Yugoslavia's position as a member of the international community and signatory to many international agreements.

The decisions of the Constitutional Court were significant in that they determined that *unilateral* secession of a republic was unconstitutional. However, in ruling that secession was possible if there was the unanimous agreement of Yugoslavia's republics and autonomous provinces, the Court's decision was controversial, given the almost unanimous legal opinion in Yugoslavia, prior to these cases being decided, that secession was illegal and unconstitutional.

In the year preceding the outbreak of war in Yugoslavia in mid-1991, federal authorities attempted to initiate a process of constitutional reform in a desperate effort to preserve the federation. On 17 October 1990, the Yugoslav Presidency submitted to the Federal Assembly a document entitled 'Concept for the Constitutional Structure of Yugoslavia on a Federal Basis'.[17] This document was a draft set of principles for further constitutional reform. Principle 11 of the draft stipulated that, on the basis of a successful referendum, each republic was entitled to leave the federation in accordance with procedures to be set out in the federal constitution. The Presidency recognized that, although a constitutional right of secession was unusual in federal constitutional structures, it was impossible not to include such a right in the light of the extent to which such a right had become a political demand within Yugoslavia.

Details of the Presidency's thinking on the actual implementation of a right of secession are found in documents considered, but not adopted, by the Presidency in early March 1991. These documents noted that the right of secession flowed from the right of peoples to self-determination. The implementation of a republic's secession was to be initiated by means of a referendum of a republic's citizens. If the referendum failed, the issue was not to be raised again for five years. A successful referendum required a simple majority of voters to cast their votes in favour of secession. An important qualification on the referendum procedure related to republics with more than one constituent people. In such republics the majority of each people had to vote for secession. If any people did not vote for secession, then areas in which that people was the majority population would remain in Yugoslavia, provided such areas bordered on the remaining part of Yugoslavia. In effect this provided for the possible partition of republics following a secession referendum. In cases of partition, the Federal Assembly was to determine the appropriate territorial division as a precondition to formal legislation validating the secession and partition.[18]

The proposals failed to proceed to implementation. However, they were significant because they illustrated that no republic was irrevocably opposed to secession. Rather, the dispute was over whether republics could secede within the confines of existing republic borders, or whether these borders would need to be abandoned and replaced with borders that more closely resembled territorial divisions along national lines.

Canada

Canada represents the most recent case of judicial analysis of the right of secession from the perspective of a state's constitutional law. The debate within Canada in relation to secession has occurred in the context of the possible departure of the province of Quebec from the Canadian federation. The 'Quebec question' has been a dominant theme in Canadian political debate over the past few decades, especially when secessionist provincial *Parti Québecois* governments in Quebec organized referenda on secession in 1980 and 1995, both of which failed to attract majority support.

On 20 August 1998, in *Secession Reference*, the Supreme Court of Canada handed down its decision on the Canadian government's reference to the Court concerning the legality of a future unilateral secession by the province of Quebec from Canada. One of the specific questions put to the Court was: 'Under the *Constitution* of Canada, can the National Assembly, legislature or government of Quebec effect the secession of Quebec from Canada unilaterally?'

The Court answered this question in the negative. In so doing it stressed the relevance of 'four fundamental and organizing principles of the Constitution'. These are federalism, democracy, constitutionalism and the rule of law, and respect for minorities. In the words of the Court: 'These defining principles function in symbiosis. No single principle can be defined in isolation from the others, nor does any one principle trump or exclude the operation of any other.'[19]

These principles dictate that, under Canadian constitutional law, secession requires a negotiated amendment to the Canadian Constitution. The Court ruled that

> the secession of Quebec from Canada cannot be accomplished by the National Assembly, the legislature or government of Quebec unilaterally, that is to say without principled negotiations, and be considered a lawful act. Any attempt to effect the secession of a province from Canada must be undertaken pursuant to the Constitution of Canada, or else violate the Canadian legal order.[20]

Although Canada's Constitution is silent on the issue of secession, in that it neither expressly authorizes nor prohibits it, a negotiated constitutional amendment to facilitate secession is necessary because 'an act of secession would purport to alter the governance of Canadian territory in a manner which undoubtedly is inconsistent with [Canada's] current constitutional arrangements'. Given that Canada's Constitution is an expression of the sovereignty of Canada's people, any amendment could be made to the Constitution, including the secession of Quebec, provided that such an amendment was achieved by procedures set out in the Constitution.[21]

The Court proceeded to broadly delineate the procedure by which the secession of Quebec could be constitutionally achieved. The first step would be 'a clear expression of the people of Quebec of their will to secede from Canada'. This could be determined by a referendum on secession, even though the referendum itself would have no legal effect and could not bring about unilateral secession. However, a clear referendum vote in favour of secession is important because it 'would confer legitimacy on the efforts of the Quebec government to initiate the Constitution's amendment process in order to secede by constitutional means'. The political legitimacy that would flow from a referendum that showed a clear desire on the part of the population of Quebec to secede would place an obligation on the other provinces and the federal government to enter into negotiations 'to negotiate constitutional changes to respond to that desire'. These negotiations would need to be conducted in a manner consistent with the principles of federalism, democracy, constitutionalism and the rule of law, and respect for minorities. A refusal by any party to so act would undermine the legitimacy of that party's position and could jeopardize the negotiations as a whole. The negotiations could reach an impasse, in which case, provided they had been conducted properly by all parties, it would mean, from the perspective of Canada's constitutional law, that the secession of Quebec would not be permitted because of the absence of a constitutional amendment.[22]

As to the referendum that could trigger this procedure, the Court, on a number of occasions, referred to the need that the referendum amount to a 'clear expression' of the population of Quebec in favour of secession. The Court ruled that 'the referendum result, if it is to be taken as an expression of the democratic will, must be free of ambiguity both in terms of the question asked and in terms of the support it achieves'.[23]

It is appropriate to comment on a number of issues arising out of the Court's decision on secession in the context of Canada's constitutional law. These include the following:

- the wording of any referendum question,
- the meaning of a 'clear expression' of support for secession,
- the position of Quebec's minorities on secession,
- the process of negotiations on secession,
- the content of secession negotiations,
- the appropriate amendment procedures, and
- the possibility of a successful, but unconstitutional, secession.

The Wording of the Referendum Question

The Supreme Court indicated that the referendum question would need to be 'free of ambiguity' in terms of the question asked. The Court also ruled that the determination of what was a clear question to be put to a referendum was to be established by the political process.[24] It is suggested that this requirement 'is justifiable both in terms of democratic accountability and as a requirement of fairness'.[25]

The Supreme Court's requirement that the question be 'free of ambiguity' suggests that it did not believe that the questions posed in the two previous Quebec referenda met that standard.

The October 1995 referendum in Quebec asked voters the following question: 'Do you agree that Quebec should become sovereign, after having made a formal offer to Canada for a new Economic and Political Partnership, within the scope of the Bill respecting the Future of Quebec and of the agreement signed on 12 June 1995?' It has been shown that a 'Yes' vote in response to this question was not always understood as a vote for independent statehood. This flowed from the confusion of what was meant by the word 'sovereignty' in the referendum question. Between one-quarter and one-third of Quebec voters favouring sovereignty for Quebec believed that it meant that Quebec would remain a province of Canada.[26]

The Meaning of a 'Clear Expression'

The Court expressly declined to define what was meant by a 'clear expression' by the people in the context of a secession referendum in Quebec, on the ground that this was a matter to be determined by the political process.[27] In the 1980 and 1995 referenda the Quebec government claimed that a bare majority of votes cast would have been sufficient. In the wake of the Supreme Court's decision, this position was maintained by the then *Parti Québecois* government.[28] However, a reading of the Court's judgment suggests that it does not accept this position and that more than a simple majority is required. The Canadian federal government has repeatedly rejected the Quebec government's contention, and passed legislation to the effect that, unless the federal House of Commons is satisfied that a clear majority of Quebec's *population* supports independence, it will not participate in any constitutional negotiations on secession.[29] The requirement of more than a simple majority is 'justifiable in terms of establishing procedural barriers against too easy a right to exit that may undermine the very basis of democratic politics'.[30]

In seeking guidance on what sort of majority vote would be needed to amount to a 'clear expression' in favour of secession one could turn to constitutions of existing states that explicitly deal with secession of federal units. The *Constitution of Saint Christopher and Nevis* provides that the island of Nevis can secede from the federation and stipulates the procedures for such an act. One of the requirements is a referendum for secession supported by 'not less than two-thirds of all the votes cast on that referendum' (Article 113(2)(*b*)). In the failed 1998 secession referendum in Nevis, only 61.7 per cent of votes cast supported secession. The *Constitution of Ethiopia* permits secession in accordance with procedures that require, inter alia, a referendum on secession supported by a majority vote (Article 39(4)(c)). However, both the above constitutions have a significant hurdle to overcome before a secession referendum can be held. In the case of Nevis, the Nevis Island legislature must vote in favour of secession with a majority of at least two-thirds of all the elected members of its Assembly (Article 113(2)). Similarly, in the case of Ethiopia, a two-thirds vote is required by the legislative council of the relevant unit seeking secession (Article 39(4)(a)).

The Position of Quebec's Minorities

An issue in any secession referendum in Quebec will be the position of that province's minority populations. To date the English-speaking and indigenous populations of Quebec have opposed moves towards Quebec's secession from Canada. The problem of these minorities can be illustrated by the following possible scenario. On the basis that a two-thirds majority vote in favour of secession is indicative of a 'clear expression' in favour of secession, would such a result be viewed as legitimate if it were achieved in circumstances in which significant majorities of Quebec's minority populations voted against secession? In other words, what would be the status of a referendum vote in favour of secession achieved on the strength of significant support by the French-speaking population of Quebec, but strongly opposed by the English-speaking and indigenous populations?

It could be argued that, having achieved the required threshold in percentage terms of Quebec's entire population, there is a 'clear expression' in favour of secession. The independence referendum held in Bosnia-Hercegovina in 1992 would support this view. In that case the international community interpreted the results of the referendum as legitimating secession and extended international recognition to the former Yugoslav republic following the referendum. In the referendum the Bosnian Muslim and Croat populations overwhelmingly voted in favour of independence. Of the 63.4 per cent of the population that voted, 99.4 per cent voted in favour of independence. The Serb population's boycott of the referendum was in effect a vote against independence. The referendum result meant that the vote of 62.7 per cent of the total electorate of Bosnia-Hercegovina in favour of independence legitimated the secession of that republic notwithstanding opposition to secession from its significant Serb minority population.

On the other hand it could be argued that the Quebec referendum scenario suggested above would be legitimate, but only to the extent that there would be an obligation to negotiate with a view to facilitating the creation of an independent Quebec covering those regions of the province that supported independence. Such a referendum vote would not legitimate the negotiation of a constitutional amendment to facilitate Quebec's secession within its present provincial borders. Indeed, the Court contemplated that partition of Quebec could be a result of secession negotiations when it indicated that the question of borders, discussed below, could be one of the issues in the process of negotiating a constitutional amendment on secession.

The Process of Negotiations

In relation to the course of negotiations that must follow a successful referendum on secession in Quebec, the Court rejected the idea that the other provinces and federal government had to accede to the secession of Quebec. Similarly, the Court rejected the view that a successful secession referendum in Quebec would impose no obligations upon the remaining provinces and central government. These absolutist propositions were not sustainable because of the requirement that negotiations be governed by the principles of federalism, democracy, constitutionalism and the rule of law, and the protection of minorities.[31] The Court observed as follows in relation to the course of negotiations:

> The rights of other provinces and the federal government cannot deny the right of the government of Quebec to pursue secession, should a clear majority of the people of Quebec choose that goal, so long as, in doing so, Quebec respects the rights of others. Negotiations would be necessary to address the interests of the federal government, of Quebec and the other provinces, and other participants, as well as the rights of all Canadians both within and outside Quebec.[32]

Later in the judgment the Court added that the negotiations would need 'specifically' to address 'the rights of minorities'.[33]

The Court's judgment is not clear on the issue of which parties would participate in the negotiations. In a number of places the Court refers to negotiations between the Canadian provinces and federal government. On the other hand, the Court, as quoted above, refers to the provinces and federal government 'and other participants' as being engaged in negotiations. This is a significant matter because any negotiated resolution of a Quebec initiative to secede would need to be the product of an agreement by the participants to the negotiations. It is thus necessary to determine who, apart from the provinces and central government, are to be participants to the negotiations. If there are to be 'other participants' the Court judgment does not indicate who they may be. As noted, the Court explicitly ruled that the rights of minority groups have to be addressed at the negotiations. Yet the Court does not state that such groups are entitled to participation in the negotiations. This may well indicate that such groups are by implication excluded from participation in the negotiations. If they are to be participants it is odd that the Court did not state this, given that it did specifically state that their interests are to be addressed in the negotiations. Furthermore, the judgment does not indicate what majority of participants needs to support any agreement reached at the negotiations. This may well be part of the 'content and process of negotiations' that the Court expressly stated were to be determined by the political process.[34]

The Content of Negotiations

Although the Court ruled that the 'content and process of the negotiations' would have to be determined by the political process, it did indicate some of the matters that could be the subject of negotiations relating to Quebec's secession. One was the issue of Quebec's borders.[35] This is of particular importance given that the issue of borders has generated major differences of opinion between the central government, Quebec's aboriginal peoples and Quebec's government. The Canadian government[36] and the James Bay Crees[37] have argued that Quebec's present provincial borders would not automatically become international borders following secession. The Quebec government has argued the opposite and has relied heavily on the break-up of Yugoslavia as a precedent.[38] In Yugoslavia it was held by the Badinter Arbitration Commission that existing internal republic borders became international borders following recognition of independence pursuant to the international law principle of *uti possidetis juris*. However, the Canadian Supreme Court effectively rejects the proposition that existing federal borders are sacrosanct in the context of a negotiated constitutional amendment for the secession of Quebec. It has been argued that Quebec's aboriginal communities have an effective constitutional veto on the question of borders within the context of a negotiated constitutional amendment to facilitate Quebec's secession.[39] On the other hand, the Court appears to recognize that existing borders could become international borders if an unconstitutional secession was, nevertheless, legitimated by the international community extending recognition of independent statehood to Quebec.

The Constitutional Amendment Procedures

The Supreme Court judgment makes it clear that any secession of Quebec, or indeed any agreement that may be negotiated as the result of a secession initiative by Quebec, would need to proceed by amendment to the Canadian Constitution. As the Court stated, a successful referendum in Quebec would 'initiate the Constitution's amendment process'.[40] The question of the procedure for amendment of the Constitution is one that has been the subject of wide debate within Canadian legal circles. Canada's complex and varied constitutional amendment procedures are contained in Part V (ss.38–49) of the Constitution Act, 1982.

The two major alternatives are the so-called general procedure which requires the assent of both houses of the federal parliament plus the consent of at least seven provincial assemblies which together represent at least 50 per cent of Canada's population (ss.38–40, 42), and the unanimity procedure which requires the assent of both houses of federal parliament and of all the provincial legislative assemblies (s.41). In both procedures some provinces are required by their own constitutions to have a referendum vote in favour of the amendment before it is voted upon by the provincial legislature.

Prior to *Secession Reference*, Canadian constitutional lawyers were divided over which of the two Part V procedures would apply in a case involving the secession of one of Canada's provinces.[41] The Supreme Court declined to make any pronouncement on 'the applicability of any particular constitutional procedure to effect secession unless and until sufficiently clear facts exist to squarely raise the issue for judicial determination'. The Court in its references to constitutional amendment to effect secession made no specific reference to either of the stipulated procedures in

Part V, merely noting that 'various procedures to achieve lawful secession [were] raised in argument'.[42]

It has been argued by Donna Greschner that the effect of the Court's decision is to render both alternatives within Part V as inapplicable to cases of secession.[43] Greschner refers to the Court's pronouncement on the four fundamental constitutional principles noted above as being

> a necessary part of [Canada's] Constitution because problems or situations may arise which are not expressly dealt with by the text of the Constitution. In order to endure over time, a constitution must contain a comprehensive set of rules and principles which are capable of providing an exhaustive legal framework for our system of government.[44]

This passage leads Greschner to conclude that, accepting that the Part V methods are unworkable in the context of secession, a constitutional amendment based upon the four fundamental principles is appropriate. She then argues that the Court, in ruling that the secession of Quebec could not be achieved lawfully without principled negotiations based upon the four fundamental principles, meant that

> Unilateral secession is not one that is attempted without compliance with the Part V amending formula, but one attempted without principled negotiations beforehand. Conversely, a non-unilateral secession is one preceded by negotiations and, to use the Court's phrase, will 'be considered a lawful act'.[45]

Provided Quebec lives up to its obligation to engage in principled negotiations on secession, Greschner argues that, if such negotiations did not produce an amendment to permit secession, a declaration of independence by Quebec would be lawful.

Greschner further supports her argument with compelling claims that the Part V procedures do not fit comfortably with the issue of secession because they were not designed with the purpose of creating two independent states out of one. However, whatever the merits of her arguments, her proposition that Part V does not apply in relation to secession fails to deal with the unequivocal statement by the Court that 'Under the Constitution, secession requires that an amendment be negotiated.'[46] This statement clearly means that Part V cannot be simply ignored in relation to a secession amendment.

Successful, but Unconstitutional, Secession

A final comment on the Supreme Court's decision relates to the possibility of a successful secession of Quebec even if a constitutional amendment to achieve that result was not agreed upon pursuant to negotiations between Quebec and the other provinces and federal government. The Court opined that, in the event that Quebec's attempt to secede was thwarted by a failure of any of the other parties to the negotiations to negotiate in good faith, Quebec might well find sympathy in the international community, with the result that it would be more likely that its independence would be recognized internationally than if itself it had failed to negotiate in good faith. The Court also suggested that an unconstitutional and unilateral secession by Quebec could possibly succeed if recognized by the international community. Although recognition is not necessary to achieve statehood, the Court recognized that, in the context of secession, 'the viability of a would-be state in the international community depends, as a practical matter, upon recognition by other states'.[47]

Historically, international recognition of statehood has been the major foreign policy goal of any secessionist movement.[48] The recognition of independence of the Spanish American states by the United States of America in 1822 has been described as 'the greatest assistance rendered by any foreign power to the independence of Latin America'.[49] The recognition by India, a significant regional power, of Bangladesh in 1971 was a key to the success of the latter's secession from Pakistan. Conversely, the failure to gain international recognition has been a major contributing factor in the failure of various secessions. This is confirmed by the failure of the southern Confederacy to gain British recognition of its secession from the USA in the 1860s, and Katanga's failed secession from Congo in the 1960s. The fact that only Turkey has recognized the 1983 secession of the Turkish Republic of Northern Cyprus means that the latter's secession has not, at least to date, been successful.[50]

In relation to a unilateral secession by Quebec the recognition of the four former republics of Yugoslavia serves as an instructive precedent. International recognition was extended to the republics despite the unilateral acts of secession being declared unconstitutional by Yugoslavia's Constitutional Court. Recognition was justified, in part, by allegations of intransigence on the part of Serbia and, to a lesser extent, Montenegro, who sought to retain parts of the territory of the seceding republics within what remained of Yugoslavia.

Conclusion

The domestic constitutional law of the three federal states of the United States, the former Yugoslavia and Canada indicates some common themes as to the right of secession. Although the United States Supreme Court declared that the American union is indestructible, the decision in *Texas* v. *White* is, in its essence, very much the same in effect as the various decisions of the Yugoslav Constitutional Court and the Canadian Supreme Court in *Secession Reference*. That essence is that a unilateral secession of a federal unit is constitutionally illegal. Undoubtedly the tenor of *Texas* v. *White* is more strongly anti-secessionist than is the case with the decisions in Yugoslavia and Canada. All three cases indicate, in varying degrees of detail, that the agreement of other federal units is necessary for secession to occur. Their agreement is required largely because secession is not merely a concern of the federal unit that wishes to secede but also a concern of other units in the state, and it is this concern that largely underpins the prohibition of unilateral secession pursuant to a state's constitutional law. A consequence of this, as is suggested in the cases decided in the former Yugoslavia and in Canada, is that, even if secession is agreed upon in the manner required, it may need to be on the terms that the seceding federal unit be partitioned so that territory populated by groups within the republic opposed to secession could remain within the parent state.

Notes

1 Allen Buchanan, 'Self-Determination, Secession, and the Rule of Law', in Robert McKim and Jeff McMahan (eds), *The Morality of Nationalism*, New York: Oxford University Press, 1997, p.301.

2 The question of whether states should explicitly constitutionalize the right of secession has, in recent times, generated some debate. In this debate, Daniel Weinstock is the significant proponent for the constitutionalization of secession. His most prominent critic has been Cass Sunstein. See Daniel Weinstock, 'Constitutionalizing the Right to Secede', *The Journal of Political Philosophy*, vol.9 (2001); Cass R. Sunstein, 'Should Constitutions Protect the Right to Secede? A Reply to Weinstock', *The Journal of Political Philosophy*, vol.9 (2001); Cass R. Sunstein, *Designing Democracy: What Constitutions Do*, Oxford: Oxford University Press, 2001, pp.95–114; Cass R. Sunstein, 'Constitutionalism and Secession', *University of Chicago Law Review*, vol.58 (1991).

3 Sunstein, 'Constitutionalism and Secession', p.633. Sunstein repeated the assertion in Sunstein, *Designing Democracy*, p.95.

4 *Texas* v. *White*, 74 US 700, 725 (1869). The principles in *Texas* v. *White* were subsequently reiterated by the Supreme Court in *White* v. *Hart*, 80 US 646, at 650–51 (1871); *Keith* v. *Clark*, 97 US 454, at 461–2 (1878); *Poindexter* v. *Greenhow*, 114 US 270, at 290–91 (1885).

5 *Texas* v. *White*, 74 US 700, at 725 (1869).

6 Ibid., at 726.

7 Herman Belz, 'Deep-Conviction Jurisprudence and *Texas* v. *White*: A Comment on G White's Historicist Interpretation of Chief Justice Chase', *Northern Kentucky University Law Review*, vol.21 (1993), p.129.

8 *Williams* v. *Bruffy*, 96 US 176, at 186 (1877).

9 'First Inaugural Address', 4 March 1861, in Abraham Lincoln, *Lincoln: Selected Speeches and Writings*, New York: Vintage Books/Library of America, 1992, p.291.

10 *Reference re: Secession of Quebec* [1998] 2 SCR 217.

11 Akhil Reed Amar, 'Abraham Lincoln and the American Union', *University of Illinois Law Review* (2001), p.1115.

12 Ibid.

13 'Mišljenje Ustavnog suda Jugoslavije o suprotnosti amandmana IX–XC na ustav SR Slovenije sa ustavom SFRJ', 18 January 1990, *Službeni list SFRJ*, vol. XLVI, no.10 (23 February 1990), p.593.

14 'Odluka o ocenjivanju ustavnosti ustavne deklaracije o Kosovu kao samostalnoj i ravnopravnoj jedinici u okviru federacije (konfederacije) Jugoslavije kao ravnopravnog subjekta sa ostalim jedinicama u federaciji (konfederaciji)', 19 February 1991, *Službeni list SFRJ*, vol. XLVII, no.37 (20 May 1991), p.618.

15 'Odluka o ocenjivanju ustavnosti deklaracije o proglašenju suverene i samostalne Republike Hrvatske', 13 November 1991, in Milovan Buzadžić, *Secesija bivših jugoslovenskih republika u svetlosti odluka Ustavnog Suda Jugoslavije. Zbirka dokumenata s uvodnom raspravom*, Belgrade: Službeni list SRJ, 1994, p.159.

16 'Odluka o ocenjivanju ustavnosti deklaracije o suverenosti države Republike Slovenije', 10 January 1991, *Službeni list SFRJ*, vol. XLVII, no.23 (5 April 1991), p.452.

17 'Predsedništvo SFRJ dostavilo Skupštini koncept federativnog uređenja Jugoslavije', reprinted in *Borba* (18 October 1990), p.2.

18 'Predlog ustavno-pravnog postupka za izdvajanje iz Jugoslavije', reprinted in *Nedeljna Borba* (2–3 March 1991), p.13.

19 *Reference re: Secession of Quebec* [1998] 2 SCR 217, at 248.

20 Ibid., at 272.

21 Ibid., at 263–4.

22 Ibid., at 265–70.

23 Ibid., at 265.

24 Ibid., at 294.

25 Margaret Moore, 'The Ethics of Secession and a Normative Theory of Nationalism', *Canadian Journal of Law & Jurisprudence*, vol.13 (2000), p.247.

26 Kenneth McRoberts, *Misconceiving Canada: The Struggle for National Unity*, Toronto: Oxford University Press, 1997, p.230.

27 *Reference re: Secession of Quebec* [1998] 2 SCR 217, at 294.

28 *An Act Respecting the Exercise of the Fundamental Rights and Prerogatives of the Quebec People and the Quebec State*, 2000 S.Q., c.46, s.4.

29 *An Act to Give Effect to the Requirement for Clarity as Set Out in the Opinion of the Supreme Court of Canada in the Quebec Secession Reference*, 2000 S.C., c.21, s.2. A public opinion poll conducted immediately after the Supreme Court decision indicated that over three-quarters of Canada's population believed that a clear majority meant more than 50 per cent plus one. The same poll indicated that just over two-thirds of Quebec's population thought that a higher threshold was required: *Angus Reid Poll on Reference*, 28 August 1998, available on website http://www.uni.ca/ar_ref.htm (visited on 2 January 1999).

30 Moore, 'The Ethics of Secession', p.247.

31 *Reference re: Secession of Quebec* [1998] 2 SCR 217, at 266–8.

32 Ibid., at 267–8.

33 Ibid., at 293.

34 Ibid., at 266–7, 293–4.

35 Ibid., at 269.

36 'Letter of Stephane Dion, Federal Minister for Intergovernmental Affairs to Lucien Bouchard, Premier of Quebec', 11 August 1997, in Stephane Dion, *Straight Talk: Speeches and Writings on Canadian Unity*, Montreal: McGill-Queen's University Press, 1999, p.189.

37 Grand Council of the Crees, *Sovereign Injustice: Forcible Inclusion of the James Bay Crees and Cree Territory into a Sovereign Quebec*, Nemaska: Grand Council of Crees, 1995, pp.171–227.

38 The Quebec government has relied heavily on a report it commissioned from five international law experts which stated that Quebec's provincial borders automatically became international borders upon the secession of Quebec. An English translation of the report is reprinted in Anne F. Bayefsky, *Self-Determination in International Law: Quebec and Lessons Learned*, The Hague: Kluwer, 2000.

39 Peter Radan, '"You Can't Always Get What You Want": The Territorial Scope of an Independent Quebec', *Osgoode Hall Law Journal*, vol.41 (2003).

40 *Reference re: Secession of Quebec* [1998] 2 SCR 217, at 265.

41 Jeremy Webber, 'The Legality of a Unilateral Declaration of Independence Under Canadian Law', *McGill Law Journal*, vol.42 (1997).

42 *Reference re: Secession of Quebec* [1998] 2 SCR 217, at 274.

43 Donna Greschner, 'The Quebec Secession Reference: Goodbye to Part V?', *Constitutional Forum*, vol.10 (1998).

44 *Reference re: Secession of Quebec* [1998] 2 SCR 217, at 240.

45 Greschner, 'The Quebec Secession Reference', p.22.

46 *Reference re: Secession of Quebec* [1998] 2 SCR 217, at 270.

47 Ibid., at 272–5, 289, 296.

48 James Crawford, *The Creation of States in International Law*, Oxford: Clarendon Press, 1979, p.248.

49 Samuel Flagg Bemis, quoted in Piero Gleijeses, 'The Limits of Sympathy: The United States and the Independence of Spanish America', *Journal of Latin American Studies*, vol.24 (1992), p.487.

50 Robert Jennings and Arthur Watts, *Oppenheim's International Law*, vol.1, 9th edn, London: Longmans, 1992, p.130.

Index

For Product Safety Concerns and Information please contact our EU
representative GPSR@taylorandfrancis.com
Taylor & Francis Verlag GmbH, Kaufingerstraße 24, 80331 München, Germany

www.ingramcontent.com/pod-product-compliance
Lightning Source LLC
Chambersburg PA
CBHW050714280326
41926CB00088B/3019